CW00348927

"For anyone wondering what's next book shines a light on the latest think important questions we should be conｼｲｰｩｵ about the future role of crypto, as well as exploring the arguments behind centralised and decentralised currencies. Of particular interest to me were the insights into the next stage of banking disruption and how technology and finance can be brought together to make the world a better place."

Anne Boden

Founder and former CEO, Starling Bank

"What is money? What function does it serve and what do we value? These are not existential questions for our industry — rather, they are the foundational questions to help us understand where the industry will, or should, go next. In *Intelligent Money*, Chris covers a wide range of topics, from crypto and decentralization to artificial intelligence and generative finance, and challenges us to imagine (or re-imagine) the role of government, society, and technology in the context of an evolving financial services system. A timely read!"

Theo Lau

Author of *The Metaverse Economy*

"Chris Skinner masterfully navigates the complex waters of digital banking, offering invaluable insights for the modern financial era. This book is a must-read for anyone looking to understand and excel in the fintech landscape."

Jason Bates

Co-founder, Monzo

"Filled with thought-provoking information on AI applications in FinTech, Chris Skinner's book is an educational and insightful resource in the financial industry."

Jill Castilla
President and CEO, Citizens Bank of Edmond

"*Intelligent Money* is a 'must-read' for every fintech and banker wanting to navigate the challenges of the coming decade. Having taken a fresh look at the evolution of money and its role in society and described the latest innovations in money in an accessible way, Skinner then raises a host of questions, some practical and some philosophical, facing the worlds of banking and technology, consumers and ethics, government and regulations. He then draws conclusions that are often unexpected and sometimes uncomfortable, but when presented alongside the data and Skinner's uncontestable real-world logic, make total sense. The world of *Intelligent Money* he describes is not utopian. It is not very neat or particularly pretty. But it is customer-led, exciting and optimistic."

Tony Craddock
Director General, The Payments Association

Everything you wanted to know about money, data, and information... past, present and future, the players in this world, the metaverse, future-verse.... And most important how it's going to affect you and your future. A must read for everyone that interacts in the financial ecosystem... that's everyone!!

Uzoma Dozie
Founder of Sparkle and former CEO, Diamond Bank

INTELLIGENT
money
When Money Thinks for You

CHRIS SKINNER

Marshall Cavendish
Business

Published in 2024 by Marshall Cavendish Business
An imprint of Marshall Cavendish International

A member of the
Times Publishing Group

Other Marshall Cavendish Offices:
Marshall Cavendish Corporation, 800 Westchester Ave, Suite N-641, Rye Brook, NY 10573, USA • Marshall Cavendish International (Thailand) Co Ltd, 253 Asoke, 16th Floor, Sukhumvit 21 Road, Klongtoey Nua, Wattana, Bangkok 10110, Thailand • Marshall Cavendish (Malaysia) Sdn Bhd, Times Subang, Lot 46, Subang Hi-Tech Industrial Park, Batu Tiga, 40000 Shah Alam, Selangor Darul Ehsan, Malaysia

Marshall Cavendish is a registered trademark of Times Publishing Limited

ISBN 978-981-5113-21-1 (paperback)
ISBN 978-981-5218-55-8 (e-book)

Printed in Singapore

This book is dedicated to Eddie, Freddie and Kamila.

My life, my loves and my reason for being.

CONTENTS

PREFACE

I remember moderating a panel discussion in New York way back when. It was in the early 2010s, and bitcoin had arrived. We talked about what that meant and I made a statement that you cannot have money without government. The bitcoin promoters hated me for saying that and they retaliated. They called me a statist. A statist is an advocate of a political system in which the state has substantial centralised control over social and economic affairs. I then realised I had walked into a political minefield. The people I faced are called libertarians. Libertarians believe in a free market and the private lives of citizens. In other words, they hate government and government intervention.

This argument would never have arisen if it were not for the internet. The internet allows everyone to connect everywhere, all the time, wherever you are, whoever you are and whenever you need to connect. The internet does not recognise government or countries or borders. The internet does not recognise time or time zones. The internet does not recognise money, currency or regulations. The internet is a wild west. A wild west that libertarians love.

This is why I got into trouble when I said that you cannot have money without government. It was the first time I felt that I was old, or old school, but why can you not have money without government? The main reason is that money is our main method for trading and having value. The reason we have banks is to store money and value. Banks are regulated by governments. They have licences. With no licence and no governance, you have a wild west. If your money disappears, you have no recourse, no control and no one to call.

It's just gone. This is the reason for states and state controls. It is the argument of the statist.

However, the libertarian argues a different way. The libertarian believes that you can create a system with no borders or state controls. We can have a system created for the individual and managed by individuals. The network of citizens manages everything and, in our connected and networked world, who needs centralised governance?

It's a valid question. More importantly, it strikes to the heart of what I was saying. I was not saying that you need centralised governance, but you do need governance. You cannot have money without governance, and that means you cannot have money without government. So who is the government? Is it the state or the citizen?

This is the massive friction of our times. Who controls the world or, rather, who controls my world? My world is controlled by many factors. My world is controlled by my wife and children; my mother and father; my work and my country; my friends and connections; my bank and my funding; my connections and network; my country and government; my everything.

And there is the rub. Who controls your world? If you place it in the context of libertarians versus statists, your world is controlled by governments who should not have that control because they are not qualified. Your world can, today, be controlled by your network.

Having had this debate for over a decade, the funny this is that I have never stated who the control should be. I have said that you cannot have money without government, but I have never said who the government was. The government is not necessarily the Federal Reserve, the Bank of England or the European Central Bank. But my point is, government or, if you prefer, governance? Who provides support of the system? If the system collapses, who do you call? If you lose all of your hard-earned value, who will help you? If everything goes wrong, what can you do? These questions answer my statement: you cannot have money without government.

I have seen so many examples of cryptocurrency exchange platforms that supported the libertarian dreams of money without governance collapsing, and their users collectively losing billions. It is then, at that point, that they ask, "Where's our money?"

The answer is that it's gone because you placed your investment in a platform that was unregulated, poorly managed, had no guarantees and could just as easily have been a Ponzi scheme. A Ponzi scheme involves someone taking money from one investor and giving it to another. Most of these schemes have no structure except the trust of giving to one to give to the other to get better returns on those investments. The problem is that the return on your investments is paid by the deposits of other people. It's a house of cards and, when the house of cards falls, you are at the bottom of the pit.

Therefore, the real question is how to protect our investments in a world of decentralisation? Do we need government and what government do we need? How can we trade safely and with confidence?

These are questions I have been grappling with for over ten years—since the arrival of bitcoin—and my conclusion is that you need some form of hybrid finance. You need to allow decentralised finance to trade without borders over the global network, but with some form of centralised and regulated support. When the decentralised finance fails, I want to have someone to call to get my money back. Who you gonna call? Well, it's not Ghostbusters. In other words, money without governance or government is never going to work. If there is no one to call and no way to sort out the issues, you are stuffed.

My belief is that you cannot have totally decentralised finance. What is decentralised finance?

> Full decentralisation exists only when every element of the project is out of the hands of the original team [and] the government cannot blame any single party for what happens. We have actually not had a chance to experience this with anything except Bitcoin thus far & have much to learn about how real decentralisation will actually materialize itself.[1]

---

1   Andrey Didovskiy, "Demystifying Decentralization: Separating Fact from Fiction," *HackerNoon*, 28 March 2023, https://hackernoon.com/demystifying-decentralization-separating-fact-from-fiction.

If it works, this changes everything as, historically, all finance has been centralised and we believed in governments and banks and their rules and regulations to protect us. The core concept here is belief. The belief we have that governments protect us and that banks will not lose our money. In fact, money itself is just a belief. It was invented by humans and is something that does not actually exist. We just made it up. However, the core is the belief in something that we then accept as real. We accept this government. We accept this money. We accept this system. We accept this structure.

Thanks to the network of mobile and online, this acceptance is now being fundamentally challenged. Which government do you trust? Do you trust the government of your country or do you trust the government of the network of citizens?

We have developed a financial system with regulations and governance over centuries to ensure that, if a collapse happens, you can get your money back. That's why, when we saw the 2008 financial crisis and, more recently in 2023, the collapse of banks like Silicon Valley Bank and Credit Suisse, we could call someone and get our money back. If you have a decentralised system where there is nothing behind it, except an idea of support, it does not work.

This is why this book argues that you cannot have purely decentralised finance. You need some form of centralised finance. However, just to be clear, I don't mean that centralised finance has to have a national government or a regulator backed by a national government.

In the same way that libertarians have had issues with me for the last decade, arguing that you *can* have money without governance, bankers argue that you *cannot* have decentralised finance without governance. There is a huge friction here.

Can you have an effective currency for the networked economy that is not backed by a national government? The proposal of this book is that yes, you can. Through the chapters of this book, you will find that:

- governments fail
- banks fail
- crypto fails
- everything can fail

This is why money needs to be intelligent. Artificial intelligence has grown rapidly in the last decade to become somewhat mainstream. ChatGPT is the breakout platform of this process, but there have been others. By combining artificial intelligence and decentralised finance, are we living through a transformative moment of time? Some say yes but the old school say no. Are you new school or old school? Libertarian or statist? Or can you be both?

Given that as the basis of the book, we then look at what works. What governance and financial system do we need for the networked world? How can we integrate decentralised finance and centralised finance? How can we make these systems work?

My answer is hybrid finance. We can create a financial system that is both decentralised, controlled and owned by the individual *and* centralised, regulated and guaranteed by the system. What will the system look like? Will it be the system of government or the network?

Let's find out...

AS MONEY BECOMES INTELLIGENT

In 1950, the brilliant British scientist Alan Turing proposed a test. Considering that computers back then were running on valves and electron tubes, it was a visionary test. He suggested that when a computer-generated code could be created that appeared to be human, we would have reached a true level of artificial intelligence (AI).

For many years, the test has been applied to everything from Watson by IBM to AlphaGo by Google, but none have successfully passed it. When will we really have smart machines that appear truly intelligent or human?

In 2022, OpenAI developed a system called ChatGPT that appeared to get there. ChatGPT stands for Chat Generative Pre-trained Transformer. Since its launch, ChatGPT has become all the rage online because it appears so human-like. However, ChatGPT has not passed Turing's test. Close, but no cigar. This is because ChatGPT scrapes together human content from the network and purely places it in a nice framework that appears original. Without the original human content, it would not work.

Despite this, it has sparked huge amounts of investment in AI around the world to develop the next generation of intelligence. Intelligence developments that date back to the 1950s, and have come a long way since. This book will explore those developments in the context of money, so let's start with how far intelligent money has come since the 1950s.

The first major examples of intelligent money date back to the 1980s, when computer scientists were looking at neural networking for trading. The idea was that systems could be built where, when one stock was rising and another was diving, you could pair them. Paired stock trading using computer systems quickly developed. If IBM was going up and Microsoft down, the system would automatically buy IBM and sell Microsoft. A simple concept, and one that has since developed into amazingly complex algorithms. In other words, we moved from paired trading to programmed trading to algorithmic trading to flash trading to the system we have today, forty years later.

At the same time as those developments, we saw an evolution of how this relates to you and me as people. Back in the 1990s, we discussed the idea of infomediaries. The idea was to replace intermediaries—your personal financial advisor, who you would meet face to face—with an infomediary—your digital advisor to whom you would delegate authority to deal with your money through an interface. We moved from infomediaries to personal financial management to financial dashboards to the system we have today, thirty years later.

The point being made here is that automated financial trading, whether in corporations or for individuals, is not new. It's been brewing for decades. The difference today is that the developments have moved at an extreme pace, fuelled by generative intelligence technologies.

What are generative intelligence technologies? Generative intelligence technologies, also known as generative AI or GenAI, are a type of artificial intelligence capable of generating text, images or other media, using large language generative models. This is when it starts to get complicated as large language models, or LLMs for short, are deep learning algorithms that can recognise, summarise, translate, predict and generate content using very large datasets.

Putting it simply, we have systems in the 2020s that can take data from everywhere, interpret them, regenerate such content, and answer almost any question you ask with everything from a picture to an article to music and art.

- Draw me a picture of a dog in the style of Michelangelo. No problem.
- Create a song that sounds similar to the Beatles, but influenced by Eminem. No problem.
- Write a book about intelligent money in the style of Chris Skinner...?

These systems include LLM chatbots such as ChatGPT, Bing Chat, Bard and LLaMA, and text-to-image artificial intelligence art systems such as

Stable Diffusion, Midjourney and DALL-E. The thing you need to bear in mind here is that these LLMs using GenAI can only do this by scraping content from the systems and networks—the human creation is still key. This is because systems and computers are nowhere near developed enough to reach what we call the Singularity. The Singularity is a future point in time when technological growth becomes uncontrollable and irreversible, resulting in unforeseeable consequences for human civilisation. In other words, the machine takes over.

Is this likely to happen or is it just the scary view of movies to make us afraid of technological progress? That is a tough call, but we are definitely creating more and more intelligence in the machine. However, the challenge for the machine is that the human brain and human intelligence is also complex.

An average human brain has something in the order of 100 billion neurons. Each neuron is connected to up to 10,000 other neurons, which means that the number of synapses is between 100 trillion and 1,000 trillion. In other words, your brain is basically not a LLM or an AI. It is an incredibly complex human system, developed over years, and, on top of this, your brain connections and insights are completely unique. Your brain is nothing like my brain or anyone else's. We are all unique.

Investment in GenAI surged during the early 2020s, with large companies such as Microsoft, Google and Baidu as well as numerous smaller firms developing GenAI models. These Big Tech firms want to try and create an automated version of your brain. The reason? So that you don't have to think.

What Google and others are trying to do is to recreate your brain using compute power, but that is challenging as a neural network with trillions of connections is still a long way off. For example, Google has been working heavily on developing AI over the past decade with systems that recognise cats or can play games and win against humans. Yet they are still a long way off from replacing human ingenuity and, in my view, never will. However, we *are* moving rapidly towards a world where machines have intelligence.

The good news here is that we can delegate the things we don't want to think about to the machines. Do I want to think about my money day to day? Not really. Do I want to make a payment? No, I just want to buy something.

Do I want to get a mortgage? No, I want to move to a new home. Do I want to invest in ABC Corporation? Not really, I want the return on investment. These are all the things that, with intelligent money, you can delegate to the machine. That's intelligent money.

The thing is that, in all of this discussion, we have a friction fuelled by media and movies. What does the future world of intelligent machines hold? Is it *Terminator*, where the machines take over and fight humankind, or is it *Her*, where Joaquim Phoenix falls in love with his operating system? It's up to you to decide, but this book explores those themes in the context of money and finance.

First Things First: What Is Intelligence?

As already mentioned, it is a huge challenge to develop a system that can replicate a human brain. Nevertheless, there are three defined key phases as to how this will happen. We are already moving past the first phase to the second. The first phase is when a computer system can beat a human at a game. That was something that IBM achieved when its system called Deep Blue beat Garry Kasparov, a chess grandmaster, in 1997. This phase was also surpassed when Google developed AlphaGo. Go is one of the most complex games on Earth and, in an exhibition match, AlphaGo beat the best human player, Fan Hui, 5-0 in 2015.

The thing about these events is that the systems were tasked with just one activity—to play one game. What if the system could play both chess and Go? When systems can multitask, we move to the next level of artificial intelligence, which is where we are today.

The second phase of AI is called general AI. General AI is when a system can multitask and perform several activities at the same time. Today, we now have systems that can integrate text, media, data and more and generate their own versions of those inputs. That's what ChatGPI, Bard, Midjourney and DALL-E do.

They appear super intelligent but, as mentioned, all they are doing is taking input from all networked resources and representing them in a new way. Don't get me wrong, it's very clever, but they are not *thinking*. So, this is where we are today, at the second level of machine intelligence. The machines can now appear far more conversational and creative, based on the content drawn from millions of sources.

In finance, that's great! We can have our infomediary and delegate our finance to the machine. This is why I call this intelligent money. The money is managed and directed by the machines, based on algorithms and resources drawn from a million places. However, the machine is not a human and does not have the intelligence of a human. We are still a long way away from that endgame, the Singularity, but we are moving in that direction, especially if we achieve the endgame of super AI.

Super AI is when the machines are as intelligent as us and pass the Turing Test. It is when they appear to be human, and/or perhaps even more intelligent than humans. It is when you will not be able to tell the difference between Chris Skinner and Ex Machina Skinner.

Putting this into context, there are three levels of intelligence:

- artificial narrow intelligence (ANI): AI with a narrow range of abilities
- artificial general intelligence (AGI): AI on par with human capabilities
- artificial superintelligence (ASI): AI that surpasses human intelligence

In 2022, with ChatGPT, we achieved the move to level 2. What happens in the future will be interesting, especially when we reach level 3. Right now though, we are at the start of level 2 and it is amazing. Think about this in the context of money.

Imagine Intelligent Money

AI integrated with finance creates a vision where every transaction can be displayed through your devices via your apps. This is something I have written about since the 2000s where the front-office user experience is all about devices in the internet of things (IoT) connected through apps, the middle office is the infrastructure based on cloud platforms connected through application programme interfaces (APIs) and the back office is all about data analytics, where the machines sift through petabytes of data to create personalisation. It's the apps-API-AI economy.

It means that wherever you go, whatever you do, whoever you deal with and how can be drilled down into minutiae. You can see what you bought and where—that's the easy bit. What about what you bought where, and the details of the actual product you purchased?

Today, you might get a little bit of information, such as a purchase at a store online or in a shop. You get the store name and the amount. With some apps, through Open Banking and Google API integration, you might get a picture of the store and a little more information. But what about if you could get details of every item in your shopping basket, where it came from and how sustainable it is?

Imagine the integration of AgriTech, MediTech, RetailTech, FinTech and all others through Open APIs, sprinkled with AI. Imagine going to the supermarket and buying a steak, potatoes and broccoli for dinner. Imagine that you later wonder where that steak came from, how the potatoes were grown and whether the broccoli is sustainable.

Imagine opening your financial app run by your technology provider, which has integrated all of these industries through APIs. Imagine you can now look at the fact that you paid $16.75 for these foods on 11 October at 14:36 through your contactless payment system. You swipe, and it shows each of the items you purchased. You double tap each item and it shows you the provenance of the food purchased through a blockchain-based tokenised system. It shows you how organic and sustainable each food item is through the supply chain. Imagine being able to do this for every single item you purchase anywhere. Well, soon, you won't have to imagine. It's coming.

The likelihood is that layers of information services will be laid on top, such as showing how sustainably, healthily and caringly you are living your life. Forget personal financial management (PFM); it will just be personal management—are you living a good life? Are you being good for society and good for the planet? What exposures do you have to bad lifestyle habits, such as alcohol consumption, vaping or smoking?

The issue with this vision is that because you can see all of this information, so too can anyone else with access to your digital footprint. Maybe they cannot see everything, but certainly a bank or government can. Or can they?

Imagine a world where all of that data is yours. Imagine a world where you have your own space on the network and no one else can access that space without your permission. Imagine that no one can follow your digital footprint. Along with many others, Tim Berners-Lee, the godfather of the internet, is trying to achieve that vision. He has been building a project called Solid for the last decade, which is focusing on decentralising the network.

All of these developments are moving us to a world where everything is decentralised and owned by the individual, enriched by not just big data but massive data, and only accessible to banks, governments and others on a permissioned basis. Imagine the future. Imagine that data can live as one. Imagine Generative Finance.

What Is Generative Finance?

Generative Finance, or GeFi for short, is the integration of AI into finance. This all started with ChatGPT, the LLM framework for GenAI. The general idea of GeFi is that you can integrate intelligence into everything you do with money. Today, we are part of the way there. Most challenger banks offer integration of transactions with Google Maps for example, so you can see where you were when you bought that cappuccino. Tomorrow, it will go far further.

For example, you are travelling and make a lot of foreign exchange transactions. Your GeFi app tells you that you are being irresponsible and could have saved $10 per transaction if you had paid in the local currency rather than your home country's currency. For example, you have a whole range of regular payments, and your GeFi app alerts you to the fact that three of the things you subscribe to have not been used for the past six months. For example, you arrive at the office and the GeFi app tells you that both you and your neighbour have driven to the same office for the past year. Why don't you carshare? Okay, the last example may seem like something out of *Black Mirror*, but you get the idea.

What about if we zoom out and put this into a macro picture? As a corporation, you have suppliers worldwide. I remember at one point that Apple reached almost 800 suppliers in over 30 countries. How hard is that to manage? Back then, in the mid-2010s, I enjoyed the concept of a company using real-time connectivity to manage its supply chains. Knowing that a component ordered as part of a 10,000 component order is on a ship in the middle of the South China Sea and will be delivered to the port of your choosing in the next 32 hours is kind of freaky, but realistic.

Imagine how this could change things. By way of example, back in the late 1980s, I remember a story used in a business book about how Ford's executive team was blown away by Toyota's just-in-time (JIT) processing. The team had flown to Japan to find out about the inner workings of Toyota, and discovered that Toyota paid orders on arrival if they were correct. If they were incorrect, they were rejected and sent back.

Why was this important? Because Toyota had three people employed in Accounts Receivable compared to Ford's 400 or so. When you think about embedding such intelligence into finance, payments and transactions today, you can just imagine the phantasmagorical outcomes.

An item is tracked in real time, delivered with GPS tracing and paid for with immediate effect on safe arrival—only to be eaten by your dog (which is what happened to my Amazon order yesterday).

First, we need to consider the role of money and how it will fit into this future intelligent system. A system where we may all live in the metaverse of Web3, and where money is no longer controlled by governments, but is decentralised to the network. Where cryptocurrencies are far more pervasive than government-controlled currencies, and where national borders are no longer relevant because we are one connected world.

Let's start with answering a basic question: what is money?

WHAT IS MONEY?

Many people believe that money replaced barter. It is a commonly held belief that humans evolved from nomads to farmers to city dwellers and that, as they became civilised, they bartered bread for meat. However, that proved difficult if, say, the butcher did not want meat. That's why money was invented thousands of years ago, with the oldest form of money dating back to Mesopotamia.

However, according to anthropological researchers, this history of the evolution of money is not true. Based on extensive studies of indigenous tribes, academics have found that most tribes work in a gift economy. If you need meat, the butcher gives it to you. Then, when the butcher needs bread, the baker gives it to him. It's reciprocal, with each specialist in the tribe giving what is needed to the others in the tribe. So where did this idea of barter come from? Answer: Adam Smith.

Adam Smith was a Scottish economist and philosopher who, for many, is regarded as the father of economics/capitalism. His major work was *An Inquiry into the Nature and Causes of the Wealth of Nations* (1776). In this book, he put forward the theory of how money developed, and described an imaginary scenario in which a baker living before the invention of money wanted meat from a butcher but had nothing the butcher wanted. "No exchange can, in this case, be made between them," Smith wrote.

As this sort of scenario was so undesirable, the commonly held view is that societies must have created money to facilitate trade, particularly as the evolution of barter to money is a fixture in just about every economics textbook. The belief is that people bartered precious stones, beads, fabrics and food, but it was often difficult to achieve a deal. Therefore, money was invented to simplify the process.

However, as mentioned, the idea that humans became civilised, started to barter and then replaced bartering with money is a fallacy, according to anthropologists. Anthropologists have pointed out that this barter economy has never been witnessed as researchers have travelled to undeveloped parts of the globe. In a 1985 paper, Cambridge anthropology professor Caroline Humphrey wrote: "No example of a barter economy, pure and simple, has ever been described, let alone the emergence from it of money; all available ethnography suggests that there never has been such a thing."[1]

So, what was the process instead? As explained in the *Atlantic*:[2]

If you were a baker who needed meat, you didn't offer your bagels for the butcher's steaks. Instead, you got your wife to hint to the butcher's wife that you two were low on iron, and she'd say something like "Oh really? Have a hamburger, we've got plenty!" Down the line, the butcher might want a birthday cake, or help moving to a new apartment, and you'd help him out [...] it's much more efficient than Smith's idea of a barter system, since it doesn't depend on each person simultaneously having what the other wants. It's also not tit for tat: No one ever assigns a specific value to the meat or cake or house-building labour, meaning debts can't be transferred.

Defining Money

Given the above, the first question we need to answer is this: what is money? This question comes up more and more in my thinking, especially when you look at cryptocurrencies, central bank digital currencies (CBDCs), stablecoins and such like. At its core, money is just a belief system. If people believe it is money, then it is. This is well illustrated by the fact that when a central bank replaces a banknote, for example the Bank of England phased out the old

---

1   Caroline Humphrey, "Barter and Economic Disintegration," *Man* 20, no. 1 (March 1985): 48–72. https://doi.org/10.2307/2802221.
2   Ilana E. Strauss, "The Myth of the Barter Economy," *Atlantic*, 26 February 2016, https://www.theatlantic.com/business/archive/2016/02/barter-society-myth/471051/.

£20 note in 2022, one piece of paper becomes worthless and a new version becomes worthy. When I went to my commercial bank with a pocket full of these notes, I was informed that as, at that time, the old notes were still legal tender, I could only deposit them into my account, and not exchange them for the new notes. It then struck me. Yesterday, I had believed that a piece of paper was worth £20 and yet, today, I didn't. It was worth nothing.

This is the key to what's been happening with cryptocurrencies. With the issues around Terra-LUNA, Celsius, Binance and more, the belief in bitcoin has been shaken, along with all of the other cryptocurrencies. Their value has gone through the floor.[3] So why did these currencies gain value in the first place? It's all about that belief system.

For example, Bob Diamond, the former CEO of Barclay's Bank and co-founder and CEO of Atlas Merchant Capital, recently stated, "I can't think of anyone who believes that in the future a digital version of the dollar for corporates and institutions isn't going to happen. We are definitely going to digitalise money."[4] If I were to ask whether it would be a digital dollar, a digital renminbi, a digital euro, a digital bitcoin or a digital Ethereum, the answer would be that it's your choice. It would be whichever one you believe in the most.

If Elon Musk says a cryptocurrency is good for the money, people believe it. If all of your friends are investing in bitcoin, you believe in it. If you see that the market is exploding like a tulip bubble, you believe it. Whatever you believe has value is what you believe. Diamonds are the best example. Diamonds are inherently worthless.[5] It's only because they have been hyped and marketed that they have value. It's just about what you believe.

This is well illustrated by Professor Niall Ferguson in his 2008 book *The Ascent of Money: A Financial History of the World* in which he discusses the fact that money sits at the heart of our economic systems. Without money, countries, businesses and organisations would not be able to trade. The fact we have created a global belief system that can trade is the essence of humankind.

---

3   The value of most cryptocurrencies dropped by more than 80 per cent between 2021 and 2022.
4   Shazlim Amith, "Bob Diamond: Digital Currencies Will Play a Major Role in Finance," Coin Edition, 10 January 2023, https://coinedition.com/bob-diamond-digital-currencies-will-play-a-major-role-in-finance/.
5   Stephanie, "10 Reasons Why Diamonds Are Worthless You Should Know," A Fashion Blog, 23 December 2022, https://www.afashionblog.com/why-diamonds-are-worthless/.

What you then realise is that money is the glue that allows the progression and innovation of humankind. Underpinning this glue is the trust that you are good for the money. Replace "trust" with "belief" and you get the idea. Money is meaningless unless you believe it has value. That's the core point. If you believe it has value, you can create infrastructures and mechanisms, like banks and bank networks, to enable the movement of funds fast, frictionless and now almost free.

So how do we define money? According to the Bank of International Settlements (BIS), the major regulator owned by the world's central bank, the key features of money are that it is:

- a store of value
- a medium of exchange
- a unit of account

Above this, money needs to be:

- fungible[6]
- durable
- portable
- recognisable
- stable

Many people in finance believe that money backed by a central bank is the best way forward. It's the most trusted because the belief is there. I am not so sure about this as we have seen currency collapses in many countries, such as Zimbabwe and Venezuela, when the belief in the government and central bank disappears.

Beju Shah, Head of the Nordic Centre, BIS Innovation Hub, speaking at a presentation about money beliefs

---

6   Fungible, or fungibility, is a key concept in finance. It means that one item can be replaced by another. I can replace beads with shells and shells with rocks. Non-fungible is the opposite. You cannot replace one asset with another. Hence, when you hear discussions about non-fungible tokens, the difference is that they cannot be exchanged or replaced by something else, whereas fungible tokens can. In the latter case, I can replace a dollar with a euro; in the former case, I cannot.

This is why it is so difficult to agree on what money is. Your money may be dollars but I can't use those in Europe, so my money is the euro. Your money is the yuan, but I cannot use those as mine is the rial. Money is purely what you believe it to be and, more importantly, what your neighbourhood and government believe in.

This view is changing today as you have statists—those who believe in the power of the state and are centralists—versus libertarians—those who believe you can avoid intermediaries like banks and the state, and deal peer to peer in a decentralised way. Statists are saying that money is fiat currency while libertarians are saying that it's whatever they want to trade in. Then there are people in between, who are just not sure.

It is similar to the story of an economist, logician and mathematician who meet on a train. They see a purple cow out of the window and the economist says, "Look at that! All the cows here are purple!" The logician says, "No, there are cows here and, yes, one is purple." Then the mathematician says, "No, there is one cow here and, on this side, the cow is purple."

No wonder we talk about a confusion of economists, and a friction in our belief systems.

I accept that today this piece of paper is worth £20, €20, $20 or whatever. I accept that bitcoin is worth $30,000 today but was worth $70,000 yesterday, and a few years ago it was worth $20,000. These things are worth whatever you believe in and trust. Trust is the belief in a system, and that system is whatever you believe in.

A Dystopian or Utopian Future? Money Is the Core

There are lengthy discussions about our future worlds, as portrayed by *Star Wars* and *Star Trek*. From hoping that the force is with you to boldly going where no one has gone before, *Star Wars* and *Star Trek* offer two vastly different views of the future. *Star Wars*, as per its title, is all about the fight for supremacy and who wins and loses; *Star Trek* is a utopian view of the future, where we focus on the betterment of humankind.

Perhaps the most striking realisation is that one has money and the other one does not. One is dystopian and one is utopian. Money exists in *Star*

Wars in the form of Imperial credits but it doesn't exist in *Star Trek*. Could we have a future world where humans are motivated by something other than wealth?

Reputation is the core of what you earn in the utopian world of *Star Trek*. Could we create a world where the betterment of humanity—and your contribution to that goal—is recognised in reputational credits? It may be idealistic, but which world would you rather live in? A world of harmony or a world of war?

The problem with a world of harmony, where money does not exist, is that it creates a question about motivation. Why would you get out of bed in the morning if there were no reward? If there were no reward, what would motivate you? If you cannot see a return on your investment of work, what would be the point?

In *Star Wars*, the reward is beating the bad guys; in *Star Trek*, the reward is being recognised as a good person. Both reward, but one gives an Imperial credit whilst the other gives a reputational credit. Credit where credit is due, you need incentives in either world as this is what makes us human. We live to strive, to work, to get better, to get more, to earn, to invest, to build wealth.

It's Not Money as We Know It

We have just had a recent past that has been very troubled with the pandemic. This meant that, for two years, I was locked in my room. It was bad and sad, but I was lucky to spend most of it with my two little boys who were four years old when the pandemic started. The reason why I mention this is that when you have children, you start to question everything. It makes you think about things. I found myself asking a lot of questions about money, finance and technology. For example, our world does not exist in the way that we see our world. Our world has no countries; we made them up. Our world actually has no borders; we created them. The internet doesn't recognise countries, and that's a huge issue for regulators, companies and financial institutions. How do you deal with the world connected through the network of currencies that doesn't recognise regulations and borders?

Albert Einstein famously made the point that time does not exist. It's true. Just think about it. If you cross the border from Afghanistan into China, you have to put your clock forward $3\frac{1}{2}$ hours, the largest time change of any border in the world, simply because Chairman Mao combined China's five time zones into one in 1949. We simply made time up, and now we talk about real time and doing everything transparently, interconnected globally, immediately on demand. That changes the way we should think.

We also have issues when thinking about money because money does not exist. We simply made it up. The US dollar doesn't exist. It was invented. The same is true about the euro and the Chinese yuan. In fact, right now there's a big debate around dedollarising the world. Should the dollar stay as the reserve currency of the world? What happens if it doesn't? What would we do? How would that change how we bank and how we think? Asking these questions makes you realise that the way we grew up is not the way our children will grow up. And it's not the way of the future. We will have to think differently.

THE MOVE TO INTELLIGENT MONEY

There appears to be three monetary and financial systems developing. The first is centralised, the second is distributed and the third is decentralised. The second and third models overlap somewhat as a decentralised financial system has points of control, or nodes, but they are part of the distributed network. Therefore, I am just going to talk about centralised versus decentralised identity, financial systems and data systems.

The two variants—centralised versus decentralised—highlight the difference between analogue and digital, or physical and digital. The physical, analogue structures that are centralised are well understood and embedded in society. They have formed over centuries, have national governments at their core and fiat currencies as their modus operandi. In contrast, the digital, networked structures that are decentralised are completely misunderstood and are still emerging. They are forming right now, have purely networked governance and whatever currency the networked believes in as their value exchange.

This is the clear dystopia of where we are today. What's the utopia? The utopia is obviously where traditional governmental structures live in harmony with the new networked structures. Can that be achieved? I'm not so sure. The major challenge is that government structures are created to control behaviours, activities, trade, finance, society and thinking. Many now accept that the networked world, which recognises no borders, no controls and no government, will not live that way.

I have always said that you cannot have money without government. In the physical world, that is obvious. You need governments to issue currencies and back them with regulations. But what does this mean in the networked world? In the networked world, you cannot have money without governance. But who is the governor of the networked world currencies? The Federal Reserve? The European Central Bank (ECB)? We, the people? Elon Musk?

The important point here is that a dual system is developing. The first is familiar, where we have money managed by government; the second is emerging, where we have money managed by governance. The latter is our new digital world of money, and we are wondering how this can be governed. Specifically, we are wondering how it can be governed in a way that can be trusted.

This is the critical point: you cannot have money without government, but it doesn't need to be a national government. It doesn't have to be the Federal Reserve or the ECB. It could be that we, the people, create a globally networked currency that works for the benefit of us. That is what is happening in this battle between analogue, physical and centralised versus digital, networked and decentralised.

There are two paths to the future: One is already set and is known—fiat currency; the other is developing, emerging and unknown—digital currency.

What Is a Fiat Currency?

Fiat derives from the Latin word meaning "let it be done" in the sense of an order, decree or resolution. Fiat money is a type of currency that is not backed by a commodity, such as gold or silver. It is typically designated by the issuing government to be legal tender. In other words, it is centralised. Throughout history, fiat money was quite rare until the twentieth century, but there were some situations where banks or governments stopped honouring redeemability of demand notes or credit notes, usually temporarily. In modern times, fiat money is generally authorised by government regulation.

Fiat money generally does not have intrinsic value and does not have use value. It has value only because the individuals who use it as a unit of account—or, in the case of currency, a medium of exchange—agree on its value. They trust that it will be accepted by merchants and other people.

Fiat money is an alternative to commodity money, which is a currency that has intrinsic value because it contains, for example, a precious metal, such as gold or silver, which is embedded in the coin. Fiat also differs from representative money, which is money that has intrinsic value because it is backed by and can be converted into a precious metal or another commodity. Fiat money can look similar to representative money (such as paper notes), but the former has no backing, while the latter represents a claim on a commodity (which can be redeemed to a greater or lesser extent).

Government-issued fiat money banknotes were first used during the eleventh century in China. Fiat money started to predominate during the twentieth century. Since President Richard Nixon's decision to suspend US dollar convertibility to gold in 1971, a system of national fiat currencies has been used globally.

Fiat money can be:

- any money that is not backed by a commodity
- money declared by a person, institution or government to be legal tender, meaning that it must be accepted in payment of a debt in specific circumstances
- state-issued money which is neither convertible through a central bank to anything else nor fixed in value in terms of any objective standard
- money used because of government decree
- an otherwise non-valuable object that serves as a medium of exchange (also known as fiduciary money)

What Is a Cryptocurrency?

In contrast, *crypto*, like *encrypted*, means that something is packaged in a way that is secret and secure, and can be shared digitally without breach. A cryptocurrency is a digital currency that works this way, and is designed to work as a medium of exchange through a computer network that is not reliant on any central authority, such as a government or bank, to uphold or maintain it. It is a decentralised system for verifying that the parties to a transaction have the money they claim to have, eliminating the need for traditional intermediaries, such as banks, when funds are being transferred between two entities.

Individual coin ownership records are stored in a digital ledger, which is a computerised database using strong cryptography to secure transaction records, control the creation of additional coins and verify the transfer of coin ownership. Despite their name, cryptocurrencies are not considered to be currencies in the traditional sense, and while varying treatments have been applied to them, including classification as commodities, securities and currencies, cryptocurrencies are generally viewed as a distinct asset class in practice. Some crypto schemes use validators to maintain the cryptocurrency. In a proof-of-stake (PoS) model, owners put up their tokens as collateral. In return, they get authority over the token in proportion to the amount they stake. Generally, these token stakers get additional ownership in the token over time via network fees, newly minted tokens or other such reward mechanisms.

Cryptocurrency does not exist in physical form (like paper money) and is typically not issued by a central authority. Cryptocurrencies typically use decentralised control as opposed to a CBDC. When a cryptocurrency is minted, created prior to issuance or issued by a single issuer, it is generally considered centralised. When implemented with decentralised control, each cryptocurrency works through distributed ledger technology (DLT), typically a blockchain, that serves as a public financial transaction database. Traditional asset classes like currencies, commodities and stocks, as well as macroeconomic factors, have modest exposures to cryptocurrency returns.

The first cryptocurrency was bitcoin, which was first released as open-source software in 2009. As of March 2022, there were more than 10,000 other cryptocurrencies in the marketplace, of which more than 70 had a market capitalisation exceeding $1 billion.

What Are Stablecoins?

Stablecoins are a form of digital currency typically pegged to fiat currencies, such as the US dollar; baskets of currencies, such as cryptocurrencies; and/or commodities, such as gold.

Stablecoins differ from traditional digital records of money, such as bank deposit accounts, in two primary ways. First, stablecoins are cryptographically secured.[1] This allows users to settle transactions near-instantaneously without the fear of double-spending or having an intermediary, such as a bank, that deals with all of the process. Instead, the technology does it for you. On public blockchains, this also allows transactions to take place 24 hours a day, 7 days a week, 365 days a year.

Second, stablecoins are typically built on DLT standards that can be programmed. This means that stablecoins work as unique blocks that, when placed upon a blockchain, can become smart contracts to create payment and other financial services. Smart contract is a concept that came out of the blockchain technology known as Ethereum. As this technology lends itself to the corporate and governmental world, it is extremely popular for businesses and banks.

What is a smart contract? As defined by IBM:

Smart contracts are simply programs stored on a blockchain that run when predetermined conditions are met. They typically are used to automate the execution of an agreement so that all participants can be immediately certain of the outcome, without any intermediary's involvement or time loss. They can also automate a workflow, triggering the next action when conditions are met.

What Will Be the Digital Currency?

It is difficult to answer this question, which may seem strange when we spend so much time talking about payments and finance. My answer usually returns to "a basket", but a basket of what? A basket of dollars, mixed with euros and yuan? A basket of dogecoins, bitcoins and Ethereum? No, a basket of both.

This is the outlook where people can choose what constitutes their basket of currencies. They will choose to invest and store coins as value of their choice. Some may like yuan, some dollars, some bitcoins and some Shiba Inu. It will be their choice entirely.

---

1 Cryptography is a method of protecting information and communications through the use of codes so that only those intended to use the information can read and process it.

Some come with more risks—dogecoin being a good example, regardless of Elon Musk's backing— and some are more stable, which is why most people and countries like the US dollar. Why is the US dollar the world's main currency? Because the United States is the main superpower. That status only emerged in the twentieth century and, specifically, when we removed the gold standard and the Bretton Woods agreement.[2] The thing is, the world is now changing. Do we need a new agreement? Do we need a new currency standard? And if so, what would it be?

Some say it's bitcoin, but bitcoin is destroying the planet. For example, a 2022 report titled Revisiting Bitcoin's Carbon Footprint, conducted by climate and economic researchers across Europe, estimates that "bitcoin mining may be responsible for 65.4 megatons of CO_2 per year ... which is comparable to country-level emissions in Greece (56.6 megatons in 2019)."[3]

Furthermore, a paper produced by the Massachusetts Institute of Technology (MIT), a well-respected institution, states that "a single Bitcoin transaction uses the same amount of energy as a single US household does over the course of nearly a month."[4]

Meanwhile, others argue that this narrative is wrong: "bitcoin's climate footprint pales in comparison to the digital technology industry, representing only 2.3% of total emissions. Compared to the global banking and gold mining industries, bitcoin only consumes 40% as much energy as either."[5]

The MIT paper discusses the pros and cons of proof of work (PoW) versus PoS. Ethereum has moved to PoS and found that its energy usage reduced by 99 per cent immediately. The opening paragraph of the paper gives away the sentiment:

---

2   The Bretton Woods Agreement aimed to bring uniformity to global exchange rates by fixing the currencies of 44 countries against the value of the US dollar. In turn, the US dollar was pegged against the price of gold. For more information, see James Chen, "Bretton Woods Agreement and the Institutions It Created Explained," Investopedia, 21 March 2022, https://www.investopedia.com/terms/b/brettonwoodsagreement.asp.

3   Alex de Vries, Ulrich Gallersdörfer, Lena Klaaßen and Christian Stoll, "Revisiting Bitcoin's carbon footprint," Joule 6, no, 13 (March 2022): 498–502. https://www.sciencedirect.com/science/article/pii/S2542435122000861.

4   Amy Castor, "Ethereum moved to proof of stake. Why can't Bitcoin?" MIT Technology Review, 28 February 2023, https://www.technologyreview.com/2023/02/28/1069190/ethereum-moved-to-proof-of-stake-why-cant-bitcoin/.

5   Christopher Barnard and Graham Laseter, "No, Bitcoin is not destroying the planet," Washington Examiner, 10 December 2021, https://www.washingtonexaminer.com/opinion/no-bitcoin-is-not-destroying-the-planet.

Last year, Ethereum went green. The second-most-popular crypto platform transitioned to proof of stake, an energy-efficient framework for adding new blocks of transactions, NFTs, and other information to the blockchain. When Ethereum completed the upgrade, known as "the Merge," in September, it reduced its direct energy consumption by 99%. Meanwhile, Bitcoin continues to chug along, consuming as much energy as the entire country of the Philippines.[6]

So what was the Merge? The Merge was when Ethereum moved from PoW to PoS in September 2022. It was a major move, and sets Ethereum apart from most other crypto platforms.

It was known as the Merge because, for almost two years, a separate PoS blockchain, called the Beacon chain, whirred alongside the original Ethereum chain for developers to test, improve and test again. The key here is that it addresses mining issues related to the climate emergency. If you've heard of bitcoin being a climate destroyer, that's because PoW requires proving you've mined the coins; PoS doesn't. In short:

- PoW is a decentralised consensus mechanism that requires members of a network to expend effort solving an arbitrary mathematical puzzle to prevent anybody from gaming the system.
- PoW is used widely in cryptocurrency mining for validating transactions and mining new tokens.
- Due to PoW, bitcoin and other cryptocurrency transactions can be processed peer to peer in a secure manner without the need for a trusted third party.
- PoW at scale requires huge amounts of energy, which only increases as more miners join the network.
- PoS was one of several novel consensus mechanisms created as an alternative to PoW.
- With PoS, cryptocurrency owners validate block transactions based on the number of coins a validator stakes.

6   Amy Castor.

- PoS was created as an alternative to PoW, the original consensus mechanism used to validate a blockchain and add new blocks.
- PoS is seen as less risky in terms of the potential for an attack on the network, as it structures compensation in a way that makes an attack less advantageous.[7]

Needless to say, there is a major conflict between those who believe in PoW and those who believe in PoS. PoS requires those who validate blockchain blocks to have a stake in the game, with a minimum of 32 Ethereum (around $55,000). PoW only ensures that you invest in the compute power to mine a bitcoin which, in itself, is fairly complicated. The difference, therefore, is compute power versus the depth of your wallet. The former requires power usage and the latter does not. More importantly, a key here is that PoS requires a person or company to identify themselves versus PoW, which does not. In other words, a more centralised view versus a decentralised view, and the whole vision of bitcoin was to avoid any centralisation. The first line of Satoshi Nakamato's 2008 paper is that bitcoin would be "a purely peer-to-peer version of electronic cash [that] would allow online payments to be sent directly from one party to another without going through a financial institution".[8] Therefore, why would you want the system to be backed and validated by central authorities that *stake* their capital to back the network?

Can Bitcoin Be the Future Digital Currency?

Going back to that MIT paper, PoW is a huge issue due to the amount of compute power required to mine coins. As I've already said, the paper states that one bitcoin uses the same amount of energy that a US household uses over a month. Yet this is a highly debatable comment. The figure the paper quotes comes from the Digiconomist's Bitcoin Energy Consumption Index, which estimates that one bitcoin transaction takes 1,449 kWh to complete, or the equivalent of approximately 50 days of power for the average US

---

7 For more information, see Scott Nevil, "What Is Proof of Work (PoW) in Blockchain?" Investopedia, 27 May 2023, https://www.investopedia.com/terms/p/proof-work.asp.

8 Satoshi Nakamoto, "Bitcoin: A Peer-to-Peer Electronic Cash System," Bitcoin White Paper, November 2008, https://bitcoinwhitepaper.co/.

household.[9] To put that into money terms, the average cost per kWh in the United States is close to 12 cents.[10] That means a bitcoin transaction would generate an energy bill of $173.

And here's the fundamental point: a bitcoin *transaction* does not cost any energy compared to *mining* a coin. And, on top of this, *mining a coin* takes up a lot less energy than *running a centralised monetary system* with central banks, banks and affiliated institutions involved.

That is why there is a lot of contradictory research on this subject. For example, according to the Cambridge Centre for Alternative Finance (CCAF), bitcoin consumes around 110 terawatt hours per year—0.55 per cent of global electricity production—or roughly equivalent to the annual energy draw of countries like Malaysia or Sweden.[11] Similarly, Cambridge University's discussion of bitcoin basics makes this even clearer:

> The popular "energy cost per transaction" metric is regularly featured in the media and other academic studies despite having multiple issues … transaction throughput (i.e. the number of transactions that the system can process) is independent of the network's electricity consumption.[12]

Another very useful paper comes from the FIM Research Centre for Germany, which notes that:

> Today's PoW cryptocurrencies do, indeed, consume an amount of energy which may be regarded as disproportionate when compared to the currencies' actual utility. However, we also argue that the energy consumption associated with a widespread uptake of PoW cryptocurrencies is not likely to become a major threat to the climate in the future.[13]

---

9   Digiconomist, "Bitcoin Energy Consumption Index," https://digiconomist.net/bitcoin-energy-consumption.
10 U.S. Energy Information Association, "Electric Power Monthly," https://www.eia.gov/electricity/monthly/epm_table_grapher.php?t=epmt56a.
11 Cambridge Judge Business School, "Cambridge Bitcoin Electricity Consumption Index: Bitcoin network power demand," https://ccaf.io/cbnsi/cbeci.
12 Cambridge Judge Business School, "Cambridge Bitcoin Electricity Consumption Index: FAQ Bitcoin Basics," https://web.archive.org/web/20210504080905/https:/cbeci.org/faq/.
13 Johannes Sedlmeir, Hans Ulrich Buhl, Gilbert Fridgen and Robert Keller, "The Energy Consumption of Blockchain Technology: Beyond Myth," *Business & Information Systems Engineering 62* (June 2020): 599–608. https://link.springer.com/article/10.1007/s12599-020-00656-x.

Admittedly, it uses a lot of energy, but how much energy *should* a monetary system consume? That's a really good question that Nic Carter, a partner at Castle Island Ventures, a US venture firm investing in public blockchain start-ups, has tried to answer. He concludes:

> There are countless factors that can influence Bitcoin's environmental impact — but underlying all of them is a question that's much harder to answer with numbers: Is Bitcoin worth it? It's important to understand that many environmental concerns are exaggerated or based on flawed assumptions or misunderstandings of how the Bitcoin protocol works. That means that when we ask, "Is Bitcoin worth its environmental impact," the actual negative impact we're talking about is likely a lot less alarming than you might think.[14]

A key aspect here is to compare bitcoin with other assets, not countries, in its energy consumption. This puts things into far more context. Rather than saying bitcoin uses more energy than Denmark, why not say that bitcoin uses *far less* energy than banks?

Furthermore, research by ESG analyst and investor Daniel Batten has found that around 52.4 per cent of all bitcoin mining relies on renewable energy for its power needs, and this trend is expected to continue to grow in the coming years as traditional energy sources become more and more expensive.[15]

In other words, there are two extreme views. One is that bitcoin is destroying the planet because of its energy usage for mining; the other is that the issues bitcoin has created will be solved. Personally, I believe that the bitcoin PoW model is unsustainable. This view is supported by those in the banking industry who dismiss bitcoin as a speculative asset class, and not a currency of the future. To explain further:

1. **Governments do not recognise it as a currency** and, when you're dealing with money, 34 per cent of all transactions is tax—corporation tax, personal tax, value added tax, employment tax, national insurance

---

14 Nic Carter, "How Much Energy Does Bitcoin Actually Consume?" *Harvard Business Review*, 5 May 2021, https://hbr.org/2021/05/how-much-energy-does-bitcoin-actually-consume.
15 Daniel Batten, "Bitcoin by energy source," Batcoinz, 2023, https://batcoinz.com/bitcoin-by-energy-source/.

tax, etc. When a third of all payments are government taxes and governments do not recognise your currency, then it is not a valid token of exchange.

2. **It is not a store of value** as you cannot predict the price of a bitcoin due to the fact that its supply does not match demand. That is why it has such sudden drops in value, due to the supply and demand structure of bitcoin. There are, in other words, no monetary controls of the monetary supply. Unlike with US dollars, where the Treasury might regularly burn billions of dollars of physical notes to reduce supply when demand weakens, you cannot do that with bitcoin. This means that if I hold a dollar's worth of bitcoin today, I cannot guarantee that, in a year or two, it will still be worth a dollar. It might be worth $1,000 or it might be worth nothing. That is not a store of value and, to be a valid currency, you have to have certainty about its value in the future as a store of value.

That is why the future must be PoS, whereby everything is backed by something that has trust.

The Competition to Create a Global Currency

I often refer to Bob Diamond's quote about a future digital version of the dollar. While I am not a bitcoin fundamentalist or promoter, and believe it has far too many technical flaws today to ever be a reliable global currency, I do believe that there will be a global currency in the future.

A banker pulled me up on this at one of my recent presentations, saying that he was surprised that I was promoting the idea of a future global currency as no nation would recognise such a currency. Currencies—money—are all about government and the economies of nation states. For a global currency to take off, you would have to remove the walls of the nation states.

While I would argue that this point is true, the phenomenon is already happening whether nation states like it or not. The internet is global and the internet is demanding a global currency. The internet does not recognise nation-state borders and, as the network grows more and more pervasive through the IoT and mobile network, the internet is demanding that we create a global value transfer mechanism that is fast and free.

In theory, bitcoin offers that promise but, due to scalability and cost, does not make sense in its current form. However, there will be bitcoin 2.0, 3.0, 4.0 and more iterations, validations and corrections over the next decade, and eventually there will be a digital currency for Planet Earth. This digital currency may be tied to a basket of fiat currencies—the dollar, euro, yuan, yen and pound— and those fiat currencies may also become digitalised, so you would have a double digital currency. A currency of currencies. A currency recognised by the G20 as a valid cross-border exchange mechanism that can be taxed, even with a network that does not recognise nation states or borders.

This will be challenging but seems inevitable given the fact that the trend towards globalisation is unstoppable. We talked about globalisation a lot ten years ago as the BRICS[16] emerged, but that discussion seems to have died down since the global financial crisis hit. Everyone wants to retreat to nation states and domestic focus, as evidenced by the votes for Brexit and former US President Donald Trump. However, I think that globalisation is creeping upon us no matter how much we resist or ignore it. That is what our globalised network of digitalisation gives to us: a global platform for talking, trade and commerce. If you have a global platform for trade, then, inevitably, you have to a have a global currency to support such global trade.

One currency for Planet Earth also makes sense as we talk about becoming a multiplanetary species. It might not be a topic of conversation for you, but it certainly is for NASA, Elon Musk, Jeff Bezos and Sir Richard Branson. The agenda for building human life on other planets is well under way, with the colonisation of Mars planned by 2040. If we end up being a species living on a harmonised Planet Earth, then a currency for Planet Earth also makes sense. It makes sense, regardless of the dismissive views of nation-state bankers.

---

16 BRICS is the grouping of five emerging economies: Brazil, Russia, India, China and South Africa. In August 2023, the group announced the admission of six new countries in 2024: Iran, Saudi Arabia, Egypt, Argentina, the United Arab Emirates and Ethiopia.

DECENTRALISED VERSUS CENTRALISED

A global basket of digital currencies will become the norm. The question that is open to debate is which currencies will be in the global basket. Most likely it will be stablecoins based on a basket of dollar, euro and yuan CBDCs, combined with a mix of bitcoin, Ethereum and other choice cryptocurrencies.

The core of this discussion is what we value. If you are a believer in central governments, then you want CBDCs. However, not everyone wants to have the nanny state on their shoulder, telling them what and what not to do. People who fall into this category are libertarians, and they would far prefer a basket of cryptocurrencies. This sets out the stall of libertarians versus statists. It is a debate that has gone on for years and there is a constant friction between the two sides.

The challenge today is that the people have a weapon. The weapon is the internet. Those who understand the network, and know how to use its power, can fight against state controls. This covers everything from the dark web networks to using cryptocurrencies to encrypted apps to things you would never discuss with your family or friends. The network enables this. The question is whether it allows it?

The network does not recognise countries or country borders, so how can countries with borders control it? The network does not recognise regulations and rules, so who sets the rules and regulations? The network places power in the hands of the people, but do the people know how to use that power? With great power comes great responsibility—are the people responsible?

These questions have been bubbling in my mind for over a decade, ever since Satoshi Nakamoto's white paper that created bitcoin. Can we really create a world without intermediaries or centralised systems?

It's funny as this is one of the things I've been proven wrong about. Thirty years ago, as a wistful youth, I felt that there was no need for intermediation. Intermediation is a perennial discussion in the financial industry: why do we have banks and brokers? We don't need them if we can deal directly through the power of the people. If the internet allows us to harness the power of the people, then governments, banks and more are unnecessary. We can simply run the world like an Uber app or eBay, using star ratings for trust.

Unfortunately, it does not work that way in reality. In reality, we are happy to work without borders, controls, intermediation or government until things go wrong. When we lose our money, who do we turn to? If your bitcoin wallet breaks, who are you going to call?

This is why my contention is that decentralised finance (DeFi) will work fine for everyday transactions, such as day-to-day payments. On the other hand, higher value services and higher value transactions, such as loans or mortgages, will stay with the intermediated systems of banks, government and finance, or centralised finance (CeFi), because the size of risk and potential losses are too great.

This is where DeFi and CeFi work together in hybrid finance (HyFi). DeFi is for day-to-day small stuff; CeFi is for bigger and more complex things; and HyFi combines the power of the people with the power of a regulated system. It is not an either/or but an *and*. Decentralised finance where centralised governance is added when it matters. That's one view of the future.

The Balance between Control and Freedom

On the one hand, we want order and control; on the other, we don't want to be ordered or controlled. We want governance, but we don't want to be governed. We appreciate structure, but we don't want to have that structure tell us what to do. The issue is a basic one: how far can we place control in the hands of the citizen versus how much order do we need in society to avoid anarchy?

It is an age-old discussion that has come back to the fore due to where we are today with distributed networks. Specifically, when we talk about distributed data and distributed currencies. Thirty years ago, we sparked the idea that control could be distributed and decentralised, thanks to the creation of the internet. Thirty years later, we are living with the consequences. Thirty years ago, we started the idea that the media could be in the hands of the citizen; thirty years later, we are living with the idea of government, control, money and currency being in the hands of the citizen.

There are several key frictions you can see in the world today. First, who controls my data? Second, who controls my money? Third, who controls my freedom? More can be added to the list, but these are the three major concerns right now.

First, who controls my data? Thanks to the lack of oversight of government, data has become centralised in a few key players: Google (Alphabet), Facebook (Meta), Amazon, Baidu, Alibaba and Tencent. These are the Big Tech giants that have emerged in the last twenty-five years and have collated everything about my digital footprints online. There is now a huge argument against such Big Tech centralisation and a move towards decentralisation. After all, who should control my data? The answer is me!

Why should Big Tech firms have all of this information, and why do we share it with them? Well, doing so gives us benefits. These firms get to know us better and can therefore target us with more appropriate advertising and offers. Should they really have all of this information about us though? The movement towards decentralising such data is growing and is led by Tim Berners-Lee. Berners-Lee is working on the key idea of decentralising data so that it is owned by you through a project called Solid, in partnership with MIT.

Second, who controls my money? Governments control money as they run the economies of their nations. They license banks to control money on their behalf for these reasons and yet now, thanks to the network of the people, we can control our own money. We don't need to trust governments or banks to run the economy. We can run our own economy using cryptocurrencies.

Cryptocurrencies are run by the network of the people. It's a true democracy, and it is decentralised. That sounds great, but what happens when it goes wrong? When I have currency on the network that is lost, how do I get it back? Who can I call? What is Google's phone number?

Third, who controls my freedom? The answer is the people. You might have thought the answer would be the government, but the government represents the people. Interestingly, is the government the government of my nation or is it the government of the network? This is the biggest friction we have today as the network does not recognise borders or countries or governments. Can we create a world where we are all connected, and the only controls are those we create through our globally connected network?

The key is the balance between control and freedom. As I have already said, it is an age-old discussion, and the combination of smartphones and the internet seriously challenges the structure we have today and tomorrow. My view is that we will always want government and control to fall back on when things go wrong. The question then is: what government and what control?

I Lost Control (Again)

When a central banker says that the old system needs regenerating, then something obviously has gone wrong. Swiss Re's group chief economist Jerome Haegeli stated in an interview in August 2022 that "we are in a crisis" in "slow motion" thanks to food, energy and supply-chain shocks. "You need crisis times for the shift in the macro regime."[1]

By saying this, he was basically calling for a rethinking of economics and finance. A rethinking relating to everything from the call of Klaus Schwab, the founder of the World Economic Forum (WEF), for the "Great Reset" to many other economic pundits calling for change. Change will undoubtedly come; it's just a question of *what* change will come. Will it be an evolution of the existing world order (centralised) or a new world order (decentralised)?

I think it will be both. For example, what Haegeli was really getting at is that capital markets run the world but capital markets are becoming slow and expensive. Capital markets are also opaque. In parallel, DeFi is lower in cost, creates space for innovation and is transparent. Having said that, DeFi is also super risky and, longer term, will find a home with financial institutions. In other words, the traditional structure of finance with centralised oversight and

1   Michelle Jamrisko, "A 51-Year-Old Era of Global Economics May Be Dying a Slow Death," Bloomberg, 30 August 2022, https://www.bloomberg.com/news/articles/2022-08-30/a-51-year-old-era-of-global-economics-may-be-dying-a-slow-death.

intermediated exchange will remain. It just will be in a different form as you cannot have investment markets without investment oversight. When you think of all of the Ponzi schemes sold, the scams and phishers out there, the cybercriminal community, ransomware, romance fraud and more, you need someone to regulate and manage the system.

This is precisely why there is a system. You cannot have total decentralisation or total libertarianism—you need both freedom and controls. The extremes of this debate are clear to me, and they hit to the heart of finance, as finance controls what we do and how we behave. This is why the debate is at the core of what we do as we create a new world order. What is this new world order? What will it look like? How will it work?

It seems likely that we will have a world where many people will transact peer to peer using DeFi but, when it comes to the more difficult things like investing, wealth management and mortgages, people will look for centralised controls, or CeFi. In other words, the greater the risk of loss, the more control is required.

Leading on from this, can we automate the control? The DeFi community believes we can; the CeFi community believes we cannot. The whole dark web issue, where people can trade and transact in real time with zero controls, leads to anarchy, and nobody want anarchy. There has to be some control. The question is what control? It simply boils down to what type of control: government or the people?

THE CASE FOR DECENTRALISING CURRENCIES

As already discussed and defined, money is changing and changing fast. Some believe that the network of connected people, devices and things is the future; others, especially governments and central banks, need to ensure that money is centralised and controlled. Who will win is up for debate. The key question here is whether money can be unleashed on the network without governmental controls or whether only government currencies work.

Let's begin with the challenge that decentralised currencies create. As already mentioned, decentralised currencies, with intelligence, can be placed in our network of devices and the people who use them. There are no governmental borders or controls. Just the control of the network of the people.

Why Crypto Does and Doesn't Make Sense

The impact that cryptocurrencies have already had on traditional financial systems cannot be ignored even though these currencies are still in their infancy. For cryptocurrencies to become more widely used, they have to gain widespread acceptance—and greater traction— among consumers. Let's look at a specific example of the practicalities of using crypto, such as buying a small property using my crypto savings. Practically, this creates an interesting dilemma as the seller wants the money in his bank account, whereas I am trying to persuade him to sell through payment to a crypto wallet. He doesn't trust crypto wallets, and has never used them. So what's the problem?

After losing a good chunk of cash on the Mt. Gox crash of 2014, all of my cryptocurrency is now stored in a cold store on a regulated exchange for double protection. I didn't realise that the place where I was storing my funds would only allow a cash-out limit of $10,000 a day until I tried to withdraw those savings into hard cash. Therefore, to buy the property would involve making such a withdrawal every day for several weeks.

I am pretty sure that this would raise questions from the bank, government and others if they suddenly saw $10,000 going through my bank account every day. Then add that I would need to send the money through the international financial system to be converted from British pounds into euros, where major disparities of exchange rates and fees for international transfers would apply, and it just doesn't make sense.

I tried to explain this to the owner of the house and that if he had a crypto wallet, I could transfer the full amount straight away, in real time. There would be no fees for currency conversions and no one from the bank or government would be bothered about such a transfer. I received a quizzical look in response. Only afterwards did I realise that he thought I was a thief, a tax dodger and a completely untrustworthy person. I didn't bother trying to convince him otherwise, but it brought home to me the libertarian versus statist view of the world once more.

The fact that I could transfer thousands of dollars almost instantaneously across borders, without issue and in real time, is compelling. The idea of doing that through the traditional financial system, where I cash out to send money via a grinding old network that takes days to process, costs a fortune and punishes me for moving the funds across borders, just seems archaic.

However, many people simply do not trust crypto, such as my property vendor. First, they trust the old system because it is familiar and regulated. Second, they know that a bank has to be good for the money and can track and trace it. Third, they understand that if money is lost, the bank is liable for it.

While they may have heard of decentralised currencies like bitcoin, the headlines about such currencies have put them off. First, they see them as very complicated. Second, they hear about the crashes of Terra-LUNA and FTX, not to mention the hacks of bitcoin exchanges, and worry that they will lose out.

Again, it comes back to the main argument in this book: What do you believe in? What do you accept? What is money? What creates trust in value exchange? Does it require an intermediary? Who is that intermediary? The questions are long, and the answers are short. The answer is that money and value are purely what you believe in—until you stop believing in it.

Are you DeFi-ned?

Can DeFi replace CeFi? This tension is real. Can a world without borders on a global network replace the world with borders in a centralised network? It's hard to say, but it's fascinating to watch.

A CoinMarketCap paper in this space detailed the state of DeFi, and is very illuminating:

> [The vision is] to create a decentralized and trustless financial system built to be censorship-resistant and economically inclusive, while uncompromising on its capabilities and efficiency.[1]

Already, there are some interesting nuances here. "Trustless", meaning you can't have finance without trust? "Censorship-resistant" is bandied around so much but what does it mean? You cannot censor the network? You cannot regulate it? These questions are opposites of a centralised view that can be trusted and regulated.

Can DeFi really take off? Well, it is pretty obvious that some believe it can. For example, at its peak in December 2021, DeFi had garnered $247.96 billion in total value across multiple blockchain ecosystems and applications. However, and in the wake of all the macroeconomic uncertainties, geopolitical tensions, hacks, general market downturn and an increasingly bearish outlook, the DeFi space fell to a low of $67.46 billion in June 2022.

Is it now dead? Not really. For example, the paper by CoinMarketCap also discusses the $x*y=k$ constant product pool formula used by Uniswap, a decentralised cryptocurrency exchange that uses a set of smart contracts to execute trades:

---

1   CoinMarketCap and Spartan Labs, "State of the DeFi Industry Report," September 2022, https://coinmarketcap.com/alexandria/article/coinmarketcap-and-spartan-labs-state-of-the-defi-industry-report.

Uniswap V1's mission was simple, to provide an interface for users to seamlessly exchange ERC20 tokens on Ethereum. With its main focus on decentralisation, censorship resistance and security, it effectively enabled Uniswap to create a safe and secure way for users to trustlessly trade their digital assets without a centralized custodian.[2]

What is going on here is that coders, kids and developers are redesigning the financial system right before our eyes but, because most bankers, regulators and politicians are not coders, kids and developers, we have no idea what they are doing.

The Maker Protocol platform enabled anyone to generate DAI (the Maker Protocol coin), the first decentralised collateralised stablecoin collateralised against crypto assets such as ETH and BTC.[3]

So you now have a currency backed by cryptocurrency that can be traded with a trustless system, because it is back by the network. This means that it is censorship-resistant because the regulator has no role. In other words, it is the network that controls the currency.

What strikes me as I spend more and more time in this space is that the complexity of rebuilding finance for the networked, digital world is something that requires a massively renewed sense of tech and analytics that most people have little idea about. More importantly, most would not even care about what it entails, as long as it works.

So, the question is: do you leave the technologists to rebuild finance in a decentralised way that is censorship-resistant and trustless—in other words, where there is no centralised government or regulator—or do you get to grips with this space before the kids take over?

---

2   CoinMarketCap and Spartan Labs.
3   CoinMarketCap and Spartan Labs.

This Is Why Banks Are Moving into Cryptocurrencies

Banks have spent a decade saying how useless cryptocurrencies were, but their customers are now saying that they want them because they believe in them. This is why many banks such as JPMorgan Chase, Goldman Sachs, Morgan Stanley and Citibank are talking crypto for record keeping, as an asset and as a service, but not as a currency.

For example, a survey recently performed by Cornerstone Advisors found that:

- 15 per cent of US consumers own bitcoin or some other form of cryptocurrency
- 60 per cent of crypto owners would use their bank to invest in cryptocurrencies
- 68 per cent of crypto owners are very interested in bitcoin-based debit or credit card rewards

However, "eight in 10 financial institutions have no interest in offering cryptocurrency investing services to their customers—and just 2% said they were very interested."[4]

Bear in mind that Satoshi Nakamoto's white paper on bitcoin dates back to November 2008 and I just wonder where we are going with this. It's like looking back at Tim Berners-Lee's ideas of a worldwide web. His paper was published in March 1989 and laid the groundwork for today's internet. So, imagine you're in 2002, thirteen years after that paper was issued, and there's just been an internet boom and bust. People thought firms like Amazon would be trashed and the internet was just a fad. Twenty years later, we all just wish we had had a slice of that business. This is where we are right now with crypto. Trash it at your peril.

---

4   Cornerstone Advisors, "What's Going On In Banking 2021: Rebounding from the Pandemic," https://www.crnrstone.com/banking-2021.

A Shareholder Letter Sent to Amazon's Executive Chairman Jeff Bezos

March 5. 2021

Mr. Jeff Bezos
Executive Chairman
Amazon.com. Inc.
410 Terry Avenue North
Seattle, WA 98109

Dear Mr. Bezos,

Thanks for making Amazon a great company! We thought you would like to know how it has benefited our family.

Back in 1997 when you made Amazon public, our son, Ryan, was 12 years old and a voracious reader. For his birthday, , 1997, we bought two shares of your new book selling company, which was all we could afford at the time. Within a year or so, the shares split 2 for 1, then 3 for 1, then 2 for 1 again, giving him 24 shares. The shares were in our names because of his age. We meant to put it in custody for him but we never got around to it but he knew they were for him.

Several times over the years, Ryan would want to cash in the stock but we always said we would "buy" it from him and then eventually turn around and give it back to him as a "gift". It was kind of a running joke in the family.

Due to the exponential growth in value, we decided to split the stock between ourselves and both of our children, Ryan and Katy.

This year Ryan is buying a house and would like to sell some shares. After searching for the original certificates, we needed to convert the paper shares into digital before selling them. We noticed that the first share certificate was a very low number, issue #   . I can't image how many more shares have been issued since that date!

Included is a copy of the   :h certificate of Amazon on   , 1997 - 24 years ago. Those two shares have had a wonderful influence on our family. We all enjoyed watching Amazon value grow year after year and it's a story we love to tell others.

Congratulations on a great career as CEO of Amazon. We can't even imagine how hard you and your team have worked to make Amazon the most successful and inventive company on the planet. Now may you have time to relax and catch up on things you want to do, like space exploration!

We cannot wait to see where Amazon delivers next! Next Day to Mars!

Sincerely,

Mary   and Larry

Mary   and Larry

P.S. We wished we had bought 10 shares!

Just as many bankers never imagined the idea that we would be able to fly a helicopter from a spaceship on another planet 300 million miles away—we just did that on Mars—they never imagined that people would want to break away from the traditional financial system, but they do. They demonstrably do. And they are. They demonstrably are. Dogecoin, Coinbase, bitcoin, Ethereum and more demonstrably show this. The death of cash and branch demonstrably show this. GameStop and eToro demonstrably show this. Stripe, Square, Adyen and Klarna demonstrably show this. COVID19 turbo-charged this.

All of these demonstrate clearly the seismic shift from industrial to digital. It is why central banks are clambering to launch CBDCs and why they are asking themselves what things banks should do.

The indifference of banks towards the digital natives and the digital world will ultimately lead to a new world order of the banks that do understand the needs of the digital natives and the digital world. It does not mean that banks will be disrupted, destroyed or disintermediated. It just means that banks built for digital needs will acquire the customers of banks that are not.

The Need for Money to Decentralise

The old world structures reject cryptocurrencies whilst the new world structures accept them en masse. Take Gen Z and the fact that many of them have invested heavily in cryptocurrencies.

> [...] a survey by financial group Charles Schwab found that 51% of UK investors under 37 now trade cryptocurrencies, double the 25% of whom that buy or hold equities; while a report by the UK regulator FCA found that new crypto investors in the last year "tend to skew more towards being female, under 40 and from a BAME background".[5]

I have had several people from countries that are blocked from crypto approach me to buy bitcoin, Ethereum, XRP and more for them, and often they are female. For some reason, they trust me. And there's the key point once again: trust. Someone once told me that bitcoin "is just a Ponzi scheme". I replied that the US dollar is also just a Ponzi scheme, if you think of it that way.

Think about it. Why do you believe that piece of paper in your hand has value? Let's say it's a $50 note that you are holding. Why is it worth $50? It's just a piece of paper. If the US government were to announce that, from tomorrow, all $50 would no longer have any value, you would then realise that it's actually just a piece of paper. It has zero value. Its only value is what you and the merchant believe it's worth. It's just a construct.

---

5   Isabella Pojuner, "Gen Z ride into "Wild West" of cryptocurrency amid recession," Sifted, 26 April 2021, https://sifted.eu/articles/cryptocurrency-gen-z.

The US dollar only has meaning because we believe that the United States has a strong and stable currency, backed by the US government. Before that construct, we believed that the world was tied to the gold standard. Before that, it used to be the king. It used to be the pharaoh. We only believe in the constructs of our society, our world, our governments and our financial institutions for as long as we believe in them. I have said for many years that countries don't exist, companies don't exist and governments don't exist. We just created them.

In the past, people cut up and carved the world into countries with borders, with little ability to travel across those borders and, if you did, you would find a whole new world of language, commerce and currency. Networking is removing the world of countries and borders. The network is taking over. Today, we can connect with anyone, anywhere, anytime; we all speak the same language—basic English; and we can all transact using the network of currencies. This last point is a critical one.

The whole complex structure of banking was created for cross-border transacting between countries with trust. It is a complex structure due to the very nature of physical borders and country rules. SWIFT exists to overcome this, as do Mastercard and Visa, but we now have a whole new construct being developed: the networked economy. In the networked economy, no one cares about countries, borders and governments. They care about ease of transacting, ease of work, ease of dealing with each other and ease of moving through the network.

Banks were created to overcome the difficulties of moving around the global network of physical entities. Can they evolve to deal with the global network of digital entities? Based on what we are seeing with cryptocurrencies, probably not. I guess that then brings us to the hardest question: can governments evolve to deal with a global network of digital entities?

What's Worth More: Army Coin or Swiftycoin?

We teach our children to read and write. It's a priority. Why don't we teach them to understand money? Surely financial literacy is as important as basic literacy? Some people get this, and some people don't. I woke up to this realisation big time after reading a few articles. For example, Claer Barrett made a valid observation about her young niece in the *Financial Times*:

> I am all for giving children early exposure to money and payments, but what worries me is the invisibility of digital transactions versus the physicality of notes and coins. Do children realise that actual money is being spent, or think this "magic card" simply makes everything possible?[6]

When banking is invisible, do people realise that they are actually spending real money? If physical notes and coins have gone, do you know you are transacting real cash? I'm sure, as an adult, that we understand this but what about kids?

---

6   Claer Barrett, "Vanishing cash means 'digital literacy' is vital," *Financial Times*, 2 December 2021, https://www.ft.com/content/495c5b53-f39b-47cd-9402-f2ac58a2dd78.

A dad says he was stunned when his 11-year-old daughter unknowingly ran up a £4,500 bill on a gaming app. Steve Cumming initially gave the schoolgirl permission to spend £4.99 for the game, called Roblox, on his debit card. It was only when he checked his balance months later after setting up internet banking that he saw hundreds of transactions ... his daughter thought she was spending monopoly money on the game and was shocked to find out what happened.[7]

This is not an uncommon experience and begs the question: how are we educating our children about money? Do they know it is the controlling factor in our lives? How should we teach them?

> Singapore's financial regulator has reportedly suspended Bitget, a crypto exchange that is mired in a row involving South Korea's biggest boyband, BTS ... after it got into a high-profile dispute for promoting the digital currency Army Coin, which is named after the band's followers, who are known as the BTS army.[8]

When I was a teen, I was fanatical about David Bowie. If there had been a Bowiecoin, would I have invested? Damn right I would have. In fact, I would have spent every penny I could scrape together buying Bowiecoin. Thank goodness it was not around back then. The thing is that it is around today. What do our kids know? Do they understand that Army Coins are just a creation? What's worth more: Army Coin or Swiftycoin?

In another article in the *Financial Times*, journalist-turned-teacher Lucy Kellaway lamented that her class thinks money is a game too, namely, a cryptocurrency game.

> "I'm up over £100 in one day, bitches!" a boy in the centre crows. Others proclaim their gains in a conversation peppered with the words shiba inu, dogecoin and Elon Musk. Their form tutor, a recent history graduate,

7   Dave Burke, "Horrified dad finds £4,642 gaming app bill having let daughter spend £4.99," *Daily Mirror*, 4 July 2020, https://www.mirror.co.uk/news/uk-news/horrified-dad-finds-4642-gaming-22300564.
8   Vincent Ni, "Singapore suspends crypto exchange over row with K-pop band BTS," *Guardian*, 5 December 2021, https://www.theguardian.com/technology/2021/dec/05/singapore-suspends-crypto-exchange-row-k-pop-bts-bitget.

looks on with a growing sense of unease. "Isn't trading cryptocurrencies just like gambling?" she asks them. [...] The student in the middle gives her a scornful look. "Nah Miss," he says. "It's investing."[9]

Someone asked me to explain the difference between gambling and investing, and there is little difference to be honest. The value of an investment may go down as well as up and you may not get back the money you invested. It should not be assumed that the value of investments always rises. You should ensure that you have the financial capacity to bear the risk and only invest an amount you are willing to lose.

In other words, investing is gambling. That's why we call it casino capitalism. But what does this mean for our kids, who don't even know that money exists? After all, it's just a tap, a click, an invisible thing. If I trade an invisible thing, then it's like magic, isn't it? And magic is just something that has been made up—an illusion. And an illusion is something that doesn't exist, does it?

Cryptocurrencies Are Hard to Use

Another justification for decentralised currencies to be fee-free and immediate is because the traditional banking system is full of overheads. By way of example, my bank received a refund from a retailer but, due to the account being in British pounds and the retailer trading in Polish złoty, the refund lost a lot of value. Over £170 to be exact on a purchase that was over £2,500. Sure, the £170 was a mixture of exchange rate costs and fees, but a straight reversal of a transaction should not have incurred such costs and punitive rates. It immediately made me think of buying any future purchases with bitcoin, as this would incur zero fees. Or would it?

I do most of my trading via Coinbase, and it charges fees. In fact, it charges up to 5 per cent if you take on board all charges, although the average commission is 1.49 per cent. Coinbase is one of the oldest and largest regulated exchanges out there, and one of the first crypto exchanges to go for an initial public offering (IPO). Its valuation shot to $85 billion on its first day of trading,

9   Lucy Kellaway, "Crypto in the classroom: Lucy Kellaway on the kids' new craze," *Financial Times*, 18 November 2021, https://www.ft.com/content/6ff0f503-f20b-45d5-b2d3-7f93da184e8c.

as the share price rose to over $329 per share. It's easy to use and simple to deal with, and offers financial insurance schemes on trading, unlike many unregulated exchanges.

There are a lot of exchanges out there, and working out which is best for you is not easy. There are also a lot of sites that look into them all, and give advice as to which you should use. Yet these sites often only look through a narrow lens.

Generally, rising to the top alongside Coinbase is eToro. Originally a site for social trading, it has expanded over the years, and now offers crypto trading as well as traditional stock and equities trading. If you are into crypto, the costs are negligible—eToro charges no fees for sending or receiving transactions—but it does charge a conversion fee of 0.1 per cent, which is set to market rates. Binance is popular, particularly with US traders, because it is also low cost. In general, fees are 0.1 per cent on spot trading and 0.5 per cent to buy or sell. The list goes on.

I have to admit though that all of these services are not as easy to use as some claim. Nevertheless, you need to consider why and what you are buying cryptocurrencies for: to hold (hodl) or to use. Use? Who uses crypto? Well, I do. In fact, I used the Binance app to buy a Watford football shirt and similarly used Coinbase to buy an Ethereum domain.

Crypto: Tax It, Regulate It, Subsidise It

Even if cryptocurrencies could be used easily, you have to come back to what it is being used for. If it is for payments, savings and investments, then you need to consider a quote from former US President Ronald Reagan: "If it moves, tax it. If it keeps moving, regulate it. And if it stops moving, subsidize it."

Reagan said this in the 1980s when referring to the government's view of the economy, but let's apply it to cryptocurrencies today. Initially irrelevant but now mainstream, many banks are incorporating cryptocurrencies into their portfolio of services. From custodial services at State Street to trading with JPMorgan to paying by crypto with Revolut and Stripe, the digital coin world has grown rapidly and become mainstream. Or is it? Crypto is not an overnight success. It's been a fifteen-year burner that exploded in 2020 thanks to the pandemic. During the pandemic, the largest currencies, namely, bitcoin and Ethereum, exploded with rises of over 600 per cent.[10]

Some would claim that there was a direct correlation between Covid, lockdowns and crypto purchases, although it has not been proven. What is proven is that a wild and wacky idea of creating a digital currency that could be traded globally governed by the network and not by a government has come true.

If It Moves, Tax It

This is the reason why so many governments have tried to ban trading in digital currencies and digital exchanges in recent times. They can see it going mainstream. More importantly, they want to tax it. For example, I received an email from Coinbase in January 2022:

> We're writing to let you know about a notice HM Revenue and Customs (HMRC) issued to Coinbase under Paragraph 1, Schedule 23 to the Finance Act 2011. This notice requires us to provide information on your Coinbase account to HMRC.

> The notice requires the disclosure of customers with a UK address who received payments of more than £5,000 in fiat currency out of electronic stored value payment services provided by CB Payments LTD during the 2019 and 2020 tax years.

The same is true in most economies. Some governments have banned bitcoin, or are trying to, or think they can, whilst governments are asking central banks to create their own coins, or CBDCs. Neat. Or is it?

If It Keeps Moving, Regulate It

What governments want to do is tax and regulate cryptocurrencies, and replace rogue currencies with their own. It's a great idea but is it workable?

---

10   Hadar Y. Jabotinsky and Roee Sarel, "How the Covid-19 Pandemic Affected the Cryptocurrency Market," CLS Blue Sky Blog, 26 March 2021, https://clsbluesky.law.columbia.edu/2021/03/26/how-the-covid-19-pandemic-affected-the-cryptocurrency-market/.

Perhaps. After all, investing in cryptocurrencies today is pretty speculative and, as most government representatives underline time after time, if you invest in such currencies, be prepared to lose all of your money. But then they would say that, wouldn't they?

Nevertheless, I agree with the notion that a regulated cryptocurrency system is a safer system. Instead of losing money to hacks or CEOs who die with their passwords, you would have a system you could trust. That's what all monetary systems come down to: trust. After all, if things fail, you want some way to get things back to normal.

If It Stops Moving, Subsidise It

If cryptocoins fail, how do you get your money back? You don't, unless it is regulated. That's the point. Gradually, governments will tax and regulate any crypto market, and form the hybrid system of finance that is both centralised and decentralised. There will still be those who will try to avoid such government actions, who trust the network and who do well outside the system. However, when they lose everything, they will be spitting feathers, wondering why they didn't put their money in a system that was insured.

The Wild West of Crypto

The year 2022 proved a testing year for everyone, but particularly for those in the cryptocurrency space. The Wild West of crypto is completely decentralised with no regulations. It needs governance which, as stated earlier, could be the government of the people through the network of citizens but seems more likely to be through a *regulated* exchange that is *approved* for trading by a national government.

This is because trillions of dollars of people's savings are being traded in this space, a space that is full of scams and jokers, and where there is no way of recovering lost funds. That's something I learnt years ago with Mt. Gox when I lost a small amount of bitcoin (although today that small amount would have been a large amount). Since then, as I have watched the Wild West of crypto, I have seen more and more of these sucker scams, scams that give the crypto world a bad name.

There was the story of the CEO and founder of Quadriga, a crypto exchange in Canada, who died whilst travelling overseas. As the only person who knew the exchange's password, it meant that all traders and investors were blocked and lost their funds. Next, there was the story of Ruja Ignatova, the self-named cryptoqueen, who raised billions in her digital currency OneCoin—and then disappeared. Then there was the BitClub Network that allegedly scammed people out of over $700 million, only for it to turn out to be a pyramid scheme.

Here is the core point that I keep returning to: you need trusted intermediaries to allow people who don't trust each other to trade, and that is what banking does. Banks exist as regulated and licenced institutions to ensure you can trust them to transfer funds without losing them. That's it, folks. That's what it's all about, and crypto is learning this, just as every FinTech has. Banks exist for a reason, are regulated the way they are for a reason and operate the way they do for a reason. And that reason is all about trust.

This means, for me, that cryptocurrencies—whether bitcoin, Ethereum or anything else—are emerging into a regulated world of exchanges and institutions that have licenses and operate much in the same way as banks. Unfortunately, due to a lack of regulations, the mistakes made by Mt. Gox, Quadriga and the BitClub Network were repeated by others in 2022.

The Rocky Road of Cryptocurrencies

As I have just said, 2022 was a particularly bad year for the cryptocurrency world. In this one year alone, several major cryptocurrencies and their exchanges collapsed, including Terra-LUNA, Celsius and FTX, losing investors billions of savings and reinforcing the image of the Wild West of crypto. The key spark that ignited this implosion was the failure of Terra-LUNA in May 2022.

Terra-LUNA was meant to be a stablecoin. Stablecoins are backed by real assets, such as real US dollars, and are therefore meant to be much more, well, stable. How did Terra become unstable? More importantly, having peaked at $120 per coin in April 2022, how could it lose 98 per cent of its value in under 24 hours the following month?

Basically, because there was a downturn in all cryptocurrencies during April and May 2022 but, more importantly, because Terra-LUNA was not the same as other stablecoins, which are backed by real assets. Terra-LUNA was issued as an *algorithmic stablecoin*. This means that it used blockchain technology to print money using smart contracts, similar to the way Ethereum's smart contracts work. The aim of the algorithm was to ensure that Terra-LUNA's value remained at $1 per coin.

The thing is that the smart contracts could only be executed whilst the currency had the belief of investors, and investors started withdrawing funds. The knock-on effect was that the algorithm could no longer execute contracts to maintain parity with the US dollar, and the price dropped to 70 cents and then 20 cents. In other words, the more people withdrew funds, the harder it became for the algorithms to keep the coin stable.

The stabiliser at this point was meant to be the Luna token. When Terra-LUNA dipped below $1, it could be swapped for Luna tokens (at a small profit). In theory, that was meant to keep the value of both stable. The issue was that people lost faith in Luna tokens at the same time that investors were withdrawing money from Terra-LUNA. As a result, the price of the "sister" token dropped from about $86 at the start of the week to just $0.003 on Friday 13 May. This meant that Luna crashed at the same time as Terra-LUNA in a death spiral. Essentially, investors rushed to liquidate their digital assets quicker than the "algorithmic stabiliser" could deal with.

This immediately raised questions amongst crypto watchers. Specifically, how could a cryptocurrency using the technologies that are meant to create stability drop from a market cap of $40 billion to $500 million overnight and, if that is the case, could that happen to bitcoin and others? Is this market just a massive Ponzi scheme or does it have substance?

Within the financial community, I am sure many will be sitting with smug smiles on their faces. The Germans call it *Schadenfreude*. I call it a sucker punch for those who do not investigate the markets well, and do not understand the risks. If you invested your life savings in a system you do not understand, it is no wonder you lost that money. Equally, why are you investing your life savings in something you don't understand? Markets have risk. They go up and down. Only invest what you are prepared to lose. That's something the financiers understand well.

Does this mean a flight to safety, the rise of CBDCs and the end of bitcoin and other cryptocurrencies? No. It is just another bump on the rocky road to creating DeFi. Many have never experienced these bumps, but they occur often. The website 99bitcoins.com tracks the media predictions of its expected doom, and there have been many since 2010. Yet the idea still lives. Why? Because there is a friction between national government-issued coins and networked coins. It is quite hard to send cash over the internet and, with the four-pillar model of cards or the percentage-plus costs of intermediaries, it makes absolute sense to try to move to a networked system that is fast and free. That is what DeFi is trying to achieve.

I am very aware of the faults and virtues of both systems—fiat currencies and cryptocurrencies—and believe the endgame will be a hybrid model of CBDCs, stablecoins and cryptocurrencies. The issue with Terra-LUNA was not the structural faults of such systems; it was the structural faults of Terra-LUNA and the fact that too many people believe that these currencies are all about hodling (keeping them as an investment) instead of what currencies are really about, which is allowing the exchange of value to buy and sell products and services.

That is where the real fault lies, and it is nothing to do with a Ponzi scheme. It is all about creating currencies that work for value exchange in a networked world. The issue is that there are so many examples of decentralised currencies and systems that have failed. Terra-LUNA is just one, and was quickly followed by Celsius Network and then FTX.

The Failure of Celsius Network

In 2017, Alex and Krissy Mashinsky, a husband and wife team, created Celsius Network. Celsius came to my attention when Simon Dixon, a crypto friend who focuses on this space, started regularly tweeting about them. This is because he got wrapped up in this platform as a significant Celsius investor.

Simon Dixon, CEO of prominent Celsius investor BnkToTheFuture, said this morning that he secured up to $6 billion in investor liquidity to solve Celsius' liquidity woes — only to watch the deal fall apart after Celsius refused to show its financial records to potential investors [...] "The only reason you wouldn't pursue [a lucrative round of investment] is there's something else going on," Dixon opined.[11]

Dixon was right, but then he does know what he is talking about. As a former investment banker, he has spent the last decade being committed to talking crypto, and has become a wise voice in this desert. So when he started highlighting something dodgy in the Celsius network, what exactly happened?

It all arose with the crypto crash of 2022. Prices for bitcoin and company were down over three quarters during 2022 compared to 2021. As an increasing number of investors sold their holdings, the exchanges they used came under stress, and several restricted withdrawal of funds. Celsius hit the headlines when it *stopped* crypto withdrawals, swaps and transfers between accounts on its platform altogether in June 2022 due to the extreme market conditions. "We are taking this action to put Celsius in a better position to honor, over time, its withdrawal obligations," the firm wrote in a blog post.[12]

As a key investor, Dixon tried to pull a rabbit out of the hat. However, the CEO, Alex Mashinsky, refused to provide any insight into the company's accounts and so the rabbit jumped. This created many questions and, within a few weeks, the company filed for bankruptcy protection. The company admitted it had a $1.2 billion hole in its balance sheet, making it one of the highest profile casualties of the crash in crypto markets.

At the time, it was reported that the company had around 300,000 investors, with over $20 billion in crypto assets on the platform. Since then, there has been an on-going argument as to what money lies where and with whom. Celsius is not alone. Other exchanges, like Voyager Digital, also froze customer accounts and a few of these, including Voyager Digital, have since declared bankruptcy.

---

11 Jack Kubinec, "Celsius Lost Potential $6B Bailout After Refusing To Show Financials, Investor Says," Blockworks, 12 July 2022, https://blockworks.co/news/celsius-lost-potential-6b-bailout-after-refusing-to-show-financials-investor-says.
12 "A Memo to the Celsius Community," Celsius [blog], 13 June 2022, https://celsiusnetwork.medium.com/a-memo-to-the-celsius-community-59532a06ecc6.

Celsius's issues became clear when the "stablecoin" Terra-LUNA failed, wiping out $40 billion worth of market value and dragging down the price of bitcoin. Celsius lost almost $16 million from its investments in Terra-LUNA, but had also lent to companies like the now bankrupt hedge fund Three Arrows Capital ($75 million), according to bankruptcy filings.

Add this to the failure of many other cryptocurrency ventures and it is no wonder that I call cryptocurrencies a Wild West. That's why I agree with Dixon who demands a better regulatory structure in the space.

But why is Celsius so controversial? First, it is accused of being a Ponzi scheme. For at least two years before its collapse, the cryptocurrency lender operated what could resemble a Ponzi scheme, the Vermont Department of Financial Regulation alleged in a court filing. The filing accused Celsius of running on fumes long before the crypto winter and "kept its massive losses, asset deficit, and deteriorating financial condition secret from investors".[13]

Second, the filing went further and accused the company of using its native token, CEL, to prop up the balance sheet. The filing then added another nail in the coffin, stating that Alex Mashinsky repeatedly announced that the firm had robust health even as it was booking "catastrophic losses".

Celsius Network co-founder and CEO Alex Mashinsky speaking at the Web Summit 2021

---

13 Andrew Smith, "The U.S. Regulator Alleges Celsius for Misleading Investors," Coin Republic, 13 September 2022, https://www.thecoinrepublic.com/2022/09/13/the-u-s-regulator-alleges-celsius-for-misleading-investors/.

FTX? Short for FinTech eXplosion

In November 2022, cryptocurrency exchange FTX collapsed over a period of ten days. This came as a major shock as the founder of FTX, Sam Bankman-Fried, had been the poster boy of cryptocurrencies, appearing on the front page of leading magazines like *Forbes* and *Time*, and considered a golden child by most media and followers. After all, he had built a company supposedly worth $32 billion by January 2022 at the young age of thirty, and was lauded as one of the wealthiest young entrepreneurs in the world.

However, it turns out that the glowing external image hid a bad management structure inside. FTX had a fund run by Alameda Research, and it later emerged that much of the FTX investments were being used by Alameda to make the company's investments look good. In other words, a Ponzi scheme.

When these rumours came to light, customers started withdrawing funds rapidly. A little like a run on the bank, there was a run on the exchange and FTX suddenly found itself in the middle of leverage and solvency concerns. In other words, it could not cash in its currencies fast enough to meet the demands for payment from its customers, thus leading to its collapse.

Bankman-Fried tried to negotiate a bailout by rival Binance that quickly fell through. He was soon arrested on charges of fraud, extradited to the United States and released on a $250 million bond, which was then revoked in August 2023 amid witness tampering allegations. At the beginning of November 2023, he was found guilty of fraud and money laundering after a month-long trial.

The *Financial Times* commented on the collapse of FTX, and made the statement that you should never let a good crisis go to waste.

A near-existential disaster seems to have hit the cryptosphere: FTX, a big exchange that enjoyed a $32 billion valuation in January, has collapsed with an $8 billion hole. FTX's founder, Sam Bankman-Fried — hitherto crypto's friendly face — is mired in allegations that his firm misplaced or misused client money. Confidence in the wider crypto market — its stock-in-trade — has been badly hit, with bitcoin tumbling in value. The time for politicians, policymakers and regulators to put protections in place is now.[14]

Another Day, Another Crash

I stumbled across a discussion about Nomad, a cross-chain bridge, that had just had almost $200 million of crypto assets hacked:

> The cross-chain token bridge Nomad was exploited, with attackers draining the protocol of virtually all of its funds. The total value of cryptocurrency lost to the attack totalled near $200 million. Nomad, like other cross-chain bridges, allows users to send and receive tokens between different blockchains. Monday's attack is the latest in a string of highly-publicized incidents which have drawn the security of cross-chain bridges into question.[15]

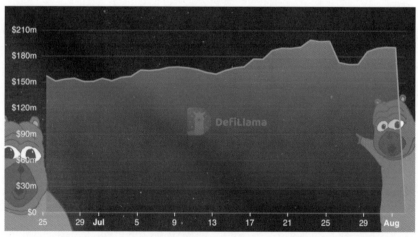

The Fall of Nomad

You may be wondering what they are talking about. Starting with the basics, Nomad describes itself as "a cross-chain communication standard that

14 *Financial Times*, "FTX's collapse underscores the need for regulating crypto," 23 November 2022, https://www.ft.com/content/c3e58d27-0a77-479f-bf52-b492efebc72f.

15 Sam Kessler and Brandy Betz, "Crypto Bridge Nomad Drained of Nearly $200M in Exploit," Coindesk, 2 August 2022, https://www.coindesk.com/tech/2022/08/02/nomad-bridge-drained-of-nearly-200-million-in-exploit/.

enables cheap and secure transfers of tokens and data between chains".[16] The key to this is that a cross-chain bridge allows interoperability between different blockchains and blockchain tokens. It is like a foreign exchange service but, in this case, it allows the exchange of information, cryptocurrency or non-fungible tokens (NFTs) from one blockchain network to another. It enables the flow of data and tokens across what would otherwise be siloed sets of data on different blockchains.

In particular, a key characteristic of a cross-chain bridge is that it enables users to exchange one cryptocurrency for another without having to change it into fiat currencies first. For example, bitcoin and Ethereum are the two largest cryptocurrency networks and have vastly different rules and protocols. Through a blockchain bridge, bitcoin users can transfer their coins to Ethereum and do with them what they otherwise could not do on the bitcoin blockchain. This can include purchasing various Ethereum tokens or making low-fee payments.

The problem with this is that this just reinforces the Wild West of crypto, following the collapse of Celsius Network and FTX. The thing is, when I delved deeper, it turns out that Nomad appeared to have done something really, really stupid. The platform had messed up a routine upgrade, and set the exchange of token contracts to a trusted root file identifier that started with 0x00. This meant that anyone could send a request to exchange tokens with an identifier starting with 0x00 and it would be accepted. As Sir Jon Cunliffe, Deputy Governor for Financial Stability at the Bank of England, stated: "unbacked cryptoassets are highly volatile, given that they have no intrinsic value."[17]

This is what the traditional financial system has always maintained, with central bankers claiming that you can lose all of your money if you place it into decentralised financial systems, and that these systems have no backing or value. But what is the banking and value of centralised systems? The belief in a central bank currency and government-issued currency? Either why, I've always maintained that *you cannot have money without governance.*

---

16 Nomad, https://app.nomad.xyz/.
17 "Reflections on DeFi, digital currencies and regulation," a speech by Sir Jon Cunliffe given at Warwick Business School's Gilmore Centre Policy Forum Conference, November 2022, https://www.bankofengland.co.uk/speech/2022/november/jon-cunliffe-keynote-speech-and-panel-at-warwick-conference-on-defi-digital-currencies.

"Cryptocurrencies combine everything you don't understand about money with everything you don't understand about computers."

John Oliver, comedian, writer, producer, political commentator, actor and TV host

Caveat emptor.

The Crypto House of Cards

The combined impact of Terra-LUNA, Celsius, FTX, Nomad and more crashing in 2022 has had everyone asking whether the house of crypto is falling apart like a house of cards. According to Wikipedia:

House of cards is an expression that dates back to 1645 meaning a structure or argument built on a shaky foundation or one that will collapse if a necessary, but possibly overlooked or unappreciated, element is removed.

In particular, following the collapse of FTX, critics are accusing cryptocurrencies of being Ponzi schemes where the funds of new investors are given to existing investors as profit. So how can cryptocurrencies be frauds?

Well, let's get back to basics. The core of all financial markets is belief. The more people who believe in the value of something, the more valuable that something becomes. A good example are diamonds. Diamonds actually have zero value but clever marketing has made us believe that they are desirable and highly valuable commodities. So things are only valuable if you *believe* they are valuable, which brings us back to crypto.

When Terra-LUNA collapsed in May 2022, a house of cards began to fall. The first knock-on effect was Celsius, a now bankrupt cryptocurrency lending company. Then we had the FinTech explosion caused by FTX, a now bankrupt cryptocurrency exchange. A fourth major cryptocurrency lending company, Genesis, quickly followed FTX early in the following year.

Consequently, people are wondering if this marks the end of cryptocurrency and bitcoin but, as the *Economist* points out:

To take out crypto entirely would require killing the underlying blockchain layers. They could either give way first, kicking the stool out from underneath everything else. Or the industry could unravel from the top down, layer by layer like a knitted scarf.[18]

What's happening at the moment is the unravelling of the froth on top of blockchain structures, which have foundations in bitcoin and Ethereum. However, those foundations have some very useful basics and use cases, such as the use of smart contracts and decentralised finance. Therefore, for me, the idea that the whole house of cards could unravel is not feasible. Nevertheless, the belief in cryptocurrencies has taken a big knock due to the unravelling of the froth on top: Terra-LUNA, Celsius, FTX and Genesis.

As US Senator Elizabeth Warren said, "with Bitcoin, there's nothing that backs it up [...] It's just belief." This is where her argument fails, however. She believes that the belief is in a government-backed coin, not just one that is made up. The thing is that bitcoin, and cryptocurrency in general, is made up by the people, for the people, and not by the government, for the government. This is the core of the argument. What back-up does the US dollar have over bitcoin? The belief of the people. But if more people believe in bitcoin than the US dollar, what does the CBDC have as its advantage?

Going back to the Ponzi reference, a Ponzi scheme is only a Ponzi scheme if you are using customer funds to re-invest in pumping the value of your fund. That's the mistake that both Sam Bankman-Fried and Do Kwon, the co-founder of Terra-LUNA, made.

"Whenever you have a business that fails, as the facts emerge, there are typically lessons learned that can inform other companies in that industry, as well as the broader public, about where risks lie and how similar risks could be avoided in the future," Deborah Meshulam, a partner at D.L.A. Piper and a former official with the Securities and Exchange Commission, said. "We're in very early days."[19]

18 *Economist*, "Crypto goes to Zero," 24 November 2022, https://www.economist.com/finance-and-economics/2022/11/24/how-crypto-goes-to-zero.
19 Sheelagh Kolhatkar, "Will the FTX Collapse Lead to Better Cryptocurrency Regulation?" *New Yorker*, 23 November 2022, https://www.newyorker.com/business/currency/will-the-ftx-collapse-lead-to-better-cryptocurrency-regulation.

So were FTX and its brethren Ponzi schemes or just creations of businesses that people believed in? To be honest, both are one and the same and, if you take this viewpoint, you could claim that the US dollar, euro and yuan are also Ponzi schemes. You only believe in them whilst others believe in them. Likewise, a Ponzi scheme only falls apart when you find it is a house of cards.

Image from the *Washington Post*

Has Crypto Failed?

I have enjoyed the rise and rise of the libertarian dream of ungoverned finance. However, following the year of reckoning, which led to the failures of exchanges and currencies in the crypto world, it's rather ironic that libertarians are now saying that we need regulations. The critical word here is "regulations". To me, it's more than just needing regulations; it is about governance and government. As I've always said: you cannot have money without governance. Do we need central banks and nations to regulate digital money or can we create a governance structure that is truly decentralised?

This became the big debate of 2023 and will continue to be moving forwards. It is very easy to say "the network is the government" or "the people are the government", yet, when push comes to shove, everyone says that we need a proper government. Is that a central government, a central bank, a national government, a major agency or something else?

As evidenced throughout this book so far, it's hard to say. There are pros and cons for both sides. For example, if you have a national government with a central bank that authorises the operation of cryptocurrencies—such as El Salvador or the Central African Republic—is that a good thing? It may or may not be, as the Central African Republic's bitcoin venture failed, which I will come back to later. In these countries, bitcoin has been recognised as legal tender by the government and seen as something positive. On the downside, after the crypto freeze of 2022 crept in, perhaps these governments are now asking whether it was a good thing to have done.

Then think about it with the boot on the other foot: does it matter to citizens? Whether the CFA franc, the other currency of the Central African Republic, or the Salvadoran peso is the preferred currency, the point is two-fold: what do you believe has value and why?

Why do you believe the CFA franc or Salvadoran peso is worth anything? Because the government says so. Then you find the economy in a meltdown, like Zimbabwe's was a few years ago, and you realise that the currency is worth nothing. So the government subsequently tells you that the US dollar is what's worth it. The US dollar has been the world's most stable currency for the past few decades, which is why half of the US dollars issued are circulating as currency overseas. What would happen if we stop believing in the United States?

The fundamental difference between the franc, peso, dollar and bitcoin is that the first three are backed by governments, regulations and licences. Bitcoin is not—but it could be. According to Brad Garlinghouse, CEO of Ripple, the United States will soon follow Singapore, the European Union (EU), Brazil and Japan with crypto legislation and regulations.

If this happens, some crypto currencies will become legal tender with legal backing and legal recognition. Without such legal recognition, crypto will remain in the wild and so, when the libertarians tell me they want their money back, I come back to my basic tenet: you cannot have money without government. Which government do you want on the network of money? After the crypto freeze and collapse, I'm guessing people will be far happier having a government they recognise behind the money and not some flaky networked economy that seems more like a Ponzi scheme than a real economy.

Having said that, as Bloomberg points out, it is hard to imagine Satoshi Nakamoto or Vitalik Buterin working for Goldman Sachs or JPMorgan Chase. In a piece by Tyler Cowen, he asks:

> What about crypto as a means of owning and trading one's online data? Or as a means of affirming one's online identity? How about lower-cost remittances made using crypto? Who has the knowledge to conclude that current attempts to build out DAOs — Decentralized Autonomous Organizations — are going to fail? The point is that no regulators or commentators have the knowledge to understand which of these projects is going to succeed or fail.[20]

In other words, if I interpret these things personally, it is purely what the network believes that determines the governance. It is not the government of the United States, India, China or anywhere else. Let the people decide. But, equally, let the people cry if it all goes wrong.

Are Cryptocurrencies Securities?

There is another huge debate around whether cryptocurrencies are securities or not. Should they be regulated by the US Securities and Exchange Commission (SEC) or not? This came to a head in 2023, as the SEC decided to take legal action against Ripple and Coinbase, charging them with operating unregistered securities exchanges. Interestingly, the SEC stated in the same year that bitcoin is not a security because it is anonymous. My belief is that this debate will rumble along for some time as this is nothing new. There have always been issues between those who are regulated and those who are not. It is a constant battle between authority and liberty; government and governance; structure and anarchy. Then what happens is that those who want to evade or avoid governance find ways to escape. We see this everywhere with tax avoidance, and even banks and governments use offshore firms to do this. We are now seeing this with cryptocurrency.

20 Tyler Cowen, "Beware the Danger of Crypto Regulation," Bloomberg, 3 January 2023, https://www.bloomberg.com/opinion/articles/2023-01-03/ftx-collapse-beware-the-dangers-of-crypto-regulation.

For example, as the US government questions and probes deeper and deeper into crypto operations, the more we see alternative places opening for crypto operations.[21] The issue always comes back to trust, security, certainty and governance. This is the argument that Ripple, Coinbase and others are having with the Federal Reserve and the SEC but, underlying all of these discussions, are the following questions: Who do you trust? What is certain? How do you govern?

These are fundamental questions at the heart of finance and life. Can I rely on you to look after my money? Can I rely on you to reimburse me if it is lost? The answer for most banks is yes. As banks have a licence from a government and guarantee they will cover any losses, you can trust banks to look after your money. You may not like them, but you can trust them.

When it comes to cryptocurrencies, however, the world is far fuzzier. Who can you trust and why? Personally, I'm far more comfortable with Ripple and Coinbase than with dogecoin or Shiba Inu. Why? Because the former do work actively with governments to try to create a regulated cryptocurrency marketplace while the latter have no management or organisation to do anything of that nature.

I guess this is the core of where I would argue between centralised versus decentralised. First, is there a management board behind the investment you are making? Second, can you contact them? Third, is it clear how you can get your money back? Fourth, who is their guarantee, their regulator, their oversight? If you cannot answer these questions, should you really feel confident about giving them your money?

It's a little bit like buying something on eBay. If you don't know the provenance, should you buy it? By way of example, I've purchased quite a few autographed documents over the years and then discovered at a later date that they are fake. If there's no provenance, there's no trust.

Coming back to whether cryptocurrencies are securities, security requires trust and, if there's no trust, there's no security. This was emphasised by Brian Armstrong, CEO of Coinbase, when interviewed in various media about the pros and cons of DeFi versus CeFi:

21 Amelia Isaacs, "Coinbase open to London move if regulatory confusion remains in the US," AltFi, 18 April 2023, https://www.altfi.com/article/10622_coinbase-ceo-crypto-could-be-20-of-global-gdp-in-20-years.

We need to have decentralized protocols so that we can have a more global, fair and free financial system. I don't think those are going to be regulated because there is no central authority for bitcoin or Ethereum [but when FTX collapsed] we started to think that what had happened validated our strategy over the last ten years of being built in the United States, trying to embrace compliance and not trying to cut any corners. How can we make sure that people understand that Coinbase is not like FTX? [...] ultimately, Coinbase stands to be a huge net beneficiary of this because it's going to bring an increased focus on compliance and trust, which is what we've been doing for the last ten years [...] I would say the regulation and consumer protection should probably happen with the centralised actors, the custodian and the exchange.[22]

Brian Armstrong, co-founder and CEO of Coinbase

Can You Regulate Crypto?

Can you regulate cryptocurrencies when they are already out in the wild? It is interesting to see how countries and regions are now responding to all of the interest in cryptocurrencies. For example, the EU is the latest to make a move with DAC8. DAC8 is the new eighth directive on administrative cooperation. This new directive is all about tax transparency rules for any platform or service provider offering transactions in cryptoassets for people resident in the EU.

22 Chris Skinner, "Brian Armstrong, CEO of Coinbase, presents the reasons why crypto needs regulation," Finanser [blog], 15 March 2023, https://thefinanser.com/2023/03/brian-amstrong-ceo-of-coinbase-presents-the-reasons-why-crypto-needs-regulation.

The rules, which are proposed to come into effect in 2026, will require all service providers, of whatever size and wherever located, to report on cryptoasset transactions carried out by clients residing in the EU. It will also require financial institutions to report on e-money and central bank digital currencies.

DAC8 is designed to complement the recently implemented Markets in Crypto-assets (MiCA) Regulation and anti-money laundering rules. These rules will provide the conditions for access to the EU market for cryptoassets, replacing existing national rules governing issuance, trading and custody of such assets.

In addition, DAC8 will include additional provisions requiring the reporting of tax rulings for high-net-worth individuals and minimum levels for penalties for non-compliance with the DAC.[23]

The directive is rather controversial as it covers NFTs and companies trading cryptocurrencies outside of the EU on behalf of EU investors. It will be interesting to see how this pans out because countries like Cyprus, Malta and even Germany are currently quite crypto-friendly for investors.

What will the new rules mean? As far as the cryptoasset and related sectors are concerned:

- Subject to some limited exceptions, all cryptoasset service providers or operators, irrespective of their size or location, will be required to report on transactions of clients resident in the EU.
- The proposal covers both domestic and cross-border transactions. In some cases, reporting obligations will also cover NFTs.
- Rather like the Common Reporting Standard (CRS), it will be necessary to carry out due diligence on cryptoasset users to determine their residence and whether reportable.

---

23 Simmons + Simmons, "DAC8: reporting rules on crypto-asset transactions," 14 December 2022, https://www.simmons-simmons.com/en/publications/clbnn5iq900c0tsb4fdn8oa14/dac8-reporting-rules-on-crypto-asset-transactions.

- The report will include details of the user and of reportable transactions effected during the previous calendar year and will be made within two months of the end of that year. The first reporting period is expected to be 2026.
- There will then be an automatic exchange of the reported information between the relevant authorities.

To some extent, these measures link in with the MiCA regulation that regulates professional cryptoasset service providers and requires them to be registered in the EU. Non-EU operators that are MiCA regulated will report in the EU member state where they are registered. Non-EU operators that are not MiCA regulated will need to register with an EU member state for DAC8 reporting purposes. Other measures covered in DAC8 include the following:

- An extension of the scope of the automatic exchange of advance cross-border rulings to include those that apply to high-net-worth individuals (who hold a minimum of €1,000,000 in financial or investable wealth, or in assets under management but excluding a main private residence). This will include rulings issued, amended or renewed between 1 January 2020 and 31 December 2025 provided they are still valid on 1 January 2026.
- An extension of the scope of the automatic exchange of information on certain payments to include dividends that are not paid or cashed in a custodial account
- An extension of the CRS requirements to include reporting on e-money and central bank digital currencies
- Establishing a common minimum level of penalties for the most serious non-compliant behaviour, such as complete absence of reporting despite administrative reminders
- Improvements to the processes for administrative cooperation among EU member states[24]

---

24 Andrew Knight and Aki Corsoni-Husain, "European Commission proposes an eighth directive on administrative cooperation (DAC8)," Harneys, 15 December 2022, https://www.harneys.com/our-blogs/regulatory/european-commission-proposes-an-eighth-directive-on-administrative-cooperation-dac8/.

What we are seeing in the EU is a region trying to implement rules where rules do not work. Cryptocurrencies do not recognise countries or borders. It will be interesting to see how this plays out. And it becomes even more interesting when you look at spin-offs of the cryptocurrency network, such as NFTs.

What Does NFT Stand For?

A non-fungible token, or NFT for short, is a term that most mere mortals do not understand. As I explained earlier, fungible means that something can be replaced by something else. For example, if I give you a dollar, you can give me a kilo of bananas. The bananas are worth a dollar and they can be exchanged easily because they are fungible. In other words, they replace each other. $1 is worth 1 kg of bananas.

What happens if you own a Picasso painting? I can give you $100 million for the painting. However, the painting is non-fungible because it is unique and not interchangeable. In other words, a non-fungible item cannot be replaced by anything else.

This is the core reason why NFTs are taking off in art, music, film, entertainment and more because, if you have something unique, you want to secure it as a unique item that can never be replaced. In the olden days, this was done through forms and certificates to provide provenance and history. Today, it is achieved digitally through an NFT. If you have a token for that Picasso painting, it cannot be replaced by anything except a sale of that token to someone else. That token is unique, as is the painting, and secures its provenance forever.

How Do NFTs Work?

When you create an NFT, it is registered on a blockchain, the most widely used today being Ethereum. Once on the blockchain, it registers a unique address that belongs to you. I recently did this using MetaMask and OpenSea. MetaMask generates the blockchain address on Ethereum and OpenSea stores the NFT asset, in this case a digital painting. I can tell you that it was by no means easy to do so, right now, NFTs are for people who love technology. It's not for the average John or Jane on the Clapham omnibus. However, bear in mind that you needed to be a rocket scientist to create a website in the 1990s and yet, today, anyone can do it. It will get easier.

What's Worth Picking Up at the NFT Supermarket?

As stated above, a lot of the interest today is in the arts: music, paintings, photographs, poetry and books. For example, NFT Studios has created a movie studio specifically for the NFT market. The company talks extensively about building Web3 solutions and, specifically, Building the Metaverse one block at a time. Blockchain, Web3 and the metaverse all go hand in hand with cryptocurrencies, as these are the foundations of the next generation internet. These technologies may work in tandem with the physical network of stores, companies, airlines and the things we do physically, with the physical things for physical activities and the digital things for digital activities.

In 2021, NFT Studios announced its debut cinematic project *A Wing and a Prayer*, the first NFT-funded film of all time. As Niels Juul, film producer and co-founder of the company, put it:

> As a producer, my biggest frustration is from the finance side, it is an ordeal. The studios are mainly doing big franchise films, an independent film can take years and years. It's hard getting investors for films and productions, especially at the development stage, with the Hollywood system. We want to democratise it.[25]

That sums up NFTs beautifully. Art is hard to fund so let's crowdfund it.

The thing is, right now, there is a lot of frivolity around NFTs and people investing unwisely. However, the people doing that are most likely the people who bought crypto in the early 2010s, which means they are rolling in it and do not care what they spend.

These developments possibly cloud the market for NFTs as it makes this space look stupid. It's not stupid. It's an evolving means of creating a new way to deal with digital creativity.

---

25 James McQuillan, "Scorsese producer Niels Juul to spearhead NFT-funded film," Blockchain Gamer, 18 December 2021, https://www.blockchaingamer.biz/news/16878/scorsese-producer-niels-juul-to-spearhead-nft-funded-film/.

Will NFTs Become like Art Collecting?

Possibly. I personally collect a lot of rare art, books, comics and autographs, and the issue with all of them is: (a) is it an original and not a replica? and (b) can you prove it? Proving both can be hard, but I tend to keep all packaging and certificates with everything I buy, so it has its provenance held intact. With NFTs, I won't have to do that, but a bigger question leads on from this: in 300 years, will anyone be able to read my NFT? The issue here is that, as with art from the 1700s and 1800s, if something is sold many times, can you find the complete history and prove its provenance? I'm fairly certain that, in one or two centuries' time, we won't only find that NFTs cannot be tracked and traced, but we won't even have the technology to read them. So, could this be yet another fad?

In summary, NFTs are really about securing digital ownership of a unique asset. It does not have to be art—you could make NFTs of diamonds, rare wines and more. It's all about having a token that is uniquely linked to an asset that is a one-off—whether that asset be physical or digital—which cannot be exchanged without a clear sale on the blockchain.

"So you can't own the precious physically, but you
can pay to have your name listed as its owner
in an online distributed database."

NFTs and Crypto Are All about Beliefs

A constant theme of this book is trust and beliefs. I apologise if it is getting repetitive but this determines whether you accept cryptocurrencies and decentralisation or would rather stick with centralisation and fiat currencies, whether digital or physical.

This was well illustrated by a scene in *South Park*, the irreverent cartoon, where an NFT is being pitched by Vic Chaos to Denny's Applebee's Max customers. One line really resonated with me: "If you believe in NFTs, then I believe in NFTs, then they believe in NFTs, and we make all kinds of f**king money."

The reason why the line works so well is that money and finance, markets and companies, countries and laws are all about beliefs. That's the underlying fundamental. If you believe that this contract with this currency authorised by this government will work, then it does. If you don't believe it, then it does not.

This theme is a critical underlay of everything in the financial system. What is it we value? Why does it have value? How is it traded? Who can you trust to trade it? These questions strike at the core of cryptocurrencies, but they also strike at the core of banking. Why do you need someone to store value? Who can you trust to store value? Where can you trade your store? How do you trade your store?

The questions always come back to the same fundamentals, but the fundamentals are changing. For decades or even centuries, we have built a system of trust based on government regulations of trusted intermediaries. This is changing. We are now building a new system of trust based on networked regulations of trusted platforms.

This is groundbreaking and revolutionary and, for all of those who think it is irrelevant, it's not. We are seeing a rapid change from physical assets to digital assets, from government currencies to networked currencies, from traditional banks to open finance and from industrial structures to digital innovations.

Our world is changing rapidly before our eyes and it's all about what we trust, who we believe in, what we believe in and why. I have been shocked by the impact Elon Musk has made on dogecoin, Shiba Inu and others. We suddenly create ecosystems out of nothing because a few believe that these ecosystems are worth believing in. That is what NFTs and crypto are all about. The new generations believe that they have value. Of course, like most central bankers and been-around-the-block elders, I worry that they will all lose their money in a Ponzi-style networked scam but, hey, if you believe in it and I believe in it, then they will believe in it.

Crypto Is Not Going Away

It is very easy to portray the whole cryptocurrency marketplace as a scam, a Ponzi scheme, the Wild West, a minefield. In some ways, it is. There are plenty of things out there designed to rip you off. There are also techie people who have good ideas that are then poorly executed. Perhaps Terra-LUNA is one such example. One thing I am certain of is that not every crypto entrepreneur has created a platform out there to rip everyone off. Most of them are doing this with sincerity but flawed designs.

Nevertheless, this means that there are many things out there—whether flagrantly unlawful or frightfully flawed—that will lose the average Joe or Jane a lot of money. Does the average Joe or Jane care? Who knows? What I do know is that all of the flak that the cryptocurrency market receives is unwarranted. Things are happening to change the global financial construct.

THIS IS THE KEY POINT!

For all the haters, bitcoin has changed things. Ethereum, supported by large numbers of corporate and financial developers due its smart contract capability, has changed things. Other currencies building on these concepts, such as Cardano and Polygon, are changing things further. Eventually, you will end up with blockchain-based cryptocurrency worlds that support global trade and Web3.

How did you miss this? You missed it because you weren't looking, you didn't understand it, you trashed it as something irrelevant and you didn't take it seriously. This came home to me as I read a *New York Times* article focused on Cory Klippsten.[26] Klippsten told everyone that Terra-LUNA was a scam and Celsius was a "massive blow-up risk". Then, when those crypto

26   David Yaffe-Bellany, "The Crypto Market Crashed. They're Still Buying Bitcoin," *New York Times*, 2 August 2022, https://www.nytimes.com/2022/08/02/technology/crypto-bitcoin-maximalists.html.

projects collapsed (causing a crash that wiped out about $1 trillion in value), he declared, "Crypto is a scam."

The thing is that Klippsten differs from most crypto haters in one crucial respect—he runs a bitcoin company. He also stated, "The only future for non-Bitcoin crypto is to seek to be co-opted by banks and governments and become part of the existing system."

DeFi versus CeFi: it's your choice. This point was emphasised by Jimmy Song, a crypto podcaster: "Bitcoin is decentralised, digitally scarce money. Everything else is centralised. There's a world of difference between a censorship-resistant, self-sovereign money versus a gambling vehicle."[27]

There's the rub. Not every crypto scheme is a scam. Some are, some aren't. Sorting out the wheat from the chaff is your job today. Tomorrow, there will be a regulatory system in this space. I've always said you cannot have money without government. The crypto folks always interpret that as "you cannot have money without a *national* government". This is not true. It is purely that, without governance, you cannot have a currency, as money only exists if it has trust.

Governance can be the network, and that's the point being made by many experts here. If the cryptocurrency community can create a global network that is censorship-resistant, but with strong governance, then self-sovereign money can, will and does exist.[28]

If that is the case, what are banks doing about it? Interestingly, many are gearing up to be crypto exchanges, crypto vaults and crypto services. For all the denigration and fear of cryptocurrencies, the banks and regulators are now stepping up to the mark. This point was emphasised when Bank of America underlined concerns about Ethereum:

As the so-called "Merge" approaches, during which the Ethereum blockchain will transition from proof-of-work to proof-of-stake, Bank of America has released a research report delving into the matter. In it, the bank noted how Ethereum had lost market share to other

---

27 David Yaffe-Bellany.
28 Self-sovereign is where individuals or businesses have sole ownership over the ability to control their accounts and personal data.

blockchains like Solana and Binance Smart Chain due to its inherent scaling limitations.[29]

The Crypto Crept In and Is Not Creeping Out

The International Monetary Fund (IMF) noted that, in emerging markets and developing economies, the advent of crypto can accelerate what the IMF calls "cryptoization", when cryptoassets replace domestic currency and circumvent exchange restrictions and capital account management measures. In other words, creating a situation that could have a potentially profound impact on financial stability.

Cryptocurrency Regulations by Country

Source: Thomas Reuters 2022

Although outright bans on cryptos around the globe are somewhat rare and are diminishing, some jurisdictions are emerging as staunch advocates. Many regions, however, fall somewhere in the middle as regulations are slow to keep pace with the immense popularity of cryptos—a risk, in and of itself.

29 Gavin Lucas, "Bank of America: Ethereum won't remain dominant if it doesn't scale," CoinGeek, 2 August 2022, https://coingeek.com/bank-of-america-ethereum-wont-remain-dominant-if-it-doesnt-scale/.

In many countries, cryptos appear to be at a legal and regulatory tipping point, according to a report by Thomson Reuters.[30] Nevertheless, the IMF and Thomson Reuters note concerns about financial stability and vulnerable customers, together with the persistent misperceptions about financial crime, which are forcing policymakers to consider significant action. Having said that, policymakers have to balance these considerations with the benefits that could be derived from the more widespread adoption of cryptos.

This is why some countries are welcoming cryptos with seemingly few regulatory concerns. Cryptos' borderless nature makes this even more challenging, as is evidenced by the near-overnight relocation of crypto firms out of China, after the country clamped down on crypto activity in 2021 after many years of trying to stop bitcoin mining.

The clear message is that there is an urgent need for a coherent, comprehensive and global approach to the regulation and oversight of cryptos. The need for policymaking cooperation globally is recognised, even though cryptoassets account for only a small portion of overall financial system assets, but they are growing rapidly. Further, direct connections between cryptoassets and systemically important financial institutions and core financial markets are rapidly evolving, opening the door to the potential for regulatory gaps, market fragmentation or arbitrage.

Without a coherent international approach to cryptos, there is a danger that they will fail to achieve their potential, and the world will lose the considerable benefits they could bring. Equally, without an international approach, the dark side of cryptoasset trading may grow out of control.

Cryptocrime Is Why Cryptocurrencies Were Invented

Upon reading, the following headline annoyed me: "Using crypto for crime is not a bug—it's an industry feature".[31] In an opinion piece in the *Financial Times*, columnist Jemima Kelly talked about being heckled for saying that crypto is all about crime:

---

30 Susannah Hammond and Todd Ehret, "Cryptos on the rise 2022 — a complex regulatory future emerges," Thomson Reuters, 5 April 2002, https://www.thomsonreuters.com/en-us/posts/investigation-fraud-and-risk/cryptos-on-the-rise-2022/.

31 Jemima Kelly, "Using crypto for crime is not a bug – it's an industry feature," *Financial Times*, 26 April 2023, https://www.ft.com/content/83b5932f-df6f-47a6-bf39-aa0c3172a098.

Crypto enthusiasts argue that it's wrong to claim that it enables crime because the technology itself is "neutral" so cannot be blamed for any illicit activity. But this simply isn't true: crypto was designed as a censorship-resistant payment mechanism that operates outside the traditional financial system and beyond the remit of regulators.

To back up her assertion, she quoted Binance's former chief compliance officer who allegedly stated, "We see the bad, but we close 2 eyes." Furthermore, she quoted Stephen Diehl, co-author of *Popping the Crypto Bubble* (2022), saying, "These exchanges know exactly what they're doing. They're basically creating a dark transnational payment network and, not surprisingly, that will be used by criminals. They're purpose-built for that."

The article went on to cite various figures and accusations that may be right or wrong. Why did the piece annoy me? Well, for two reasons. First, Kelly quoted Chainalysis's annual report on cryptocrime, and missed a key line in the report:

The share of all cryptocurrency activity associated with illicit activity has risen for the first time since 2019, from 0.12% in 2021 to 0.24% in 2022.[32]

So, 0.24 per cent of all cryptocurrency accounts is for criminal activities. In contrast, the banking system launders trillions of dollars a year, estimated to be over 1 per cent of all banking activity. Which is more efficient?

Second, although Kelly did quote the Chainalysis report, she failed to mention the opening sentence:

Every year, we publish our estimates of illicit cryptocurrency activity to demonstrate the power of blockchains' transparency – these kinds of estimates aren't possible in traditional finance – and to teach investigators and compliance professionals about the latest trends in cryptocurrency-related crime that they need to know about.[33]

32 Chainalysis, "The Chainalysis 2023 Crypto Crime Report," February 2023, https://go.chainalysis.com/2023-crypto-crime-report-demo.html.
33 Chainalysis.

In other words, criminal activity is far easier to track and trace digitally than through the banking system, where physical documents are used to open accounts and allow nested companies to hide their connections.

That's what really annoyed me because most mainstream media paints a picture of everything to do with crypto being bad, because banks are good. It's all claptrap. The fact is that most digital currencies can trace crime far more easily than most banks.

For instance, how could Chainalysis produce the following graphs for its report if there is no way to track and trace what is happening in the cryptocurrency space?

Total Cryptocurrency Value Received by Illicit Addresses, 2017–2022

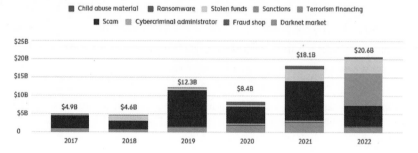

YoY Per Cent Change in Value Received by Crime Type, 2019–2022

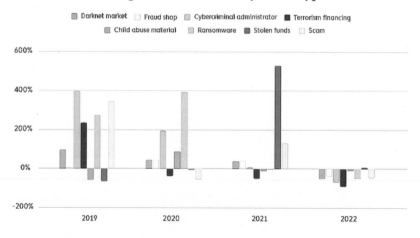

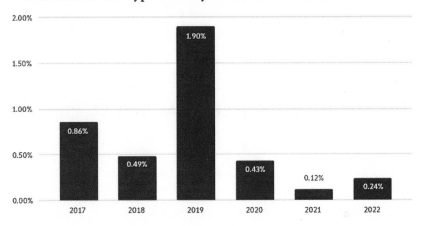

Illicit Share of all Cryptocurrency Transaction Volume, 2017–2022

In general, it appears to me to be media collusion with government and finance to say that crypto is bad while blockchain is good.

THE ARGUMENTS FOR CENTRALISING CURRENCIES

The argument made by libertarians against statists and the state is why do we need a state-backed currency? The answer lies in why money was invented in the first place, a subject I return to often. Money was invented by governments to control society. If you have no government behind a currency, what does that mean? The answer is that it means the network controls society.

This always brings me back to eBay and Amazon and the fact that reviewers and star ratings control the network. If you have 5 star reviews, then you are worth it. If you have 3 stars or lower, then you are not. We have these review mechanisms on Uber, IMDb and other services now, so how much notice do you take of them? If, like me, you think, "Meh, this has a 3-star review, don't bother," you've discovered the new regulator. It's called The People. Can The People replace The Government? Well, that's the question we are all grappling with when we look at DeFi versus CeFi.

Why a Central Authority?

It amazes me how many people misread, half-read or assume things based on what you say. When I say you cannot have money without government or governance, many assume I mean we have to have a national government authority involved that is centralised. This is a false assumption, as there is no mention of nationalism or centralisation. The proposition purely means a governance that can be trusted, whether centralised or decentralised.

Sir Jon Cunliffe of the Bank of England, for example, has claimed that "unbacked cryptoassets are highly volatile, given that they have no intrinsic value."[1] Yet they do have value if you believe they do.

---

1   "Reflections on DeFi, digital currencies and regulation," a speech given by Sir Jon Cunliffe at Warwick Business School's Gilmore Centre Policy Forum Conference, November 2022, https://www.bankofengland. co.uk/speech/2022/november/jon-cunliffe-keynote-speech-and-panel-at-warwick-conference-on-defi-digital-currencies.

Those who say cryptocurrency or Bitcoin have no value are wrong. They have at least the value of their utility to be used in future blocks to securely transfer money and assets, and to keep assets safe by not being transferred in the first place. Blockchains likely create and capture more value than just transfers, as an NFT is economically more valuable than simply its ability to be transacted. DeFi solutions like Chia Offers create trading opportunities that could not exist with previous financial technology. Storing value is a legitimate use case for those who want certainty around inflation and issuance of monies. Indeed, as with many emerging technologies, there are likely to be economically valuable uses of blockchains that have not even been thought of yet.[2]

The issue is that most associate the word "governing" with centralisation and the state. To put this into context, why do you think banks have so many regulations? Do you think they asked for them? Do you really believe that they want a strict, structured system with regulatory handcuffs to make sure it is safe? Or is it more likely that it has ended up this way because this way works?

In other words, as I've said so often, you cannot have money without government. It's a bit like you cannot have medicines, hospitals, airlines or other areas without some form of government to license those involved, and regulate and monitor their activities. This is a debate that I have had with the cryptocurrency community for over a decade, and their reply is always the same—you're a statist. The thing is, I have never said that the form of government is a nation state. The government could be the network of citizens, which is what bitcoin has promised.

However, when you have things on the network that break the trust of that network, you have a house of cards. This is why the gradual crumbling of Terra-LUNA, Celsius, FTX, Genesis and more is a challenge to the community. They break the people's trust and the people lose their money. This is why you need money with government.

---

2   Gene Hoffman and Misha Graboi, "Cypherpunks in Sportcoats: The Fundamental Value of Cryptocurrencies and Blockchains," Chia, 8 June 2022, https://www.chia.net/2022/06/08/valuing-blockchains/.

When I use the words "government", "governance" and/or "governor", I don't mean a regulator, state or national government. I mean a structure to provide oversight to ensure that people don't lose their money. Without such controls, you just have Ponzi schemes.

Nevertheless, and I learnt this one way back with Mt. Gox, Terra-LUNA, Celsius, FTX, Genesis and more were not the foundation stones of our next world of money. They were just *schemes* and poorly managed exchanges for cryptocurrencies. When you come back to the core of blockchains, the foundations are still stable.

You just need to define what the governmental system is. Is it the network and connectivity of citizens that is censor resistant and controlled by algorithms or is it the citizens ruled by a nation state, which regulates and monitors activities? Millions of people believe in the former; billions of people are run by the latter. Until there is stable, non-volatile cryptocurrency, it will probably stay that way for the foreseeable future.

How Central Banks Have Responded to DeFi

Central authorities exist to exert control and maintain law and order. Cryptocurrencies threaten this structure. With the rise of cryptocurrencies, particularly the impact of bitcoin, central banks and governments have tried for years to ban them, get rid of them, stop people investing or trading in them—and lost. They are still trying, but it is a losing battle because decentralised systems and currencies on the network of citizens are very hard to control and regulate. They don't recognise governments, borders or rules. They are out there in the wild and, even if a government does find a way to crack down on them, they move to what most refer to as the dark web.

The dark web is not visible to search engines, and requires the use of special anonymising browsers called Tor to be accessed. Because it is anonymised and invisible, it cannot be tracked or traced. It has been around for years, with the most famous dark web case study being the Silk Road, a place to buy and sell illegal substances and even contract assassinations and killings. That one got caught but don't be fooled. Silk

Road 5.0 is out there somewhere today, and is far more hidden and harder to find than ever before.

Governments have two key worries as a result. First, how do they find those who are illegally trading on the network? Second, how do they stop them? Sex and crime fuel most illegal online trade, but you need to find a way to finance such ventures. Decentralised currencies on the dark web is where that's at. However, for most people on Main Street, it is far too difficult to deal with, so we don't. We use Main Street stores with Main Street products using Main Street currencies, rather than diving into the Dark Street.

Nevertheless, as governments and regulators try to deal with these issues, they also realise that they need to respond with a legitimate alternative. Recognising that so much traffic has moved onto the network, they have also acknowledged that trying to pay with card and cash online is not the easiest thing to do and so, partly due to the pressure of digitalisation and the rise of illegal currencies (in their eyes), their response has been to develop government currencies that are digital.

What Is a CBDC?

A CBDC is the digital form of a country's fiat currency or, in other words, a digital form of the paper notes and coins you have in your pocket or purse today. Almost every government is developing a digital version of its currency to ensure that it can regulate digital activities and exclude DeFi from its structures. This is because if you trade in a DeFi structure, it's hard to tax and control it, which is an enema for governments. To date, almost half of these digital versions are in advanced development or at pilot or launch stage.

Countries exploring digital versions of their currencies

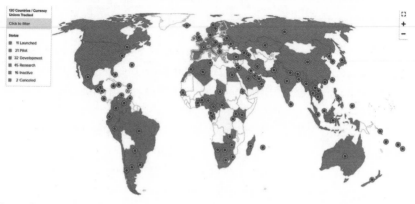

Source: The Atlantic Council

The key features of central bank currencies include:

- **Integrity:** the currency must be safe, for all and at no or at ultra low cost. As entire economies go digital—and cash dwindles away—monetary policies need to anchor to digital technology.
- **Resilience:** It is not healthy to rely on single foreign sources for critical infrastructure (for example, the energy crisis during the war in Ukraine). A digital form of money must be based on a digitally resilient critical infrastructure recognising cross-border transactional needs.
- **Integration:** The currency must be universally available to all, anywhere, at all times, without the need of a bank account.
- **Singleness:** Money must be held in digital cash as well (but stablecoins don't comply).
- **Security:** There must be a dedicated design since new risks emerge on digital infrastructure.
- **Privacy:** The CBDC must be as close as possible to cash in terms of complete neutrality about data. In other words, it must bear similar core characteristics of anonymity. However, no CBDC can be truly "as private as cash" because it can't be a hundred per cent anonymous.

Due to these features, there are now several different CBDC concepts. Some directly complement cash with a digital currency, some would be available directly to citizens without the involvement of a bank while others could only be distributed by commercial banks. Each model has pros and cons, so here is a quick review of the main structures banks are developing for CBDCs. Bear in mind that there are very few in existence right now as most are at the stage of proof of concept.

Retail CBDCs

Retail CBDCs are meant to be used by you and me and any other consumer. They are designed to be used just like cash digitally. Three different retail digital currencies are being developed: direct, indirect and synthetic.

1. A direct CBDC

A direct CBDC is available to everyone, managed directly by a country's central bank. As the Reserve Bank of India (RBI) described it:

> In this model, the CBDC represents a direct claim on the central bank, which keeps a record of all balances and updates it with every transaction.[3]

As with many other payment developments in India, such as Aadhar and the Unified Payments Interface (UPI), the issue with this structure is that it allows the government to track and trace every payment made by every citizen in real time or, as some call it, surveillance capitalism. While sweeping surveillance has long been considered a disadvantage in the eyes of citizens and advocates of civil liberties, the RBI believes that the advantage of a direct CBDC is that "the central bank has complete knowledge of retail account balances." It does also note the disadvantage that a direct CBDC "marginalises private sector involvement and hinders innovation in the payment system." Furthermore, the RBI warned that the retail CBDC "model is designed for

---

3   Reserve Bank of India, "Concept Note on Central Bank Digital Currency," 7 October 2022, https://rbi.org.in/Scripts/PublicationReportDetails.aspx?UrlPage=&ID=1218#CP4.

disintermediation ... has the potential to disrupt the current financial system ... and will put additional burden on the central banks in terms of managing customer on boarding, KYC and AML checks which may prove difficult and costly to the central bank."[4]

In short, a direct CBDC would be a straightforward path to increased financial surveillance and government control over the payments system.

2. An indirect CBDC

An indirect CBDC, or intermediated CBDC, tries to lessen the risks of disrupting the current financial system by allowing retail banks to distribute the central bank currency. This means that existing providers of consumer accounts provide and maintain the wallets used for CBDC holdings.

As explained by the Federal Reserve: "An intermediated model would facilitate the use of the private sector's existing privacy and identity-management frameworks; leverage the private sector's ability to innovate; and reduce the prospects for destabilising disruptions to the well-functioning U.S. financial system."[5]

Note that the Federal Reserve says that this CBDC model reduces the prospect of disruption to the existing financial system, but it will not eliminate it. This is because the existing retail banks may manage customer accounts with CBDCs, and therefore the government cannot monitor monetary movements and transactions. However, the retail bank now has a direct liability to the central bank for those currencies.

Potentially, for this reason, there is a heightened risk of a bank run given that customers could move deposits from one CBDC account to another in real time and seamlessly within apps. Equally, as an indirect CBDC does not remove the ability of a government to know where those currencies are going, it essentially makes it a direct CBDC with extra steps.

3. A synthetic CBDC

A synthetic CBDC isn't a CBDC at all, but rather a stablecoin. A stablecoin is a cryptocurrency backed by central bank reserves. It is pegged to government

4   Reserve Bank of India.
5   Federal Reserve Board, "Money and Payments: The U.S. Dollar in the Age of Digital Transformation," Board of Governors of the Federal Reserve System, January 2022, https://www.federalreserve.gov/publications/files/money-and-payments-20220120.pdf.

currencies, short-term securities or commodities in an effort to stabilise its value. Whilst traded, the central bank holds reserves on a one-for-one basis against the stablecoin.

The issue here—as evidenced by Terra-LUNA, a supposedly stablecoin that was unstable—is that the safety and soundness of those reserves depend on where they are held. For instance, traditional banks generally hold their reserves at the central bank in what is known as a master account. However, access to master accounts is usually limited to regulated banks only.

If, in this model, the synthetic CBDC were opened to enable access to stablecoin issuers, then a synthetic CBDC would be just like all of the other stablecoins that already exist, thus essentially defeating its purpose.

Wholesale CBDCs

Wholesale CBDCs are not designed for consumer or retail use. Instead, they are restricted to financial institutions for use during interbank settlement. So a wholesale CBDC is just a way for banks to pay money to other banks. What benefit does that provide? Most banks can already perform interbank settlement fast, securely, reliably and easily through the Depository Trust & Clearing Corporation (DTCC), the US clearing and settlement system, and T2, the ECB's system. Nevertheless, such systems are being considered.

CBDCs in the Works

With technological advances ushering in a wave of new private-sector financial products and services, including digital wallets, mobile payment apps and new digital assets such as cryptocurrencies and stablecoins, the Federal Reserve and other central banks around the globe are exploring the potential benefits and risks of issuing a CBDC.

The Digital Dollar

As a first step to foster a broad and transparent public dialogue about CBDCs in general, and about the potential benefits and risks of a US CBDC, the Federal Reserve issued "Money and Payments: The U.S. Dollar in the Age of Digital

Transformation" in January 2022. To date, the Federal Reserve has made no decision on issuing a CBDC and would only proceed with its issuance with an authorising law.

The Federal Reserve sees many benefits in a digital dollar. For example, it could provide households and businesses with a convenient, electronic form of central bank money, with the safety and liquidity that would entail; give entrepreneurs a platform on which to create new financial products and services; support faster and cheaper payments (including cross-border payments); and expand consumer access to the financial system.

It also notes the disadvantages, stating that a "CBDC could pose certain risks and raise a variety of important policy questions, including how it might affect financial-sector market structure, the cost and availability of credit, the safety and stability of the financial system, and the efficacy of monetary policy."[6]

As a result, if and when a digital dollar is introduced, the Federal Reserve will ensure that it will:

- provide benefits to households, businesses and the overall economy that exceed any costs and risks
- yield such benefits more effectively than alternative methods
- complement, rather than replace, current forms of money and methods for providing financial services
- protect consumer privacy
- protect against criminal activity
- have broad support from key stakeholders[7]

The Digital Euro

The EU kicked off formal proposals for a digital euro in June 2023. The proposals focused on ensuring cash would not be replaced but instead would be complemented by a central bank-issued digital version of the euro. The proposals are summarised as follows:

---

6   Federal Reserve Board.
7   Federal Reserve Board.

- **A legislative proposal on the legal tender of euro cash** to safeguard the role of cash, ensure it is widely accepted as a means of payment and remains easily accessible for people and businesses across the euro area
- **A legislative proposal establishing the legal framework for a possible digital euro** as a complement to euro banknotes and coins. It would ensure that people and businesses have an additional choice—on top of current private options—that allows them to pay digitally with a widely accepted, cheap, secure and resilient form of public money in the euro area (complementing the private solutions that exist today). While the proposals—once adopted by the European Parliament and Council—would establish the legal framework for the digital euro, it will ultimately be for the ECB to decide if and when to issue the digital euro.

The emphasis made as this was announced is that it would not be a government project to track and trace people. The ECB and national banks would have no identity details of those who use the digital euro. Critics fear, however, that it will give governments a way to snoop on buying behaviour. At the extreme end, conspiracy theorists portray the digital euro as a covert plan to phase out cash and monitor people's shopping habits.

Nevertheless, Mairead McGuinness, Commissioner for Financial Services, Financial Stability and Capital Markets Union, writing in the *Financial Times*, has argued that the benefits far outweigh the negatives:

Like the physical euro, the digital euro could be used anywhere in the eurozone. It would have a similar function to cash — providing access to a reliable and easily accessible form of payment, but digitally. So, first, it would ensure that the euro continues to play a key role in our lives.

Second, a digital euro could support financial inclusion. People without bank accounts or other vulnerable groups rely heavily on cash, which can put them at risk as cash is used less. The digital euro would give everyone a digital option to pay — and it could even be used without a bank account.

Third, a digital single currency could support innovation. Europe's current payment systems are national or international — we don't have truly European options, and are overly reliant on companies such as Visa, Mastercard, or PayPal.[8]

The Digital Yuan

China's plans for a CBDC have been developed over the last decade, starting in 2014, and a trial in four cities was launched in 2020.[9] The four cities were Shenzhen, Suzhou, Chengdu and Xiong'an. By September 2022, the trial had been expanded to over 23 cities across China, including Beijing, Shanghai and Tianjin. The system runs in apps just like normal money, is compatible with the nation's major payments processors—Alipay and WeChat Pay—and is known as the digital yuan, or electronic Chinese yuan (e-CNY).

According to Deutsche Bank research,[10] the introduction of the e-CNY by the People's Bank of China (PBOC) serves two different but related goals. The first, longer-term goal is to create a digital currency that can compete with other digital currencies, such as bitcoin, stablecoins and other CBDCs, while ensuring that the renminbi continues to be the dominant currency in China. The second, more immediate goal is to reshape China's current payments system by providing a cash-like digital payment method: accessible to all, low cost, anonymous (to a certain extent) and facilitates competition among payment service providers.

The e-CNY is fully backed by the PBOC and put into operation by payment service providers. It allows greater anonymity and includes better personal information protection, yet still keeps sufficient records for tracing illegal activities such as money laundering and tax evasion. The PBOC created the e-CNY with four guiding principles, namely:

1. e-CNY will be a liability of the PBOC.
2. The digital wallets that hold e-CNY will not be considered to be bank accounts as they only require a mobile phone number to work.

---

8   Mairead McGuinness, "The case for a digital euro," *Financial Times*, 28 June 2023, https://www.ft.com/content/52c5f8e3-c2bf-4450-a1bf-fe3fa7060404.
9   Jonathon Cheng, "China Rolls Out Pilot Test of Digital Currency," *Wall Street Journal*, 20 April 2020, https://www.wsj.com/articles/china-rolls-out-pilot-test-of-digital-currency-11587385339.
10 Deutsche Bank, "Digital yuan: what is it and how does it work?" 14 July 2021, https://www.db.com/news/detail/20210714-digital-yuan-what-is-it-and-how-does-it-work.

3. No interest can be paid on e-CNY.
4. Only banks can convert e-CNY into bank deposits and vice versa.

An important consideration behind the e-CNY's guiding principles is aimed at preventing the disintermediation of banks. By defining e-CNY as narrow money (M0 in bank parlance) and banning interest payments, the PBOC sees only a limited amount of e-CNY in circulation to replace cash, and not to replace bank deposits.

Interestingly, the trials and tests around e-CNY have been disappointing. For example, the PBOC gave away millions of dollars in digital yuan in several cities, such as Beijing and Shenzhen, to encourage citizens to use the virtual money but it did not succeed. Transactions using the currency totalled just 100 billion yuan ($14.5 billion) by the end of August 2022. Compare that with Alipay whose app processes around $1.6 trillion per month on average—more than a thousand times the digital yuan's monthly transaction volume at that time—and you get the idea.

Britcoin

The Bank of England has been working for some years on the idea of Britcoin, with the claim that it would "anchor the value and robustness of all monies circulating in the UK."[11]

> "The question is not whether but how we should develop the machinery
> for tokenised transactions to settle in central bank money."
> **Sir Jon Cunliffe**, Deputy Governor, Financial Stability, Bank of England

The vision for the digital pound is that it would work like cash and hold its value, but would not accrue interest or become a tool of speculators. The person leading those efforts is Tom Mutton, head of the central bank's CBDC project, who has stated that a digital pound may end up running on software that is not a blockchain, the distributed database technology

---

11 "The shape of things to come: innovation in payments and money," a speech given by Sir Jon Cunliffe at the Global Innovate Finance Conference, April 2023, https://www.bankofengland.co.uk/speech/2023/april/jon-cunliffe-keynote-speech-at-the-innovate-finance-global-summit.

underpinning cryptocurrencies and used by several digital coins issued by central banks.

In 2023, the Bank of England trialled several different versions of ledgers, including public blockchains similar to those underpinning cryptocurrencies like bitcoin, to see which option might work best for a UK CBDC. It will now spend two to three years evaluating the technology and policy requirements before making a final decision. The earliest that an eventual CBDC could appear is in the second half of this decade.

CBDCs in Reality

In the meantime, we should bear in mind that some CBDCs are already operating. For example, Nigeria released its CBDC, the eNaira, in October 2021 to widespread interest. However, a year later, it had had barely any usage within a country full of crypto-curious investors, with the result that it may need to be redesigned and relaunched.

To put this into context, even though Nigeria suffered a severe shortage in the supply of newly designed naira paper notes, people in the country do not want to use the eNaira and, instead, prefer cryptocurrencies. With a total cryptocurrency transaction volume amounting to $400 million, Nigeria ranks third after the United States and Russia in the use of such currencies. According to a 2020 online survey by Statista, 32 per cent of participating Nigerians used cryptocurrencies, the highest proportion of any country in the world.[12]

Why is this so? Nigerians enjoy trading and make over a million cryptocurrency transactions per month (figures as of 2020) but, more than this, many African nations do not trust governments or government-issued currencies. Just look at Zimbabwe as an example or, on a wider horizon, Venezuela. It is why El Salvador and the Central African Republic adopted bitcoin as legal tender.[13] Another reason is that citizens are learning that they

---

12 This figure is disputed by Sahara Reporters, which claims that Statista only surveyed a few thousand Nigerians out of a population of 212 million. See Elizabeth Ogunbamowo, "Fact Check: 32% Of Nigerians Don't Own Bitcoin As Twitter CEO Claimed," Sahara Reporters, 25 August 2021, https://saharareporters. com/2021/08/25/fact-check-32-nigerians-dont-own-bitcoin-twitter-ceo-claimed.
13 The Central African Republic's bitcoin experiment failed within a year. The reasons are multiple but relate to the nation's challenging economic conditions, scepticism surrounding its motives, limited access to technology and unfulfilled promises that related to its adoption. As a result, the legal tender status was repealed in March 2023.

can move money freely and easily, with no fees or intermediaries, across borders and peer to peer, in real time. These are the major advantages of decentralised money.

Meanwhile, central banks, governments and regulators are still trying to encourage more adoption of CBDCs. For example, when the Jamaican government launched its own CBDC, the JAM-DEX, in summer 2022, it ran a consumer incentive to reward the first 100,000 Jamaicans who signed up for the JAM-DEX with a J$2,500 ($16) deposit. However, only 36,000 people took advantage of the scheme, so it was extended to people who didn't have bank accounts through the use of know your customer (KYC). Despite this, it still did not succeed. Following the disappointing response to its initial launch, the Jamaican government introduced two further incentive programmes in March 2023 to increase the adoption of the JAM-DEX.

These illustrations of centralised versus decentralised currencies clearly delineate between trust in the government and trust in the network. It appears today, particularly in nations with unstable economies and rife corruption of those who are in power, that the citizens would prefer control of their money through a democratic network rather than a dictatorial machine.

In 2022, the CEO of JPMorgan, Jamie Dimon, was asked by the US Congress how a central CBDC would impact the bank's ability to deploy capital. He replied, "If it is properly done, it will be fine, but I don't trust it will be properly done. You're not going to have the Federal Reserve running call centres. There's a lot more to banking services than the actual token that moves the money."[14]

Bingo. Mr. Dimon's answer reminded me of a quote from the famous American philosopher Yogi Berra: "In theory, there is no difference between theory and practice. In practice, there is."

Do We Need CBDCs?

CBDCs are a response to cryptocurrencies, with the claim that the security and operation of such tokenised digital currencies would be far more secure, robust and trustworthy than those issued by the network of citizens. That

---

14   Chris Skinner, "How would a CBDC impact your ability to deploy capital?" Finanser [blog], 30 September 2022, https://thefinanser.com/2022/09/congress-to-jpmc-how-would-a-cbdc-impact-your-ability-to-deploy-capital.

claim is challenged by those in the DeFi community, who believe we can easily create distributed value networks without centralised control. It is a friction and challenge.

This is why HyFi comes to light. In HyFi, you have the traditional financial system run by banks, backed by governments, and with infrastructure created over the past fifty years. It is known, trusted and used by everyone. Then we have a new financial system, run by technologists, backed by the network, with infrastructure created over the past fifteen years. The issue is that the latter is unknown, trusted by some and used by a few. The two are in conflict and I wonder which will win. But then, does there need to be a winner?

For example, SWIFT, a messaging service used by thousands of banks to send money overseas quickly, accurately and securely, is trying to enable cross-border digital currency usage worldwide. The idea is that SWIFT would connect all of the world's CBDCs for easy payments and settlements. Is this actually needed? After all, we have cryptocurrencies already allowing global seamless real-time currency exchange worldwide and, more importantly, at no cost.

SWIFT and the banking community would claim that it is. The issue is that cryptocurrencies are not run by banks and governments. However, given this context, it's like trying to close the stable door after the horse has bolted. Cryptocurrencies are out there: they are real, they are being used and they allow real-time exchange, globally, with no issues.

The core issue is whether someone can track and trace your activities. This is the reason for justifying the use of cryptocurrencies for everyday trade, and banks with their CBDCs for longer-term saving and investing. In other words, the HyFi model.

Today, we can use crypto to trade and transact globally, in real time, with no one knowing what we are doing. Such currencies can easily work around the government and the regulatory system. That is the key attraction of crypto trading. It is also the issue, as there is no government or regulatory system so, if the funds are lost, you have no comeback. Nevertheless, if we need currencies that are global and real time, that's what cryptocurrencies provide.

The Issue with CBDCs

A widely held belief is that CBDCs would allow governments to invade consumers' privacy by enabling every payment transaction to be tracked and traced. According to Big Brother Watch, there are seven key issues with CBDCs, including the issue of privacy:[15]

1. **It is a solution looking for a problem:** There is insufficient evidence to support a national CBDC, which would transform the financial landscape, endanger privacy and a range of human rights, create security risks, and could irreversibly redefine the relationship between citizen and state.

2. **It invades privacy:** General surveillance of CBDC transactions would be inevitable, given the context of the current legal landscape, particularly around counterterror law, anti-money laundering law and investigatory powers law.

3. **Digital money would control people's lives:** The potential to program the public's personal finances or welfare payments could lead to financial control, an invasion of privacy and potentially a breach of the right to protection of property. Depending on the limitations set, it could also pose a serious threat to a range of other fundamental rights, from freedom of expression to freedom of assembly and protection from discrimination.

4. **Everyone would be identified:** It is impossible to issue a CBDC without a comprehensive digital identity system. Combining digital identity and CBDCs poses a serious risk of surveillance, security breaches, hacking/ identity theft and discrimination.

5. **It would promote data exploitation:** Providers of CBDCs would be able to use personal data to develop marketing activities and tailor products and services. Exploiting personal data in this way would endorse mass surveillance and exploitation of the public's sensitive personal data, giving unlimited access to the companies who want to sell and market to the public.

---

15 Big Brother Watch, No Spycoin, https://bigbrotherwatch.org.uk/campaigns/no-spycoin/.

6. **It could pose security risks:** A centralised CBDC system would create a huge platform of population data and, as such, would provide hostile states and criminals with a large target to focus cyberattacks upon. Specifically, combining digital identity and CBDCs creates a serious risk of security breaches, hacking and identity theft, and a successful breach would put the entire population at risk.
7. **It is undemocratic:** The decision to develop a CBDC should not be made by a central bank and government. It should be made in consultation with the citizens and jointly planned and implemented.

Central banks tend to dismiss such concerns, saying that a CBDC would not threaten privacy, and point out that privacy is a top priority. This is a matter of trust and belief once more. Who do you trust? What do you believe in?

This, in fact, creates the argument for a stablecoin. The argument is that stablecoins could improve efficiency in the payments sector, but would need to be backed by high quality and liquid assets to meet regulatory standards. This is where central banks see their key role, which is to ensure that new forms of money are robust, uniform and trusted. Therefore, if you combined a central bank structure with a decentralised structure, there may be a solution.

IS HYBRID FINANCE THE SOLUTION?

The net-net of everything covered so far in this book—the move to decentralise, the movement of governments to centralise, the breaking of banking by tech, the consolidation of tech by banks—is that we are seeing a whole rearrangement of the old world to be fit for the new world. It is that metamorphosis from analogue to digital and from industrial to networked. This demands a new form of finance—hybrid finance, or HyFi.

CeFi, DeFi? No, It's HyFi with WiFi!

As already mentioned, HyFi combines CeFi with DeFi, where DeFi works for the small things—general payments and transactions—whilst CeFi is required for big things such as investments and loans. HyFi allows both to work seamlessly together. What does this mean?

The issue with DeFi is that it is unregulated. When your payment fails, who do you call? This is the crux of the issue between DeFi and CeFi. If there is no control, how can you manage it? People do tell me that the network is the control. Really? What happens when the network fails?

This hit home a long while ago, when I realised that I didn't have Google's phone number, but it goes beyond this. These days, we spend hours on calls because we don't have access. I need to discuss a questionable payment on my bank card so I call the bank and the reply is, "We are experiencing a high volume of calls at the moment, please wait or use our website." My flight has been changed so I need a refund. I call the airline and the reply is, "We are experiencing a high volume of calls at the moment, please wait or use our website." I can no longer make my doctor's appointment so I need to make a new appointment. I call the surgery and the reply is, "We are experiencing a high volume of calls at the moment, please wait or use our website."

We have moved to a world where everything is automated, but you have to have a control mechanism. The big mistake we are making with digitalisation is believing that everything can be automated. Almost every business believes that it can take this route because it saves money. It's all about saving costs. What they fail to understand is that yes, it can cut costs, but what about the customer? When the automation fails, who does the customer call?

This hits at the heart of the discussion about DeFi and CeFi. I'm all for decentralised finance, peer-to-peer payments and cryptocurrencies. However, in a similar way to automated flight bookings, taxi rides, lost payment transactions and more, what happens when the technology doesn't work? You need a better control system that, ideally, can resolve issues as fast and as easily as possible. You can decentralise as much as you want but if you don't have the controls and access to problem resolution, you have a broken system. That is why you need HyFi.

Banks Need to Be Ready for Hybrid Money

Over the past years, the financial industry has had a weird relationship with the cryptocurrency industry. The former was launched hundreds of years ago; the latter just over a decade ago. Maybe that's why. When the cryptocurrency markets began to emerge, the financial markets said that cryptocurrencies didn't matter. Then the technology, namely blockchain, mattered but the currencies didn't because they needed to be regulated and managed by us. Now we have come to the stage of approving such new financial currencies and offering products and services to deal with them.

This is what surprises most banks. Having rejected cryptocurrencies for years, most banks have moved into custodial services and trading in such currencies over the last few years. This was due to pressure from clients and media, and it means that we are now living in a world where, whether you like it or not, cryptocurrencies are here to stay. The question is: here to stay, but in what form?

It is most likely in the form of HyFi. HyFi is decentralised banking but with a central authority to protect users against losses. It's not necessarily a government or a central bank, but a trusted authority that ensures bad actors are squeezed out of the system and that users get their money back. The authority can just as easily be a network of citizens, like the way in which we use eBay or other services based on user ratings, or it could be a regulatory service or government. It's your choice, but I trust the latter more than the former.

The reason why this is so important is that it has been clear over the past decade or so that a global network of mobile and internet demands a global currency. That is obvious. The less obvious answer is what currency. Interestingly, the nub of the answer to that question was delivered by Bob Diamond, former CEO of Barclays Bank and co-founder and CEO of Atlas Merchant Capital. He is also an incredibly astute investor and banker. Interviewed in the *Financial Times* in 2023, he stated that digital currencies are the way forward: "I can't think of anyone who doesn't believe that in the future a digital version of the dollar for institutional and corporate use isn't going to happen and be far more efficient."[1]

This is a key endorsement of where we are going but, note, it is not an endorsement of a particular currency. It is an endorsement that we will need a digital currency as our future course. Will the dollar be the dominant currency of the network and the future, or will it be the euro or yuan? Or will it be something else like—uh-oh, bitcoin?

Now, I'm very aware how much bankers hate bitcoin, but there is an emerging view that cryptocurrencies need to merge with fiat currencies, and this is the core of the HyFi argument. If you could have a CBDC merged with a cryptocurrency, what would that mean?

When travelling around Europe, you have a digital euro; in the United States, you have a digital dollar; and in China, you use a digital yuan. Then you go onto the network, and you use a global coin. How is a global coin regulated and managed? Well, the answer is that it's obviously a global coin regulated

1   Laura Noonan, "Bob Diamond says digital currencies to have 'very important place' in finance," *Financial Times*, 10 January 2023, https://www.ft.com/content/16089458-3aa9-4f20-82ec-4de47b4b2dd4.

and managed by global business with a global basket of governmentally regulated currencies. In other words, the bitcoin of the future is centrally regulated but de-centrally operated.

The core of the answer to where we are going, as endorsed by Diamond and others, is that we will have a digital currency for institutional and corporate use. Where I disagree with the Diamond camp is that it will not be a digital dollar. It will be a hybrid currency of dollars, yuan and euros managed in an integrated way as a global currency through integration in a basket of decentralised currencies, such as bitcoin and ether.

The question then for banks is how do they offer custodial and transaction services in a basket of currencies that are both centralised and decentralised?

HyFi Complements DeFi and CeFi

- DeFi: decentralised finance appeals to libertarians
- CeFi: centralised finance appeals to governments
- HyFi: hybrid finance combines the benefits of both DeFi and CeFi

HyFi combines the stability of central bank currencies with the decentralised benefits of cryptocurrencies and are, perhaps, best represented by stablecoins. The fact that stablecoins are tied to a basket of value, secured cryptographically and recorded using smart contracts has made them attractive to many communities and, as of the end of September 2021, the circulating supply of the largest US dollar-pegged public stablecoin was almost $130 billion. Having said that, it is still a nascent concept, with a high potential for innovation. There are also several different forms of stablecoin, such as those backed by public reserves, algorithms, private markets and more. Here are the key developments at this stage.

Public Reserve-backed Stablecoins

Most existing stablecoins circulate on public blockchains, such as Ethereum, Binance, Smart Chain or Polygon. Of these public stablecoins, most are backed by cash-equivalent reserves, such as bank deposits, treasury bills and commercial paper.

These reserve-backed stablecoins are also referred to as custodial stablecoins because they are issued by intermediaries who serve as custodians of cash-equivalent assets and offer 1-for-1 redemption of their stablecoin liabilities for US dollars or other fiat currencies. In other words, you can go to the bank and ask them to cash in your stablecoin for the national currency, and it will.

The issue with these is that the full backing and soundness of some public reserve-backed stablecoins have been called into question since the collapse of Terra-LUNA, which was meant to be backed by the US dollar. Equally Tether, the largest stablecoin by circulating value, agreed to pay $41 million to settle a dispute with the U.S. Commodity Futures Trading Commission, which alleged that Tether had misrepresented its backing of real dollar reserves.

Public Algorithmic Stablecoins

Public stablecoins that use mechanisms to stabilise their price, instead of relying on the soundness of underlying reserves, are often called algorithmic stablecoins. While reserve-backed stablecoins are issued as a liability on the balance sheet of a legally incorporated firm, algorithmic stablecoins are maintained by systems of smart contracts that operate exclusively on a public blockchain.

The ability to control these smart contracts is through a governance token, a specialised token used for voting on changes to protocol or governance parameters. These governance tokens can also serve as a direct or indirect claim on future cash flows from the usage of a stablecoin's protocols.

These stablecoins are based on two mechanisms: the collateralised and/or the algorithmic. Collateralised stablecoins are minted when a user deposits a cryptocurrency, such as Ethereum, into smart contract protocols. It's a form of PoS. In contrast, the algorithmic mechanism uses automated smart contracts to buy and sell the stablecoin against a related governance token, such as the US dollar. However, these algorithmic methods sometimes fail, as evidenced by Terra-LUNA in 2022.

Institutional or Private Stablecoins

In addition to reserve-backed stablecoins that circulate on public blockchains, traditional financial institutions have also developed reserve-backed stablecoins, also known as tokenised deposits. These institutional stablecoins are implemented on permissioned, or private, DLTs, and they are used by financial institutions and their clients for efficient wholesale transactions.

The most well-known institutional stablecoin is JPM Coin. JPMorgan and its clients can use the JPM Coin for transactions to enable low-cost, real-time payments and settlement. These private, reserved-backed stablecoins are functionally and economically comparable to products offered by some money transmitters. For example, PayPal allows users to make near-instant transfers and payments within its network, and balances held at these firms are backed similarly to a reserve-backed stablecoin. The key difference is the use of centralised databases, rather than a permissioned DLT.

Use Cases and Growth Potential of Stablecoins

The most important use case of stablecoins is their role in cryptocurrency on public blockchains. Investors prefer to use stablecoins instead of fiat balances to trade cryptocurrency. This is because it allows for near-instantaneous trading without relying on payment systems that sit outside a DLT or having to use custodial holdings of fiat currencies. In other words, stablecoins provide that HyFi ability to trade digital assets from fiat currencies to cryptocurrencies. More than this, they hold the potential for payment innovations, such as programmable money and DeFi.

The programmability and composability of stablecoins currently support decentralised, blockchain-based cryptocurrency markets and services. The outcome then is that DeFi's protocols allow for market making, collateralised lending, derivatives, asset management and other services. In other words, cryptocurrency could become mainstream as a stablecoin backing for robust trading globally. This is a critical factor as, if this does become the case, the key features of cryptocurrency for near-instant, 24/7, non-intermediated payments with low fees become hugely attractive for institutional investors and mainstream investment markets. It is also especially relevant for cross-border transfers, which usually take several days with high fees.

Firms are also using institutional stablecoins to near-instantly move cash across their subsidiaries to manage internal liquidity, and to facilitate wholesale transactions in financial markets requiring things such as intraday repo transactions.[2]

Thus, stablecoins have the potential to spur growth and innovation in payment systems, allowing for faster and cheaper payments, and bring the concept of DeFi (cryptocurrencies) integrated with CeFi (fiat currencies) in a HyFi form.

FSB Says Stablecoins Are Unstable

The Financial Stability Board (FBS), an international body that monitors the global financial system, does not believe in existing stablecoins. It has warned that no existing stablecoin currently meets the standards set by central bankers and financial regulators from the G20 countries.

In a letter to G20 ministers published in February 2023, FBS Chair Klaas Knot stated:[3]

The deeply interconnected and globalised nature of the financial system is such that a multilateral, cross-sectoral policy approach is required to enhance its resilience, along with an approach focused on coordination and policy consistency.

This is my core point about a global coin being based on a basket of currencies that drives the HyFi model. The FSB, for example, clarifies between DeFi and CeFi, or traditional finance (FradFI) as FSB refers to it. The FSB's argument is that the DeFi ecosystem "has a multi-layered architecture that includes permissionless blockchains, self-executing code

---

2   In a repo, one party sells an asset to another party at one price and commits to repurchase the same asset at a different price at a future date.
3   Klaas Knot, "To G20 Finance Ministers and Central Bank Governors," Financial Stability Board, 16 February 2023, https://www.fsb.org/wp-content/uploads/P200223-1.pdf.

(or so-called smart contracts), DeFi protocols and purportedly decentralised applications (DApps)".[4]

The FSB expands on this to state that many of the DeFi products and services only interact with other DeFi products and services, rather than with the traditional financial system and the real economy. The FSB is also concerned that CeFi players are entering the market. For example, BNY Mellon, State Street, JPMorgan and others are offering custodial and trading services in decentralised currencies. What does this mean for the CeFi system?

The FSB concluded in its 2023 report that "DeFi does not differ substantially from [CeFi] in the functions it performs. In attempting to replicate some of the functions of the traditional financial system, DeFi inherits and may amplify the vulnerabilities of that system. This includes well-known vulnerabilities such as operational fragilities, liquidity and maturity mismatches, leverage and interconnectedness. DeFi's specific features may result in these vulnerabilities playing out at times differently than in traditional finance, for example as a result of the risks of fire sales related to the automatic liquidation of collateral based on smart contracts, reliance on oracles for external information or dependence on infrastructure over which the DeFi developers may not have direct control (i.e. the underlying blockchain). The fact that crypto-assets underpinning much of DeFi lack inherent value and are highly volatile magnifies the impact of these vulnerabilities when they materialise, as recent incidents demonstrate."[5]

In light of its findings, the FSB has proposed that it should proactively analyse the financial vulnerabilities of the DeFi ecosystem. Second, in collaboration with standard-setting bodies (SSBs) and regulatory authorities, the FSB should explore approaches to fill data gaps to measure and monitor interconnectedness of DeFi with CeFi and the real economy alongside the cryptoasset ecosystem. Third, the FSB will look at policy recommendations for the international regulation of cryptoasset activities to acknowledge DeFi-specific risks and facilitate the application and enforcement of rules. DeFi-specific risks may include the use of smart contracts, governance arrangements

4   Financial Stability Board, "The Financial Stability Risks of Decentralised Finance," 16 February 2023, https://www.fsb.org/2023/02/the-financial-stability-risks-of-decentralised-finance/.
5   Financial Stability Board.

(including concentrated ownership), dependence on blockchain networks and use of cross-chain bridges.

In other words, the FSB is looking at how to create an effective HyFi governance model. It recognises that digital assets and cryptocurrencies are out there in the wild but, as I say, they are literally in the wild. How can you provide effective governance of a decentralised system, especially when that system is censorship resistant? Equally, what does censorship resistant mean? It means resistance to centralise authorities. So how can you create currencies that can be transacted securely and with confidence and trust, with no centralised government or governance involved?

This is the question everyone in the payments and finance world is grappling with. Is the answer DeFi or CeFi? It's a mixture, which is what HyFi proposes and, seemingly, the FSB endorses.

Where Do We Go from Here?
As made clear so far, the centralised versus decentralised view of the world is not clear-cut and dried. Then there is a hybrid view of the world, where DeFi and CeFi can work together in harmony and equilibrium.

This is a feature of Klaus Schwab's proposition for the "Great Reset". What is the Great Reset? The basis is that the global financial system needs to be reset to reflect all stakeholders, not just shareholders. Five points need to be met in order to achieve this:
1. redefining the social contract
2. decarbonising the economy
3. digitising everything
4. implementing stakeholder capitalism
5. executing the global roll-out of the above

I guess as I was raised within the system, I am a product of the system. Therefore, I subscribe to all of the above. Having said that, there is an alternative view as the above is all about money, power and centralisation and, almost always, results in the same conclusion. You cannot have an economy that is unregulated, and you cannot have money without governance for that reason.

The system firmly believes in controls but, interestingly, never demands that such controls should be centralised. If the network can create a decentralised system, with decentralised controls that can be trusted, then so be it. The trouble is that, too often, the controls cannot be trusted in the decentralised world. People lose money all of the time, and there are far too many bad actors.

On top of this, many people are not technologists, don't understand these things and quite like to have a secure control structure around them. It's a bit like the old argument about empowerment. You can all do your own thing, but most people don't want to. They want to be told what to do. You can argue this point, but eight out of ten people just want to live happy lives and have structure. That means they want someone to tell them what to do. It's the remaining two that fight the system.

How can you break the system? Throughout history, ever since humanity became civilised, the weak have been ruled by the powerful. The Great Reset argues that the WEF, and its constituent members of government and business, can increase centralised control, but that it needs to happen in an equitable style where all stakeholders win. Stakeholders being society, community, the planet, customers, employees, government and shareholders. This is why advocates of the Great Reset argue that we will never have a system that is truly decentralised. In biology, in history, in reality, there has never been a system in which everyone owns their own destiny. They have to conform to the norms of their society, whether an ant, a bee, a lion, a tiger or a human.

In other words, it is in our blood to have controllers and those who are controlled. Without those controls, nothing works. That is why I believe in a hybrid system. There will be decentralised structures, but people will only use them for things that are liberal. If they want secure structures, they will use those that have centralised oversight.

Money over Internet Protocol

The core of what is happening is the creation of Money over Internet Protocol, or MoIP for short. If you think of MoIP, it's like Voice over Internet Protocol

(VoIP), a nascent technology in the early 2000s that is now mainstream. Does this mean that we can compare banking to the telecommunications industry from twenty-five years ago?

At that time, many of the large telco firms went bankrupt because they did not predict or see the impact of such massive technological change. An interesting article in *Forbes* put this into context:

> When Voice-Over-Internet-Protocol (VoIP) was invented in 1995, most people disparaged it as a technology that couldn't scale and wasn't a threat to the telecom giants. Then, circa 2003, the technology to scale VOIP arrived – broadband – and within a flash, most of the telecom industry's copper-wire networks became obsolete. Useless relics.[6]

That much is true. I was working for a subsidiary of AT&T back then, and remember that the AT&T folks believed the changes were not relevant. Nevertheless, I disagree with the sentiment of the *Forbes* article, which also stated:

> Anyone in the world can become members of these emerging payment networks in the span of a few hours, using equipment that costs a few hundred dollars. Banks' IT systems will never be able to compete with that.[7]

Really? If this were true, it would have happened years ago. Yet for all the FinTechs in the world, of which there are thousands, not one has destroyed or disrupted a leading bank in any country to date. In fact, I would claim any start-up that wants to replace a bank will fail. What start-ups need to do is augment and amplify banks, renovate and renew their processes, simplify and solve their technology issues. Don't try to disrupt and destroy them as you will fail.

---

6   Caitlin Long, "Banks Are About To Face The Same Tsunami That Hit Telecom Twenty Years Ago," *Forbes*, 23 September 2022, https://www.forbes.com/sites/caitlinlong/2022/09/23/banks-are-about-to-face-the-same-tsunami-that-hit-telecom-twenty-years-ago/.
7   Caitlin Long.

The point most miss here is that big banks are protected by high levels of regulation. Unlike with a telco, retailer or similar firm, it matters when things go wrong. After all, banks are as important to governments as the brain is important to your body. If it's not working, you cease to exist. This is why governments protect banks and banking more than any other industry. They are up there with airlines and pharmaceuticals and, to be clear, when things go wrong, the people want a central authority to sort it out. They want a central authority that will protect them. They want a central authority to run to when they need help. They want a central authority.

When people might die, governments take notice. When economies might die, governments take notice. When industries can kill people or economies, governments take notice. That's why, since records began, no big bank has been destroyed by tech. They just get bigger and, when threatened by tech, they take it out through acquisition or imitation.

Reputation as a Currency

A colleague recently said that the future of money was power. Well, all power is based on money, but their point was that money would be based on real power, as in the energy industries. Namely, oil, gas and electricity. These are the key industries providing energy to the world. These days you could add wind, solar and other renewable energy providers to the list, but is this the future and why is it important?

Well, because energy can be a currency. Back in 2008, people were talking about water being a currency of the future.[8] Anything can be a currency. For example, the currency of the future could be your reputation. Reputation is the key currency, as reputation creates trust. If you are trusted, you can trade. If not, you cannot. Money and investing have little to do with assets; it's all about trust. What is it that backs your investment? What is it that reinforces your trust?

This gets interesting when you consider what actually backs anything of value. When you buy something, can you guarantee it will be delivered? When you invest or buy anything, you have a belief that it is of value, but is it really?

---

8   Chris Skinner, "*The future of trading,*" Finanser [blog], 6 August 2008, https://thefinanser.com/2008/08/the-future-of-t.

Whether it is bitcoin, the US dollar, a work of art or a rare commodity, the core of any trade or transaction is your belief that it has value. That belief is based on trust. That trust is based on reputational history.

Reputation is the core of what you earn in Gene Rodenberry's utopian world of *Star Trek*. Could we create a world where the betterment of humanity, and your contribution to that goal, is recognised in reputational credits? *Star Trek*'s idea is not acquiring monetary wealth, but reputational wealth.

This shows the nature of currencies. The only reason why we accept a currency is because we trust it. The only reason why we invest in something is because we trust it. If you buy something, whether it be a Picasso painting or a book from Amazon, you trust it will be delivered. Obviously, it makes a difference when something costs $100 million as compared to $1, but the trust in the follow-through is the key.

And how is that trust built? It's based on reputation. You have to have a reputational trust to attract investment. Reputation is created by track record. Reputation is maintained through consistent actions and can be lost in a second. This is the core of all monetary and market movements and investments. Do you trust it? What's the provenance? Can you accept its reputational value?

Gene Rodenberry recognised something that I have only just realised myself. We do not trade in commodities, assets, products and services. We trade in trust, backed by reputation. Is this the currency of the future?

> "Reputation and honours replace
> economic wealth as markers of status."
> **Manu Saadia**, *Trekonomics* (2016)

MOVING FINANCE INTO THE VIRTUALLY AUGMENTED WORLDS

After all of the discussions about trust, belief, centralisation, decentralisation and the currencies of the future, we now move into a third dimension or, to be more exact, the third web. The third web, or Web3, is about to arrive and it is very different to what has come before. It brings us much closer to the vision of a virtual life in a virtual world with virtual money. Web3 demands that we have new currencies and constructs. At the heart of this debate is what will the financial world of the future be in a virtual structure? Let's first define some areas:

> Web3, as envisioned by the Web3 Foundation, will be a public internet where data and content are registered on blockchains, tokenized, or managed and accessed on peer-to-peer distributed networks.

> Web3 promises to be a decentralized, immutable version of the web, free of intermediaries and built with the same cryptographic verifiability that has given rise to cryptocurrencies, non-fungible tokens (NFTs), and new types of decentralized applications underpinned by a distributed ledger, or Dapps.[1]

The background to this is that Web1 was the basic internet structure; Web2 created commerce and social services that are now dominated by a

---

1   Scott Carey, "What is Web3? A new decentralized web, or the latest marketing buzzword?" Infoworld, 12 January 2022, https://www.infoworld.com/article/3646597/what-is-web3-a-new-decentralized-web-or-the-latest-marketing-buzzword.html.

few Big Techs; and Web3 will change all of that by using Ethereum and other services to decentralise everything, particularly finance, which will become DeFi.

The problem is that some believe that Web3 is morphing into a monster that looks, talks and acts like Web2, but with the shiny addition of the blockchain. What's the problem with this? Well, the core issue is that too much power is in the hands of too few. The power should be in the hands of the people, and yet it is in the hands of Jeff Bezos, Mark Zuckerberg and Pony Ma.

Moving on, why is Ethereum so integral to Web3?

Ethereum is by far the largest Web 3.0 and DeFi ecosystem, maintaining 30% of all full-time developers working in the space since 2017 [...] There are over 18,000 monthly active developers in the DeFi and Web 3.0 ecosystem that provide various contributions to projects. Of that tally, over 4,000 work on Ethereum, accounting for over 22% of all the developers working in the space, according to research by Electric Capital.[2]

By using Ethereum tokens on a registered ledger, the view is that we can give power to the people through decentralised finance. Yet the huge battle between centralisation and decentralisation still rages. The interesting thing is that Ethereum can enable both but, given the way Web3 is panning out, it is leaning towards centralisation rather than decentralisation.

There are some very influential people who are trying to change this outcome, such as Tim Berners-Lee.

"I've always believed the web is for everyone," wrote Tim Berners-Lee, the well-known (and knighted) creator of the World Wide Web. The web has evolved into an engine of inequity and division; swayed by powerful forces who use it for their own agendas," he added. "Today, I

2   Ruholamin Haqshanas, "Ethereum Leads Web3 Developer Count, with 700+ New Devs Each Month," Tokenist, 6 January 2022, https://tokenist.com/ethereum-leads-web3-developer-count-with-700-new-devs-each-month/.

believe we've reached a critical tipping point, and that powerful change for the better is possible — and necessary."[3]

If they succeed—and put the power into the people's hands—the structures impacted are not just Big Tech, but Big Banks and Big Gov too.

Welcome to the Metaverse

If the Web3 decentralised vision *is* realised, it will deliver the metaverse. The metaverse is the alternative world of the internet that allows you to travel without leaving your chair. It's like the holodeck of *Star Trek: The Next Generation*, where you walk through a door—in this case, a virtual one—and enter an alternative universe.

As defined by Wikipedia: "[The Metaverse is] a collective virtual shared space including the sum of all virtual worlds and the Internet. It may contain derivatives or copies of the real world, but it is distinct from augmented reality. The word 'metaverse' is made up of the prefix 'meta' (meaning beyond) and the stem 'verse' (a backformation from 'universe'); the term is typically used to describe the concept of a future iteration of the internet, made up of persistent, shared, 3D virtual spaces linked into a perceived virtual universe."

Why is this a hot topic as people have been living virtually for a while? During the pandemic, people were locked down for over a year, and transporting themselves to other worlds via the internet. The *New York Times* makes this easy to digest:

Remember hearing about "the internet"? Get ready for "the metaverse." The term comes from digital antiquity: Coined by the writer Neal Stephenson in his 1992 novel, "Snow Crash," then reimagined as the Oasis in the Ernest Cline novel "Ready Player One," it refers to a fully realized digital world that exists beyond the analog one in which we live ...

---

3   Kate Clark, "Tim Berners-Lee is on a mission to decentralize the web," TechCrunch, 9 October 2018, https://techcrunch.com/2018/10/09/tim-berners-lee-is-on-a-mission-to-decentralize-the-web/.

As a buzzword, the metaverse refers to a variety of virtual experiences, environments and assets that gained momentum during the online-everything shift of the pandemic. Together, these new technologies hint at what the internet will become next.

Video games like Roblox and Fortnite and Animal Crossing: New Horizons, in which players can build their own worlds, have metaverse tendencies, as does most social media. If you own a non-fungible token or even just some crypto, you're part of the metaversal experience. Virtual and augmented reality are, at a minimum, metaverse adjacent. If you've attended a work meeting or a party using a digital avatar, you're treading into the neighborhood of metaversality.

Founders, investors, futurists and executives have all tried to stake their claim in the metaverse, expounding on its potential for social connection, experimentation, entertainment and, crucially, profit.[4]

Profit. That's where our interest should be piqued. So why is this relevant to FinTech and Banking?

Well, payments and finance are going to be a battleground in metaverse worlds. There are virtual world payment systems. Interoperability between such worlds has not been cracked. You may wonder why it's important to do this, and the answer is customer experience. If I build up a major virtual world store of value with MetaBank but cannot transfer this to AltBank, then the customer will become frustrated. We saw this in the past with Second Life when Ginko Financial disappeared (more on that later), and it is clear that there is an opportunity here to be the MegaBank for the metaverse.

There's plenty more about the metaverse out there. Some of you may dismiss this as just gaming but I would urge you to bear in mind that gaming is bigger than the movie industry. It is the greatest marketplace now and

---

4   John Herrman and Kellen Browning, "Are We in the Metaverse Yet?" *New York Times*, 10 July 2021, https://www.nytimes.com/2021/07/10/style/metaverse-virtual-worlds.html.

well into the future, and it will demand access to virtual banking and finance. Therefore, if you dismiss it, you are missing out and losing out on one of the greatest opportunities to make money *and profit* for the next decades.

What we are going to see is a whole army of visionaries and innovators from Facebook to PayPal to Stripe to Adyen to the whole FinTech community creating an alternative financial universe. A finverse if you like. The challenge of the finverse—which will be HUGE!—is where do you find a financial service you can trust in this alternative life?

The Metaverse Will Be Worth Trillions

Citibank has stated that the metaverse will be an $8 to $13 *trillion* opportunity by 2030:

> The total addressable market for the Metaverse could be between $8 trillion and $13 trillion by 2030, with total Metaverse users numbering around five billion. But getting to that market level is going to require infrastructure investment. The content streaming environment of the Metaverse will likely require a computational efficiency improvement of over 1,000x today's levels. Investment will be needed in areas such as compute, storage, network infrastructure, consumer hardware, and game development platforms.

> [...] the definition of what counts as money in the Open Metaverse is also likely to be very different from what counts as money in the real world today. Interoperability and seamless exchange between underlying blockchain technology are critical to ensure a frictionless user experience. Different forms of cryptocurrency are expected to dominate, but given the multi-chain trend in the crypto ecosystem, cryptocurrency will likely coexist with fiat currencies, central bank digital currencies (CBDCs), and stablecoins.[5]

5   Citi GPS, "Metaverse and Money: Decrypting the Future, Citi," 30 March 2022, https://icg.citi.com/icghome/what-we-think/citigps/insights/metaverse-and-money_20220330.

The bank's views are hardly surprising, particularly as other major financial firms, such as JPMorgan Chase, are opening virtual branches in the metaverse. The question is why would you need a branch in the real or virtual world and, in a greater context, why do you need a bank?

A series of events dating back twenty years ago show the way. Back in the 2000s, a hype cycle surrounded something called Second Life, and a big lesson came with Second Life because real money was being made.

Second Life was a popular virtual world that hit the headlines in 2006 due to some users making over $1 million in real life by developing and selling properties in their virtual lives. At the time, the biggest bank in Second Life was Ginko Financial. Ginko Financial allowed people to put real US dollars into a virtual bank. The virtual dollars were called Linden dollars as the platform was run by Linden Lab. A real US dollar purchased 27 Linden dollars, and the virtual dollars could be used to buy designer label outfits as well as virtual property on the main street.

That was great but then, one day, Ginko Financial simply disappeared. It turned out, upon investigation, that the bank had been run by one player who, having taken almost a million of real money as deposits, had pressed delete and bought himself an apartment and a Ferrari. Unsurprisingly, this upset the Second Life community and, for three months, the virtual people in Second Life demonstrated outside the virtual headquarters of the Second Life operator, Linden Lab, demanding their money back.

Vittual demonstrators
in Second Life

Initially, Linden Lab stated that it just provided the platform and was not responsible for regulating such virtual banks. Eventually though, Linden Lab backtracked and said that if you want to be a bank in the virtual world, you have to be a bank in the real world. In other words, you have to have a banking licence backed by a regulator, which is typically a central bank operating on behalf of a national government. Message heard, lesson learnt.

Now we are replacing Second Life with the metaverse, but nothing has changed. In the metaverse, people will have fun, but they will also invest and exchange money and value. As they do so, they will need a metaverse bank and a metaverse coin.

Whoever owns those platforms will be regulated and managed, in the same way as real-world money. It does not mean that they are regulated and managed by a national government, as the government could be the network. It could be a cryptocurrency or a new world currency that the network endorses and accepts. After all, we only believe money is money and has value because that is what we believe.

The point is that, whether it's cryptocurrencies, FinTech, the metaverse or something else, you need governance to make finance work successfully. What governance do you need? This is where a lot of technologists, libertarians and FinTech people get it wrong. Even Bill Gates has got it wrong. Back in the 1990s, Gates said that we need banking but we don't need banks.

We need to make payments, but we don't need banks to make payments. We need to save and invest, but we don't necessarily need banks to save and invest. We need to borrow and get credit, but we don't necessarily need to go to banks to get credit. However, a core element of banks is that they are licensed and governed and provide *a guarantee of trust* that you will not lose your money. No other business does this. No other business has the insurance guarantee that ensures no losses.

This is why banks will be around for the next century or more, maybe even the next millennium, because if you store money, you need to store it somewhere that is trusted. If you're just transacting, it doesn't really matter. Decentralised finance for transacting is therefore fine, but storing savings and investments on a platform that's decentralised, and that has no guarantee or licence or backing?

Isn't the Metaverse Just a Game?

In the 2000s, there were several massive trading scandals involving investment banks, such as the major losses created by Jérôme Kerviel of Société Générale and Kweku Adoboli of UBS. And let's not forget the most infamous rogue trader of all, Nick Leeson of Barings Bank. What did they all have in common? Gaming.

You probably don't think of it like this but banking is a game. This is particularly true of investment banking and trading. You see the numbers moving on the screen; they turn red, they turn green. It's just like a game. That is the comment that both Kerviel and Adoboli made. It didn't seem real. It was just about moving numbers and charts on screens. It's much like the seductive game of online gambling, which people refer to as casino capitalism. The difference between the two is that those who gamble tend to gamble with their own money, not other people's.

Now imagine that you are a student into gaming who gets a job with MegaInvest Bank. You're trained for six months under the graduate scheme and then you get your big opportunity—to join the trading team. You join the team, are given a screen, see the numbers rise and fall, call the clients, shift millions and, over time, billions. You get the idea. The idea is that, in our age of digitalisation and screens, the line between reality and virtuality is very, very fine. What's the difference between Fortnite and Apple shares? Just a click.

Back in the early 2010s, when Adoboli's case came to light, one trader stated that the City was rife with gambling addicts whose habits contributed to a risk-prone culture.[6] Then you watch a series like the BBC's *Industry*—where investment bankers are hooked on drink, drugs, gambling and worse—and you think that it can't be real. But it is. The world of trading and investments is dominated by the lucky gamblers who win and smashed by the many who lose.

Sometimes, I wonder if we are one click away from disaster but, luckily, checks and balances are in place. When we get flash trading and flash

---

6   Peter Walker, "Kweku Adoboli's risky bets fuelled by City-wide 'addiction'," *Guardian*, 20 November 2012, https://www.theguardian.com/business/2012/nov/20/kweku-adoboli-bets-city-addiction.

crashes, the system catches up and places safeguards, brakes and blocks. Or, at the very least, we hope it does.

So, let's bring it back to reality. Imagine the City is one big gambling house, and traders are betting on thousands of companies (horses) running on tracks around the world. Pensions funds and asset managers are knocking on the bank's (bookie's) door, and the ones who win and get the best returns are happy to pay a percentage of their winnings to the bookie. The more the bookie makes, the bigger the bonus. The only difference is that most bets on a racetrack are for small beans; most bets on the City track are for the gross domestic product (GDP) of Ghana. Why Ghana? It's where Kweku Adoboli was born, with a GDP of just over $75 billion in 2022.

Banking on the Game[7]

Instead of democratising or decentralising financial markets, most customers want to "play" the markets and enjoy the thrill of quick wins and losses, just as one would in a casino. Why should we offer banks and trading services when people simply want casinos? Are customers educated about trading? Most certainly not. A good number of people fail, losing their hard-earned cash. Following regulatory requirements, some financial institutions sent customers books about the secrets to success in financial markets, but even this did not achieve the intended results, as most of those books ended up in the bin.

What about those who are not doing anything about their financial affairs? In developed markets, approximately 40 per cent of the population in the United States and approximately 45 per cent of the EU population are categorised as financially illiterate. In emerging markets from Asia and Africa, about 50 to 60 per cent of these populations do not even have access to financial services. In parts of the world, addressing issues in financial literacy and inclusion mean first addressing literacy, thus doubling the challenges for delivering meaningful financial content.

These challenges are not new. Various initiatives driven by G20, the World Bank, regulators and governments around the world aim to promote

---

7   This section was written by Matthias Kroener, founder and former CEO of Fidor Bank and co-founder of Tradelite Solutions.

financial inclusion and education, with the goal to stabilise and improve local societies. But it is difficult to make financial literacy an engaging and exciting topic that people would be interested in, especially since the topic has mostly been presented in the form of classroom theories, complex charts and boring numbers. Have you ever tried to learn about mortgages, asset allocation, inflation, loans, compound interest and capital gains without any support? It can be extremely frustrating.

Now, here is the million-dollar question: how can we deliver financial literacy as an interesting and fun activity for the user? Gaming is the solution to this dilemma. Game-based learning has long been proven to be an engaging and productive way of delivering education to learners of all levels. Video games, in particular, are an effective method to reach every corner of the world. For example, there are three billion gamers worldwide, and this number is growing.

People love games because the ultimate objective of a game is to provide the best user experience possible. Games support players' wishes to become "better" by giving concrete tasks and achievable goals that fit with the players' capabilities and offering timely reward and feedback by eliminating distractions with fun and engaging interactions. Players naturally learn and improve skills, without the obvious educational experience of "being taught" and "studying". In addition, as games are fun, easy and convenient, players are more likely to increase visits and duration per visit. Ultimately, the user experience that each game aims to offer is *flow*.

Here, "flow" refers to the state of operation in which a person performing an activity is fully immersed in a feeling of energised focus, full involvement and enjoyment throughout the process of the activity. Therefore, it is important to try to ensure that games are never too easy (and hence boring) or too complicated (and hence frustrating).

So why should financial institutions think of distributing video games to their customers? Some believe that the challenges of financial inclusion and financial education can be tackled by using video games as a method of customer acquisition, customer engagement and customer education. Video games provide an entertaining channel to create and maintain contact with the customer, increase customer lifetime value and transport the messages of the brand without being boring or frustrating. And to achieve the flow effectively, one must leave game development with the experts, namely, the game developers.

Finally, there is a big difference between video games and gamification. Video games offer no-to-low risk education, entertainment and some thrill while gamification is often a "fun camouflage" to products and services with real material risks. The two—games and gamification—may look similar, but are certainly not the same.

Take the Finverse More Seriously

Making banking fun in the virtual worlds will become a great way of giving customers service, education and capabilities. This is why bankers need to take the finverse more seriously. The strange thing is that a lot of people don't get this. For example, when talking about the metaverse and crypto, Jemima Kelly, a commentator with the *Financial Times*, stated:

> As far as I'm concerned, the hypocritical fantasy that underpins crypto also lies at the heart of the metaverse. This isn't about building a decentralised paradise where everyone can prosper and live in harmony; this is about making a small group of people rich.
>
> [...] I have always suspected that one of the reasons people keep buying into crypto — which I consider akin to a Ponzi scheme — is that they don't really understand it.[8]

Oh dear. These are ingrained old-market views. Like the extremes of how young internet-born generations feel about the world versus how older industrial-focused generations feel about the world. The younger generation thinks that everything can liberalised through the network; the older generation thinks that the younger generation is stupid, and the network has to conform to its industrial-era rules.

---

8   Jemima Kelly, "Cryptocurrencies will be as useless in the metaverse as they are now," *Financial Times*, 27 October 2021, https://www.ft.com/content/c28799d4-88bf-42b9-8ad5-53ab5647ba60.

So, here's the conflict: the network promotes freedom whilst the regulators promote government control. This is why Kelly's comments seem a little naïve because new generations using new technologies are creating new ways to interact and new ideas about how money works. Younger people will change the world. It's not going to be me.

By way of example, look at gaming. In recent years, the gaming industry has surpassed the combined revenues of the film and music industries. This is why the metaverse is so important. If you can create that holodeck, then that will be the next-generation gaming world and will be worth more than the film, music and gaming industries and all other downtime activities combined.

If you consider that statement, then currencies for metaverses make absolute sense. You may enter the metaverse with a dollar or a yuan but, once you're in, you never cash out. You need interoperability between metaverses, but you don't need dollars or yuan. It's an idea that has been around for a long time. By way of example, Fidor Bank's former CEO Matthias Kroener had the idea back in the early 2010s to bank World of Warcraft Gold. Now, he's banking on gaming. Sure, some metaverse investments will be wasted—think of Second Life and Ginko Financial—but some will be the next-generation winners.

HOW FINTECHS ARE TAKING THE OPPORTUNITY

Moving on from the metaverse, let's look generally at what is happening with FinTech. Around 30,000 new FinTech firms have launched around the world since the 2000s, with all of them looking to create new ways of doing payments, finance, investments and loans. They are embracing everything from blockchain, cryptocurrencies, APIs, apps and AI to embedded financial services, quantum computing and more. Using these technologies, they are reinventing finance. Who are they? What are they doing? Where?

By 2021, the FinTech industry had grown from almost nothing in 2010 to 38 per cent of the value of the financial market players. Every single aspect of the market has been taken apart by these new visionary players, and they are all focused on doing one thing brilliantly. Unlike banks, they are not trying to do everything. Some are innovating and doing things that have never been done, particularly in the cryptocurrency space, but most are solving the things that are broken and don't work online with banks. My advice to any start-up is to either fix what banks do badly or do things that banks don't do.

The Value of FinTech versus Banks

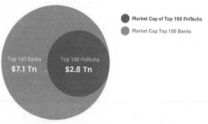

Sources: Companiesmarketcap, CFTE 2021

When we talk about FinTech, we tend to talk a lot about a few FinTech firms—Stripe, Revolut and Klarna—but what about the rest? Let's map the new global financial ecosystem of FinTech innovations.

The United States

Source: CBInsights

Europe

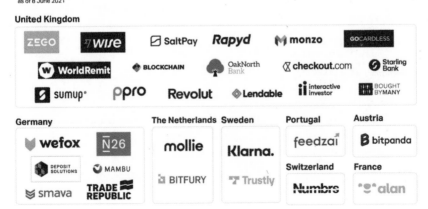

Source: Sifted

Africa

140 Financial Services Companies in South Africa

Source: Baobab Insights

Latin America

180+ FinTech companies shaping Latin America

Source: Armada Labs

China

Source: Tellimer

Hong Kong

Source: CrowdFundInsider

The above does not include the microsystems that you can see in Singapore, Hong Kong, Dubai and other city states. Nor does it include countries that are growing FinTech bubbles, such as India. India's FinTech companies are poised to become three times as valuable in the next five years, reaching a valuation of over $150 billion by 2025, according to a report by BCG and Ficci. The worldwide view is even more amazing.

A Global View of FinTech Unicorns

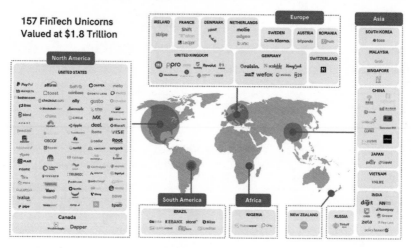

Source: CFTE

Given the number of firms worldwide, is FinTech really disruptive? Nearly every FinTech start-up says that it will change banking forever. These start-ups use the word "disruption" continuously, as well as words like "incumbent" and "old" to describe traditional financial firms. Yet, after almost twenty years of such talk, has the old incumbent been disrupted? This doesn't seem to be the case when we look at big financial firms like JPMorgan Chase or Visa.

In both cases, we see how a big old bank and the massive payments network have survived well through the past twenty years or so of *supposed* disruption. This begs the question: why are they not being disrupted? They actually are, but they recognise that there are massive barriers to disruption. The barrier for entry into a banking system is how to break a 200-year-old cartel that does not need disrupting? The barrier for entry into the card payments network is how to break a 50-year-old duopoly that does not need disrupting?

So what disruption is happening? Well, most of it is around the periphery of the system. It's not at the core of the system. When you look at the FinTech unicorns, most are tackling things in the adjacency of banking that can be tackled by the network. For example, Stripe addresses the issues of checkout online, eToro deals with how to make investing easier and Square (renamed Block) offers easy ways to take and make payments for small businesses.

The truth is that a lot of these so-called FinTech disruptors are not disrupting; they are adding. Stripe, eToro and Block have added easier ways to access payments and finance, rather than replaced them. They also use Visa and Mastercard, which have not been replaced, and accept payments from banks like JPMorgan, which are as systemically important as ever.

So, what is really happening here? There are two major factors: the existing and the new. The existing force is so well structured that it is hard to change it. It's a bit like saying "let's create a new political party" or "let's create a new car company". Obviously, it can be done—just look at the Green Party or Tesla—but it is a fragile system fighting a stable one.

And there's the rub. When you have massive infrastructure and engagement, getting people to change is hard. It's like the well-trodden line of people who say banks are bad and need to change but then not one of them changes their bank. By way of example, when Barclays exposed the LIBOR scandal, its customers said that they would close their accounts and leave the bank. Did anyone do it? Not that you would notice. When Wells Fargo got caught out with illegal account openings and signatures, customers said that they would close their accounts. Did they? Not that you would notice.

The fact is that people may dislike banks but they need banking like they need electricity. People may find FinTechs that make payments and cross-border services easier, but these are additions to banking. They don't replace banks. People may enjoy more services around the world online, but those services online are still backed by Visa and Mastercard because Visa and

Mastercard are accepted worldwide. So, the world may be changing but the traditional firms are still behind that world of change, whether you like it or not.

Are FinTechs Being Valued as a Financial or a Tech?

Chris Brendler, an analyst at D.A. Davidson, made the following comment about FinTech Affirm, a US buy now, pay later (BNPL) start-up:

> "These kind of hybrid financial technology stocks, they kind of trade like tech stocks when they're growing really fast and the financial side of their business doesn't cause any problems [...] but, if you start having higher losses or funding problems, that's when they start to perform like financials."[1]

What's the difference between a tech stock and a financial stock? About 1,000 basis points. Tech stocks trade on future market potential and see firms valued for billions when they have never made a profit and have revenues in the millions. A financial stock trades in millions when they have revenues in the billions.

This is a big frustration for those in banking, as their measurements for the investment community are all about return on equity (ROE), cost-to-income ratio, cost of funds, net interest margin (NIM) and such like. These are then stacked up against a community of equivalent financial firms and typically create a share price of almost nine times earnings. A tech firm gets price-to-earnings ratios of five times that level.

This is because technology companies grow far faster than financial firms. Therefore, if you invest in the right ones, there is far more potential. Take a company like Stripe which, in 2021, processed $640 billion in payments and was valued early that year at $95 billion. Out of all of that processing however, its profits are minimal. Based on figures of early 2023, Stripe is making profits of $100 million based on processing $1 trillion of payments.[2] That's not so healthy.

---

1   Sujeet Indap and Imani Moise, "Affirm struggles to convince investors of fintech bona fides," *Financial Times*, 10 May 2022, https://www.ft.com/content/53697164-cfd0-4a73-add4-9628b5c4c273.
2   Katie Roof and Jennifer Surane, "Stripe Is on Track to Turn a Profit With $1 Trillion in Payment Volume," Bloomberg, 16 February 2023, https://www.bloomberg.com/news/articles/2023-02-16/stripe-is-on-track-to-turn-a-profit-with-1-trillion-in-payment-volume.

But then roll this back to Amazon, which took years to even make a profit. Founded in 1994, it made a small profit in 2001 but has spent most its life reinvesting in its business model to fuel growth. That's what tech stocks do. A financial stock cannot do this, as reinvesting for growth is not seen as the priority. Shareholder payback wins over investing for the future in many cases.

The net-net of this is that FinTech stocks are valued as tech stocks at the start but, if they stumble, they start being valued more like bank stocks.

The Big Regression?

Interestingly, as the 2020s started, major changes began to be seen in FinTech and banking. Banks acquired FinTechs and vice versa. The main trends were around:

- Big Tech moving into finance, and the idea that we may see Big Tech banks like Amazon Bank
- banks getting into bed with FinTechs and liking it as they drive towards Open Banking
- digital banking sporting new technology, mainly video banking, which is a game changer
- new security threats and solutions increasing, with ransomware key
- income being generated from sustainable initiatives such as the carbon offset and renewable energy markets
- cryptocurrencies seriously starting to challenge fiat currencies

However, the biggest issue FinTech markets faced in 2022 was funding and the fact that FinTech is facing a big regression over the next few years. It started in China when the $300 billion IPO of Ant Group was dismantled. Now it has spread to Europe and the United States.

What is the big regression? It is the reversal of technological progress. It's not that people reject technology, particularly once they are aware of the benefits; it's due to governments and regulations. A big factor in the FinTech implosion is that regulators started to dismantle some of the unregulated markets that they now want to regulate. It began when peer-to-peer (P2P) lending stalled and, in some markets such as China, failed. By way of example,

Zopa, the original P2P lending innovator, gave up P2P lending at the end of 2021. Then crowdfunding leader Kickstarter started to struggle as it found it hard to kick or start. Now we can see governments putting more and more of a squeeze on everything from BNPL to cryptocurrency exchanges and bitcoin mining.

Although governments and regulators are playing a major role in this, the view of customers and users also comes into play. In the past couple of years, there has been a major shift away from things people don't know and don't understand, to a return to things they do know and understand. It's the big regression from tech insecurity to bank security.

This is illustrated well by many headlines about FinTech losses and layoffs, and storm clouds are gathering fast to demand market change through consolidation and merger. The *Economist* has even called this "a FinTech bloodbath".[3]

Where is this heading? It's heading over a cliff for some and into the sun for a few. We had very heady times, so much so that some companies became unicorns with no substance. For example, returning to the earlier themes of decentralisation and the metaverse, the poster child for such developments is a company called Decentraland.

Decentraland is a 3D virtual world browser-based platform powered by the Ethereum blockchain. Users may buy virtual plots of land as NFTs via the MANA cryptocurrency on the platform. Users can create and sell clothes and accessories to be used in the virtual world by the avatars. It was opened to the public in February 2020 and is overseen by the Decentraland Foundation, a non-profit organisation. In 2017, the platform raised $26 million in its initial coin offering (ICO) and, by 2022, it reportedly had a $1.2 billion market evaluation. Interesting for a metaverse that purportedly has only 38 active users a day.[4]

But then the valuations of FinTech firms are a little bit mad. By way of example, in 2019, N26's co-founder Maximilian Tayenthal told the *Financial*

3   *Economist*, "Who will survive the fintech bloodbath?" 13 October 2022, https://www.economist.com/finance-and-economics/2022/10/13/who-will-survive-the-fintech-bloodbath.
4   Richard Lawler, "Decentraland's billion-dollar 'metaverse' reportedly had 38 active users in one day," Verge, 13 October 2022, https://www.theverge.com/2022/10/13/23402418/decentraland-metaverse-empty-38-users-dappradar-wallet-data.

Times that "in all honesty, profitability is not one of our core metrics."[5] Perhaps that's why it's had bigger losses year after year ever since?

It reminds me of another tech start-up founder, Marc Lore. Lore is the founder and CEO of e-commerce start-up Jet.com, which was acquired by Walmart in 2016 in its attempt to compete with Amazon for e-commerce market share. He is an interesting person but has little idea about traditional corporate business. This is well illustrated by his comments to *Bloomberg Businessweek* where, over lunch, he shared a story about his teenage daughter, who had started her own online business. When his daughter said she was making money, Lore said that he was shocked. "How are you profitable?" he asked her. "Well, Dad, it's easy," she replied. "You just make sure your revenues are higher than your expenses." "Oh," Lore recalled saying. "I never really thought about it that way."[6]

A lot of technologists are highly naïve about business and finance and, for many of them, this is their Achilles heel. Most FinTechs began in the 2010s. This was a frothy period of good times and easy money. That's not now. In the early 2020s, crypto crashed, markets squeezed, inflation rose and funding did not. It is the first time that most FinTechs have experienced a recession.

This is highlighted by Tracxn, a market intelligence platform, which found that there was a 78 per cent year-on-year drop in investment volumes in the first half of 2023 compared to the same period in 2022. UK FinTechs raised £1.5 billion ($2 billion) in the first six months of 2023, down from £7 billion ($9.1 billion) in the first half of 2022. The first quarter of 2023 was the least funded quarter for UK FinTechs since 2020, at around £550 million ($673 million).[7]

The average deal fell from $32 million in 2021 to $20 million in 2022. Between July and September, a mere 6 firms graduated to unicorn status,

5 Nicholas Megaw, "Germany's N26 becomes Europe's top fintech with $2.7bn valuation," *Financial Times*, 9 January 2019, https://www.ft.com/content/d945cfa8-1419-11e9-a581-4ff78404524e.
6 *Bloomberg Businessweek*, "Can Wal-Mart's Expensive New E-Commerce Operation Compete with Amazon," 4 May 2017, https://www.bloomberg.com/news/features/2017-05-04/can-wal-mart-s-expensive-new-e-commerce-operation-compete-with-amazon?leadSource=uverify%20wall.
7 Suzie Neuwirth, "UK fintech funding ranks second globally despite drop in volumes," *P2P Finance News*, 25 July 2023, https://p2pfinancenews.co.uk/2023/07/25/uk-fintech-funding-ranks-second-globally-despite-drop-in-volumes/.

achieving a valuation of $1 billion or more, compared with 48 in the same period in 2021. Exits also stalled. There were 27 public listings in the last quarter of 2021, compared with 2 in the first quarter of 2022.

Interestingly, all technology sectors were impacted by recession and a contraction of spending in 2022. FinTech proved to be particularly vulnerable, however, because many of these fledgling firms were directly exposed to the risk of recession.

In the 2020s, global FinTech saw its biggest drop in funding in three years, as deal numbers fell to a four-quarter low.

FinTech Funding Falls to its Lowest Level Since 2017

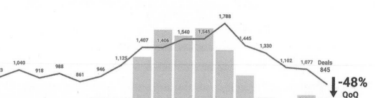

Source: CB Insights

Some forecast that this means major names like Klarna will have to downsize and challengers like Varo, a US digital bank, might even hit the wall. Some will hit the wall if they cannot get their next series of funding and, yes, this will include some major names. It does not mean that they will disappear. They will be acquired and merged because their ideas and customer base are on sale and cheap. Who are those names?

For a start, BNPL firms like Klarna are going to go through a really hard time. The *Wall Street Journal* summarises this well, showing that rising costs, delinquent accounts and late payments are creating a big squeeze on such firms. Add to this the fact that the BNPL business model is a hundred per cent reliant on consumer spending increasing, and you can see the challenge.

Another context related to BNPL is the loans and credit business. Many start-ups have been growing through a reliance on loan originations. That market will grow during this downturn as consumers will need funding. So watch out for the P2P lenders buying the BNPL failures.

It is likely that some neobanks will go belly up too. There are simply too many of them vying for business, with too many doing similar things, and too many not being disruptive but just emulating and reimagining what everyone else does.

The third area that is having a rollercoaster ride is cryptocurrency. We saw the death of Terra-LUNA, and the knock-on effect that this had, with most currencies losing half or more of their value. Needless to say, there will be huge bumps in the road ahead for bitcoin and its brethren. Hodl your breath and see how it goes.

These are the three big areas to be hit by the current climate—BNPL, neobanks and crypto. On top of this though, there will also be a serious tightening of belts as too many FinTechs are being valued as Techs rather than Fins. This means that we will see some unicorns reverting back to centaurs, and valuations reigning back from billions to millions.

Lenders that used cheap funding to provide online mortgages and BNPL loans face soaring costs and rising defaults. Neobanks that rely on transaction fees are being starved of revenues. Businesses that banked on the boom in retail investing—from crypto exchanges to online brokers—suffered as trading volumes collapse. Finally, those catering to small firms are massively exposed due to defaults on loans with these clients.

In fact, as the recession of the early 2020s hit, only a few FinTech firms had a positive outlook, namely those companies that reduce inefficiencies, and thus ought to help companies cut back in more difficult times; and firms that create new revenue lines for their clients, such as enabling a travel agent to sell their customers insurance.

The bottom line, as I have said, is that many FinTech firms struggled to survive during the early 2020s but many of these won't disappear— they will just be eaten. Unsurprisingly perhaps, Global FinTech mergers and acquisitions (M&A) experienced a sharp rise in the first half of 2022, according to a report from Hampleton Partners, which recorded 591 deals within the first six months of the year, defying the broader M&A slowdown.[8] This represented a 46 per cent increase on the same period in 2021 when there were 406 FinTech deals, as well as a 70 per cent increase (348 FinTech deals) on the same period in 2019 before the pandemic set in. Data from Dealroom reported by Sifted also pointed to another healthy year for FinTech M&A in Europe, with 190 FinTech acquisitions in Europe, versus 241 in 2021.[9] In other words, the industry has cooled and will see massive consolidation throughout the rest of the 2020s until some form of clear order returns.

Does this mean that the FinTech bubble has burst? Not at all. It just means that the wheat is being separated from the chaff, and that's a good thing, isn't it?

FinTech Schadenfreude?

People took great delight at the 2023 FinTech trade shows as they saw a lot of struggling FinTech firms holding out begging bowls to banks. Many start-ups are struggling, with their cash runway running out, and they desperately need funding and investment. The banks are smiling and would be happy if these guys went bust so that they can steal their talent and ideas. After all, around 75 per cent of all FinTech start-ups crash within two decades; the same seems to be true with cryptocurrencies crashing. With the collapse of Terra-LUNA, Celsius, FTX and more in 2022, many feel that they can cross their arms, put on a smug face and say, "I told you so!"

If you felt Schadenfreude while reading the above, you need to reassess. You're wrong. FinTech has not run out of cash. The firms that were in the too early stage or too visionary and/or had no plan, no backing and no customers have hit the wall, but thousands are still doing pretty well. For example, according to *Business Leader*, the ten largest FinTech firms in 2022 were

8   Daniel Lanyon, "Dry Powder: A fintech M&A boom is kicking off," AltFi, 13 October 2022, https://www.altfi.com/article/9980_dry-powder-a-FinTech-ma-boom-is-kicking-off.
9   Amy O'Brien, "Fintech M&A in an economic downturn: Key takeaways from the Sifted Summit," Sifted, 11 October 2022, https://sifted.eu/articles/fintech-acquisitions-sifted-summit.

Stripe ($75 billion), FTX ($32 billion), Chime ($25 billion), OpenSea ($13 billion), Brex ($12 billion), Circle ($9 billion), TripActions ($7.5 billion), Chainalysis ($9 billion), Fireblocks ($8 billion) and Carta ($7.5 billion).

Obviously one name on that list—FTX—stands out as it imploded in late 2022 but, even so, the others are all doing interesting things across interesting spaces.

It reminds me of 2001, and the dot-com boom and bust. Many today are regarding FinTech in the same way, but this space is different. Back when the internet bubble burst, newspapers and magazines ran headlines like "Will Amazon survive?". Yes, many companies did go bust—Amazon did not. Instead, the firms that were nascent in 1999, particularly those with good ideas, leadership and vision, became bigger, smarter and stronger. The same will happen with the issues FinTechs face today, and those that survive will be the Amazons of tomorrow.

CAN BANKS TAKE THE OPPORTUNITY?

For more than a decade, most bankers said that bitcoin or, for that matter, almost anything dubbed a cryptocurrency was a scam, a Ponzi scheme, and only useful for money launderers, paedophiles and terrorists. So why are banks now offering cryptocurrency services? Because their customers want them.

During 2022, almost every major bank made an announcement about offering custodial services, trading services, transaction services and more related to bitcoin, Ethereum and other cryptocurrencies. Yet, when talking to these banks, they tell me that they still hate the idea of cryptocurrencies and still believe that they are not for the public good. However, as each bank announces a cryptocurrency service, the other banks have to follow the market trend.

Banks providing cryptocurrency services, but not believing in their viability, is a fine line to tread. What this typifies is the friction between analogue and digital, industrial and networked. The old world does not recognise the new world and vice versa. The new world believes in bitcoin; the old world does not. The new world is trying to create a new financial system; the old world is trying to protect the old financial system. The new world is born on the internet; the old world was born on the railroads.

This friction is clear in so many areas that it is almost like a scene from *Les Miserables*, with the rebels putting up the barricades and the government trying to knock them down. In the book and musical, the rebels lose; in reality, they won. King Louis XVI was executed, and the government fell.

This moment in time feels like a similar shift. The shift between old world structures and new world ideas. When I ask people about what's going on, young people invariably reply that they do not believe in the old system. They are rallying against it. They are pawning the short sellers by attacking the stocks they short. They are making millions on the back of currencies they don't understand. They are bucking the system.

What about banks? Do they support assets that they don't believe have any value? Do they move into markets where they see no regulations? Do they operate under government guidance or market movements? Do they do whatever they have to do to stay in business?

It seems that the banks are doing whatever they have to do. Whilst they have CEOs who regularly spit on bitcoin, their trading desks and investment services offer to trade and invest bitcoin for you. Whilst they believe in blockchain and distributed ledger technologies, they will manage whatever digital assets the customer wants them to manage. Whilst they resist digital transformation, they invest in doing digital work.

It's a tough time and a tough moment, but it's got to be done. The inevitable march of progress is forcing banks to change, whether they like it or not; and they are changing, whether they like it or not. It is just really hard to change in order to work with things that you do not believe in. However, if the customer believes in it, you have to.

Banking Is Not Easy

A long time ago, before Google, experts predicted that telecommunications firms and retailers would acquire and buy banks, and vice versa. It did not happen and is unlikely to now. This is because banking is difficult with a heavy regulatory overhead, follows strict governmental controls and does not have the same features as other industries. These are the reasons why, despite more recent predictions, Amazon or Google has not opened a bank.

It is something that the naivety of youth does not realise. They think that banking is dumb and stupid. It's not; it's old and difficult. Sure, we can take shots at the bits of banking that don't work well and, sure, we can take bits out of the lending and payments business, but the overall landscape of banking is far more than just a loan or transaction. It's all about trust and regulations.

Today, many experts are predicting that Big Tech and FinTech will destroy and disrupt banking. Yes, they are challenging and changing banking, but destroy and disrupt it? I don't think so.

This was clearly something Bill Gates got wrong with his "we need banking but we don't need banks" comment back in the 1990s. We don't need banks to do payments and lending, but we do need banks to do banking. After all, what is banking? What are banks for? Banks are not for the things we think they are for. What they are really for is to keep money safe.

Keeping money safe may sound an easy thing to do but when you consider that many in this world are trying to steal money, it's actually a tough job. Think of all the movies and shows that you watch: how many of them are about someone trying to rip someone off, get into a bank vault, make a hustle or fake and deceive? Think about your own life and the phishing emails you receive, the fake texts you get, the friend who doesn't pay you back or the family member who constantly leans on you for help. Our lives revolve around money so any company that claims to keep money safe is offering a tough ask.

This is also the reason why banks are so heavily regulated. This is clear when you look at the latest bank scam called authorised push payment (APP) fraud. An APP "occurs when you—knowingly or unwittingly—transfer money from your own bank account to one belonging to a scammer. For example, a scammer pretends to be from your bank's fraud team and warns that you need to move your money to a safe account but it's actually an account the fraudster controls."[1]

This scam is extremely convincing. You believe that the bank has called you. You say that you will call them back. You ring the bank's telephone number, but the scammer has actually held your line and they answer pretending to be the bank. It sucks you in completely. You then authorise money to be moved, as the bank is telling you that your account has been hacked or compromised. That money is then lost forever. Since this scam emerged, the number of cases has risen rapidly and is now common in countries worldwide.

---

1   Which?, "What to do if you fall victim to a bank transfer scam," 6 April 2023, https://www.which.co.uk/consumer-rights/advice/what-to-do-if-you-re-the-v,ictim-of-a-bank-transfer-app-scam-aED6A0l529rc.

How Scams Have Soared Over the Years

Amount lost to push-payment fraud (£m)

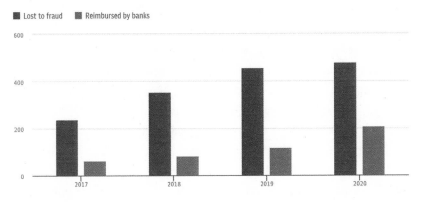

Source: UK Finance

Banks are meant to keep money safe, so how come scammers can pretend to be banks? Because banks have failed their customers, according to the regulators, so the banks are now liable for any losses made by such scams. There is also a customer duty however. Customers need to be wary of anyone who emails, texts or even calls them saying they are from their bank. Having said that, if you are called by the bank and are told to ring them back on the bank's official telephone number, well, no wonder the regulators are saying that banks are accountable.

What Would You Spend $15 Billion on?

JPMorgan Chase, one of the highest-valued banks in the world, spent $12 billion on technology in 2022,[2] rising to over $15 billion in 2023.[3] Tracking this over time, the IT budget had been increasing by around a billion dollars year-on-year, for example, it invested $11 billion in 2019, but then the figure jumped in 2023. JPMorgan is not alone. Citi, Wells Fargo, Bank of America and others are also spending billions on tech, with increasing budgets year-on-year. In fact, it almost

---

2   Joshua Franklin, "JPMorgan plots 'astonishing' $12bn tech spend to beat fintechs'," *Financial Times*, 15 January 2022, https://www.ft.com/content/e543adf0-8c62-4a2c-b2d9-01fdb2f595cc.
3   Ed Targett, "JPMorgan's technology spend to hit $15.3 billion as storage, compute volumes surge," The Stack, 30 May 2023, https://www.thestack.technology/jpmorgan-technology-spend-2023/.

seems to be a "my budget is bigger than yours" competition. JPMorgan leads the pack, but everyone else wants to announce that they have got humongous budgets for tech too. This is because many banks claim that, today, they are not a bank—they are a technology company with a banking licence.

That is simply not true, however. It is best wrapped up by Deutsche Bank, which clearly articulates that banking is *what* it does, but technology is *how* it does it today. "At its heart, our strategy empowers our businesses to control 'what' is produced, while technology has control of the 'how'."[4]

A bank is a bank, plain and simple, but now banks are trying to be FinTech banks. Banks are spending more on technology than most FinTechs are getting in investment. JPMorgan spent more on technology in two years (2018–2019) than the total investment in all of Europe's FinTechs put together in 2019. But what are the results? A new digital bank launch in Britain? A failed digital bank launch in the United States? Building an internal blockchain? A renovation of spaghetti legacy IT? Keeping the lights on?

According to JPMorgan's 2023 investments of $15 billion, the focus was to earmark new funds for data centres and cloud computing, as well as expansion into new markets like the United Kingdom and Europe. That does not necessarily impress shareholders, who are asking, what does this actually deliver and how do you measure it?

Bank structures naturally waste huge amounts of investment dollars as they are channelled down through the company. Think about the waterfall model and how this applies to banking. Think of the bank as a waterfall. The waterfall starts at the top with the CEO who says, "We're investing billions in technology this year." As the water (i.e. money) cascades from top to bottom, the main flow of water is strong and irresistible. But as that water hits the bottom, a lot of it bounces back up into the air, as spray, and does its own thing. This means that, out of that $15 billion budget, a few billion will most likely be wasted on internal conflict, politics, power bases and mistakes. That's generally how technology investments work in banks.

---

4   Patricia Uhlig and Arno Schuetze, "Deutsche Bank in strategy shift to address tech woes," Reuters, 7 October 2019, https://www.reuters.com/article/us-deutsche-bank-technology-idUSKBN1WM0U2#:~:text=FRANKFURT%20(Reuters)%20%2D%20Deutsche%20Bank,back%20the%20bank%20for%20years.

In the case of JPMorgan's $15 billion, $6 to 7 billion was spent servicing technical and process debt, such as just keeping the lights on or, more importantly, servicing the power bases of the chief information officer (CIO) and chief operations officer (COO). The other $6 to 7 billion was spent on digital transformation, partnerships, seed funding and acquisitions. In other words, don't read the top line, look at the bottom line. For example, most of the keeping-the-lights-on budget is spent on regulatory-related investments, modernisation and the retirement of technical debt. According to Tearsheet, the bank's technology spending for 2022 included:

- **Modernisation:** including migrations to the cloud, as well as upgrading legacy infrastructure and architecture, with Jamie Dimon announcing that roughly 30 per cent to 50 per cent of the bank's apps and data would be moving to the cloud
- **Data strategy:** enabling the bank to extract value in its proprietary data by cleaning it, staging it and deploying modern techniques against it
- Attracting and acquiring **top talent** with modern skills
- Following a "**product operating model**"[5]

What is a product operating model? Building a new bank using new tech? Not necessarily. In reality, JPMorgan moved its core systems to the cloud in a billion-dollar project. Then there was another project revolved around launching Chase UK, its UK-based digital bank. Finally, with only 59 million digital Chase users, JPMorgan is positioning itself as a scrappy underdog, competing against FinTech and Big Tech, whilst investing big money to ensure it stays competitive with its products and services over time. The bottom line is that, if the highest-valued bank in the world has a $15 billion budget to compete with FinTech and Big Tech, what budget do you have and what do you do with it?

---

5   Zachary Miller, "What JPMorgan is doing with that $12 billion tech spend," Tearsheet, 17 January 2022, https://tearsheet.co/new-banks/what-jpmorgan-is-doing-with-that-12-billion-tech-spend/.

Banks Spend Megabucks on Tech and Yet Are Mega Inefficient

Building on these thoughts, how can a bank spend so much on technology and yet be so inefficient? By way of example, let's take a bank cost-income ratio. That's the measure of how much a bank spends to operate, and the profit it then makes.

In 2000, German banks spent €0.777 to every €1 of income which, by 2017, had risen to €0.85 to every €1. French banks spent €0.709 in 2000, falling slightly to €0.67 by 2017. US banks spent $0.605 to operate for every $1 made and, by 2017, that was $0.57. Likewise, UK banks spent £0.48 for every £1 of income in 2000, rising to £0.687 in 2017.[6] The big US banks talk grandly about spending more than $10 billion a year on tech, and yet where are the returns? Reading the results, they are not there.

IT costs for the top US banks have jumped by billions in recent years, as the intensifying battle for talent and the growing threat from new FinTech rivals forced executives to step up spending. Cost increases at most US banks are outpacing revenue growth while banks grapple with historically low interest rates and a sharp slowdown in lending. Expenses at the five largest US banks—JPMorgan Chase, Wells Fargo, Citi, Bank of America and Goldman Sachs—were generally increased by over a fifth in 2022 compared with 2019, before the pandemic hit. In contrast, revenues only rose 10 per cent.

The question investors and shareholders are asking is how can these banks spend so much on tech and yet deliver such meagre improvements? Perhaps it is to invest in FinTech companies. Pitchbook and Sifted estimate that banks tripled their investments in start-ups between 2016 and 2021.[7]

---

6   All figures are based on statistics found at https://www.theglobaleconomy.com/rankings/bank_cost_to_income/.

7   Isabelle Woodford, "Banks made record investment in European fintech last year," Sifted, 11 October 2021, https://sifted.eu/articles/banks-funding-european-fintechs.

US Banks Are Spending More to Fend off Competition

Quarterly expenses in US$bn

■ Q2 2021   ▨ Q2 2020   ▨ Q2 2019

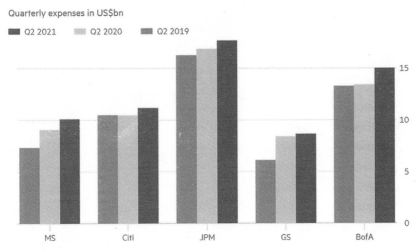

Sources: bank earnings statements; FT research

Banks Are Paying Their Employees More amid a War for Talent

Quarterly compensation costs US$bn

■ Q2 2021   ▨ Q2 2020   ▨ Q2 2019

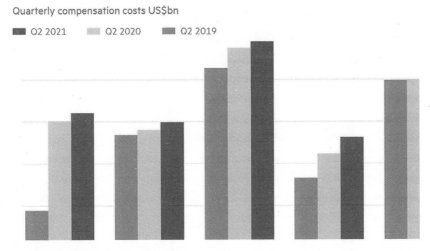

Sources: bank earnings statements; FT research

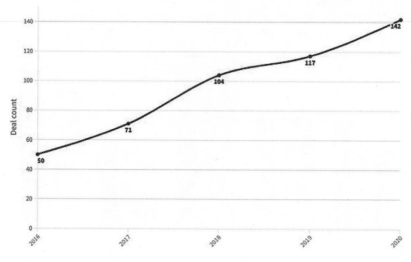

Europe VC Deal Activity in FinTech with CVC Involvement

* CVC = corporate venture capital
Source: Pitchbook

Whatever the situation, it is clear that many banks are hugely inefficient machines, but with huge budgets. They take profit from basis point differentials that are unsustainable, are challenged by many new entrants and see change as inevitable but too difficult. They are just lucky that their customers are scared of change, happy to pay more to not change and don't care about efficiency. All they care about is security and safety. A perfect marriage.

Old Banks Need an Urgent Reboot

Even with all of that investment and discussion of renewal, and building on the theme that banks are inefficient, there are more and more stories about banks messing up customer accounts, system outages, data mismanagement, issues with technology and more. These are things that banks cannot mess up. Airlines may mess up a booking, Amazon may mess up a delivery, and BT or AT&T may mess up a connection but what if a bank messes up a customer balance or a customer's access to their account? That is unacceptable.

It sits right up there with flying and pharmaceuticals. If an aeroplane from your preferred airline crashes once, it's terrible but you still might fly with them.

If one crashes every day, then you wouldn't fly with them. If paracetamol gets rid of your headache, that's good. If it gives you liver cancer, then you should not be taking it. In terms of banking and payments, if I send money to my mum, she should get that money. If it doesn't appear in her account, that's a plane crash. If it doesn't appear in her account and I call the bank but the bank still cannot sort it out, that's a terminal illness.

However, what happens if the network goes down? What happens if someone pulls the cable, and everything shuts down? What happens if nothing can move or transact between anyone, anywhere?

The thing about humanity is that we are always moving forward, onwards and upwards. We make progress every day. We innovate and invent non-stop, and the result is that the bedrock of our world today, which we take for granted, only came about in the last couple of centuries. Therefore, in the context of moving forward, onwards and upwards in banking, innovating and creating non-stop change the existing landscape. That is what is happening with banking today. Banking has only existed for a few hundred years in its current shape and form, and now it is being automated and changed. It is not an evolution of old banking. It is a completely new form of banking. In fact, it is a completely new form of everything. What this demands is a refresh, renewal and reboot of the old banking system. As demonstrated by so many IT outages in old banks, it needs to be done quickly.

Should You Have "Bank" in Your Brand?

Many challenger banks, new banks, digital offshoot banks and such like no longer include the word "bank" in their branding. Chime, Chase, Finn, Bó, Bunq, Citizens, Truist and more all provide banking services with bank licences but none of them has bank in its name. Is it a good move to not use "bank" in your branding, especially as the word is synonymous with trust?

Consumers trust banks because they are regulated and offer insurance of funds; people don't trust companies that are not regulated and offer no insurance cover. Yet this trust only develops with awareness. Many customers probably have no idea about the insurance compensation cover for their bank accounts or of the many government regulations that protect them. They just know that they have a bank account and use it accordingly. Then you have many start-ups and young investors experimenting with ideas, investing in crypto, opening accounts with FinTechs and not caring a jot about the regulations or insurance cover of where they are investing and saving.

Equally, there are so many scams out there that you only learn about through awareness and/or experience. For instance, losing thousands in a property development after using the developers' recommended lawyer instead of finding an independent legal representative; losing thousands on an unregulated exchange, dealing in crypto; and losing thousands because you trusted your partner and shouldn't have. Having said that, many people have no such issues. They make thousands in property investments and cryptocurrencies and have a partner they can trust. It's all swings and roundabouts.

What this demonstrates is that you cannot regulate trust and security—but you can try. At the end of the day, customers will decide what risk exposure they are happy with. This is the crux of the argument about whether the word "bank" matters: it is the balance between trust in securing your assets versus the risk of losing them.

This is why so many banks are starting to creep into crypto. For example, the *Wall Street Journal* reported in early 2022 that mainstream banks like BBVA and the Commonwealth Bank of Australia are allowing customers to now hold, buy and sell bitcoin and ether through digital accounts.[8] What's interesting about that statement is the use of the word "allow". Banks don't *allow* anything. Customers demand it. Banks are moving into trading cryptocurrencies because customers demand it, not because the banks are allowing it.

Many mainstream banks are trying to become hip and cool traders of the latest big things— cryptocurrencies, DeFi, NFTs and more—because customers are finding these hip and cool, but do customers want to deal with a bank that they see as anything but hip and cool? Perhaps this is the reason why banks are dropping the word "bank" from their brands in an attempt to be more like FinTechs. At the end of the day though, they are still banks and they are not hip and cool.

---

8   Patricia Kowsmann, "Bitcoin at the Bank: Mainstream Lenders Dabble in Crypto Outside the U.S.," *Wall Street Journal*, 4 January 2022, https://www.wsj.com/articles/bitcoin-at-the-bank-mainstream-lenders-dabble-in-crypto-outside-the-u-s-11641288824.

What Do Banks Need to Do to Deal with FinTech?

In January 2022, sixteen experts from Forbes Finance Council discussed what banks will need to focus on in order to compete with FinTech. They stated that banks will need to:

- become nimble and decentralised
- incentivise culture change
- combine security with blockchain technology
- lean into people-centric customer service
- provide improved transparency in lending
- expand mobile banking capabilities
- divert resources to enhance digital banking
- enable better connectivity between various services and tools
- partner with transformative FinTechs
- allow direct, secure connections between merchants and customers' bank accounts
- switch to microservices and third-party tech vendors
- speed up transactions and lower transaction costs
- leverage direct financial data and automation
- switch to an all-virtual interface
- create more customer-intimate services
- embrace 24/7 customer service[9]

These key action points build on the over forty lessons detailed in my book *Doing Digital* (2020). It got me thinking about this section's subheading—What Do Banks Need to Do to Deal with FinTech?—and how the wording is defensive. Keeping the action points in mind, let's turn the question on its head and replace "to deal with" with "embrace"—How can banks embrace FinTech and use it to leverage their services?

This reminds me of when I talked with the Financial Conduct Authority (FCA), the UK regulator, a few years ago when it launched the Regulatory Sandbox. The sandbox allows FinTech start-ups to innovate and trial in a

---

9   *Forbes*, "16 Ways Banks Will Need To Change To Survive Advances In Fintech," 5 January 2022, https://www.forbes.com/sites/forbesfinancecouncil/2022/01/05/16-ways-banks-will-need-to-change-to-survive-advances-in-fintech/.

live market environment *in partnership* with banks. Such collaboration is important. Many start-ups don't understand banking; many banks don't understand start-ups or, more clearly, technology and digitalisation. If the two can work together in partnership, then it's a win-win. If they compete and fight, it's a lose-lose.

This is the point. Most banks struggle with digital transformation and FinTechs can help them to transform. Most FinTechs are trying to help banks digitally transform by focusing on their processes and sub-processes, and using Open Banking and APIs to transform them. It's not an adversarial relationship, but a symbiotic one. Sure, there are some FinTech start-ups that want to disrupt and destroy the big old banks, but I think many more are focused on addressing a different question and opportunity—how can we use technology to make banks more effective and efficient?

When you look at the likes of Stripe, Wise, Currencycloud (now Visa) and their brethren, they are all targeting areas where banks are ineffective and inefficient and solving the issues. That's why Visa acquired Currencycloud. In fact, if you look at the likes of Plaid, Dynamic Yield, Aiia and others, they are all looking at the same questions: What's wrong with the current structure? How can we make it better, more effective and more efficient? What is the opportunity of the network and open world to improve poor bank processes?

Mastercard,[10] Visa and PayPal woke up to this a few years ago. Equally, a few banks have, too. The key to this is that FinTech is improving banking processes in most cases, and not destroying banks.

Why Old Banks Should Be Worried

There is a big difference in digital attitudes between banks and FinTechs. The big difference is that the incumbent views digital as a cost-cutting exercise—if the customer self-serves, then we don't need to serve and we save money— whilst the start-up regards it as a customer-enhancing opportunity.

Old banks focus on digital as a cost and efficiency driver and hardly ever see technology as a customer service tool. In contrast, start-ups view digital as a way to create valuable and powerful customer propositions. They use

---

10 Mastercard announced the acquisition of both Dynamic Yield and Aiia in 2021.

digital to differentiate and drive rapid customer and market share growth as the main objective. In so doing, they benefit from all of the savings and efficiencies of digital-only processes—*as a by-product*. This is a critical point. If you only look at technology as a cost-reduction process, you never get the market opportunities. If you look at technology as a market opportunity, you get the cost savings naturally as a by-product.

When you think of it this way, you can see why so many FinTech start-ups have achieved unicorn status. Why? Because they are using technology to give customers a better experience and, as they do, they get the rewards of more customers, more revenues and more investment. There's no discussion of cost reduction in the majority of start-ups. Instead, the discussion is about the customer and the customer experience.

I could spend months writing a business case for a bank executive team that would show the clear cost-benefit analysis for why the bank should invest in a particular technology. The team would rip it apart and we would spend another six months doing the process all over again. Even when I outlined how the technology would enhance the customer relationship, grow more revenue and deliver greater profit, no one listened. Yet if I could show how the bank could make a thousand people redundant, it would be all ears. In this regard, one of my favourite stories is that JPMorgan was able to fire 1,500 lawyers thanks to AI being able to do the work in a fraction of the time.[11] Now, that got the investment!

Why Do Challenger Banks Find It Hard to Challenge?

It is interesting to follow companies that have tried to challenge traditional banks. For years, supermarkets and retailers have tried to take on and replace banks but have done a rotten job. For example, UK supermarket Tesco sold its mortgage book to Lloyds in 2019, owing to "challenging market conditions", and announced that it was closing all deposit accounts in 2021. Marks & Spencer, another major UK retailer, also decided to close all of its bank branches and current accounts in the same year. Rather than

11   Hugh Son, "JPMorgan Software Does in Seconds What Took Lawyers 360,000 Hours," Bloomberg, ·
     28 February 2017, https://www.bloomberg.com/news/articles/2017-02-28/jpmorgan-marshals-an-army-of-
     developers-to-automate-high-finance.

competing with the likes of Lloyds and Barclays, supermarket banking ventures have been added to the pile of challenger banks that have failed to do much challenging.

The big retailers—Tesco, Walmart, Marks & Spencer, Sainsbury's and others—have been attacking banking for a long time. Many of them launched their own banking divisions in the 1990s and, thirty years later, are shutting them down. Why?

Well, a good example is Sainsbury's. In the 1990s, Sainsbury's presented its bank launch on the basis of research that found most consumers thought banks were "complacent", "arrogant" and "greedy". The UK retailer was going to shake this up by creating a friendly bank so how come it failed in its mission?

First and foremost is that most customers do not care about switching banks. They feel safe and secure with their current bank and switching sounds scary and difficult. This is why most customers stay with their bank longer than they do with their partner.

In addition, a lot of retail banking does not make money. This may sound strange when you hear that banks make huge profits, but the profits flow from corporate and investment banking more than from retail banking. Most banking not only makes no money but it also costs a lot of money. Why? Compliance, risk and regulation. So how do banks work? That's the bit the supermarkets didn't understand and, to be honest, most FinTech challengers also don't understand.

Banks work on a weird concoction of subsidising "free banking" for the retail consumer with high interest fees (punishments) for those who break the rules, supported by interest and charges made on corporate and institutional client dealings. Take away the commercial banking, payments and pension fund transactions and no one would ever have access to a bank account.

That is now changing. Retail banking is no longer that expensive. Neither is commercial nor investment banking. These days, accessing finance is simple and cheap. So why have supermarkets failed in this area? What did they do wrong? Why did they fail when newer entrants seem to be succeeding?

Well, it's all down to timing. The supermarket banks tried to attack incumbents in the 1990s. At that time, the cost of entry was huge. It wasn't just the cost of entry, but also regulatory barriers and the fact that supermarket managements didn't understand how banking worked.

They failed on so many fronts, the most crucial one being unable to master deposit-based banking. You would think that they would have worked that one out but they never did. They offered loans, savings and cards, but never cracked deposit-based banking. For me, that is the core issue for all challengers and entrants. If you cannot get a customer to trust you with their wages and salary, you have not got a customer. That is the problem the supermarket banks faced, and they never solved it. It's equally the issue that challenger and neobanks face. Will they be able to solve it?

If you are used purely for payments and transactions, you're a commodity that has no ties. If you are the bank with my core deposit—my salary, my income, my main transaction—then you are different. So why didn't customers switch to the supermarket banks? Brand? Trust? The core offer?

To be honest, it was for all of those reasons. Their brands were less trusted than those of traditional banks. Why? Because they are supermarkets geared up for leveraging our shopping and credit, and maximising the outlay from our wallets, rather than protecting us from those who want to steal from our wallets. Do banks want to steal from our wallets? Yes, but they are regulated to do it in a way that ensures we don't lose out big time (or so they say).

Supermarket banks and challengers are therefore faced with three big consumer barriers:

1. Can you give me a better offer?
2. Can I trust your offer is better and you have my core interests at heart?
3. Can I believe that you have done this with guarantees and government support?

What the supermarkets messed up most were the product and the offer.

What Is Open Banking?

Things have changed, however, since the days of supermarket banks. The reason why challenger banks like Chime, Monzo and Starling are taking off is that the technology structures of the 2020s are very different to those of the 1990s. We now have cloud computing, smartphones, apps and APIs.

Back in the 1990s, supermarket banks could not gain access to the data that the banks held. In the 2020s, challenger banks can. This is all thanks to regulations that have opened bank data to third-party usage and, in a nutshell, is called Open Banking.

What is Open Banking? According to Investopedia, Open Banking is the system of allowing access and control of consumer banking and financial accounts through third-party applications, usually based on plug-and-play code called APIs. The aim is to reshape the competitive landscape and consumer experience of the banking industry by allowing data to be used by third parties to provide more knowledge about our financial dealings.

In a recent discussion about Open Banking, almost everyone mentioned "customer" and "customer journeys". *Customer* is the critical factor here as customers do not care whether they are using Open Finance or not. What they care about are financial services that are easy to use, fast, safe and secure. That's what the Open Finance ecosystem can deliver. The question is how to make customer journeys fast, easy and safe using open systems.

To start with, you need *critical* mass. Without critical mass, it's not worth it. No one makes enough money, and opportunities for those offering services are severely limited. You need scale, and if that's not there, Open Finance fails.

How do you get scale? Through *common* standards that have *commonality and consistency.* This is why APIs and interoperability come to the fore. You cannot have a thousand different development structures. You need one that can plug-and-play. If you have that, you then have *conformance* for performance. You have scale, ease of use, speed and all of the other factors that will make customer journeys better. However, there is still a barrier to overcome, which is *confidence.*

Most consumers don't trust the idea of *open*, as they want to keep their data private. That is why you should not talk about Open Banking or Open Finance. Customers don't want to hear that. All they want to hear about is better, faster, easier and more secure finance. Those are the outside-in messages. The inside-out view is when we talk about Banking as a Service (BaaS)—embedded and open ecosystems and platforms. What's the customer's perspective? Focus on that first or they don't have confidence.

If they do have confidence, as the benefits are sold, you then get *consent*. Customers have to give their consent to allow Open Finance access to their data. It's their data; it's their privacy; it's their *concerns* that have to be addressed.

You can only do this using the outside-in view and sell the benefits. Your TV can download your favourite movies, your car can pay for its own parking, your groceries arrive after ordering them from your fridge door, you never miss the best offers because your apps do it for you and so on. It's all about *consideration*. Every time you allow third-party access, you get payback. That's what customers want, and they must want whatever is being offered in order to give consent.

That is the final point: you need to show *care*. Customers need to feel that you care about their money and their exposures. They need to feel that you are putting their interests first, and not your own. They need to feel that you recognise that they are the customers, and that they are in charge.

The Lego Bank Can Work

The FinTech 250 is CB Insights' annual list of the top FinTech firms in the world. In 2022, these firms were selected from a pool of over 12,500 companies.[12]

12 CB Insights, "The Fintech 250: The most promising fintech companies of 2022," 4 October 2022, https://www.cbinsights.com/research/report/top-fintech-startups-2022/.

CB Insights' FinTech 250 for 2022

Note: Companies are private as of 9/12/22. FTX was removed after declaring bankruptcy on 11/11/2022.

The list is interesting as it demonstrates the laser-focused drive that FinTechs have to solve one thing well, and doing that one thing much better than a bank, which is soft-focused on solving everything. As I said in *Doing Digital* (2020): "If thousands of new, shiny FinTech firms are doing one thing well, how can a bank compete when it is full of legacy and heritage, meaning that it does a thousand things averagely?" FinTech start-ups take a single process in a single part of the financial jigsaw puzzle, whether it be retail, commercial or investment banking; insurance; or wealth management. They then solve it with beautiful code, which is often subsequently released into the Open Finance system as an API.

Next, we have to address the thorny issue of how banks partner with these firms. If a bank does step back and determines that it wants to pick up code and software with a FinTech start-up, what is the right way to go about this? Philippe Gelis, co-founder and CEO of foreign exchange firm Kantox, summarised this well:

[Working with banks] is a fine balance between your willingness to adapt to partnership requirements and your willingness to walk away from the deal if the demands are clearly excessive, or if they put your overall business strategy or focus at risk.[13]

In his case, his firm thought that it had a deal with a bank. Then, after months of talks, the bank walked away and copied the firm's ideas. This is the challenge for a FinTech firm that desperately wants the opportunity to grow. Give away too much and you lose everything.

Looking at it from the bank's perspective, the bank wants the ideas but doesn't want to lose control. It does not really understand the concept of partnerships, as it has not entered into one before, and is learning on the way, too. The thing is, as I've said often, a partnership between a FinTech and a bank is often unequal. The bank thinks it is bigger, better and stronger, and hence treats the FinTech start-up as inferior. Now translate that to your own relationships. Could you imagine having a partner who you think is less worthy than thou? Partnerships don't work that way.

So, we have thousands of niche and specialist start-ups doing amazing things to fix the things that banks do badly online, and thousands of large and traditional banks that are struggling to keep up with all of these innovations, and either copying or acquiring code to try to maintain their positions.

What's the outcome of all this? Where's the endgame? The endgame is an Open Banking ecosystem in which BaaS is used for the integration of that ecosystem, and the BaaS provider is a fully-licenced bank. In other words, the bank does not necessarily need to partner with FinTechs. What it needs to do is orchestrate and integrate. Most FinTechs offer their code on a pay-as-you-use cloud API in the Open Banking ecosystem. Just look at Stripe, Adyen and more.

This results in the CIO becoming the Chief Conductor (CC). The leader of the Bank-as-a-Platform must be a coordinator of many distributed parts. That

---

13   Chris Skinner, "Banks and FinTech Partnerships: a Clash of Extremes," Finanser [blog], 11 July 2019, https://thefinanser.com/2019/07/banks-and-fintech-partnerships-a-clash-of-extremes.

is the CC's role. The CC must be able to see everything, from the back office (percussion) through middle office (wind instruments) to front office (strings), and get them to operate with perfect timing and in tune to the song they are playing. The CC is the head of the pick 'n' mix of all those start-ups out there that are doing one thing brilliantly. The CC then needs to select the pieces to rebuild the bank, moving away from a monolith to a Lego bank. It's down to the CC to decide which Lego pieces of apps, APIs and analytics will be the best selection for the bank and the customer.

Ten years ago, few banks understood the role of the CC or the parts in the ecosystem that enable them to deliver BaaS. Even now, most banks still do not understand this structure. Some are doing well, but too few, by far, considering how quickly the markets change.

The Lego Bank Arrives

The Lego Bank has thousands of pieces—or, if you prefer, processes—and, historically, banks have built all of their structures so that they can manage those processes internally. Bearing in mind that most old-style banks are better at dealing with risk, compliance, accounting and distribution through buildings with humans, it doesn't come as much of a surprise that when those very same banks build software, they tend to do it quite averagely. That's why 30,000 FinTech start-ups have emerged around the world in the last twenty years. Each one of these start-ups tends to start from scratch and build software that is more of an art form than just an internal development. And as I keep stating, they also tend to focus on doing just one thing brilliantly well with software, rather than trying to do thousands of things averagely.

With so many start-ups in this space, how do banks identify a good start-up from a bad one? How do banks identify a start-up that has dotted its i's and crossed its t's?

This is the due diligence that banks should have completed years ago, as customers don't want to build their own Lego Bank, even though they could. The problem for most customers is that they want the services that Stripe, Klarna, Adyen and others can offer, but they don't have the time or knowledge to do the due diligence on them. That's why someone else has to do it for them through the curation of the financial ecosystem.

A financial curator looks at the whole plug-and-play world of the financial ecosystem we have today, and works out which companies are doing well. The financial curator performs the due diligence and then brings those companies to the customer.

Don't Be a Wolf in Sheep's Clothing if You're Not a Wolf

Many people have said that banks are boring, unable to change, incapable of being truly digital and constantly being challenged by challenger banks and FinTech. Yet, here we are, with many of these challengers and start-ups begging for banks to work with them. How has this come about?

To put it simply, it's due to a recession. This recession began in the pandemic and has become rife in most economies since then. Yet, when you look at Tier 1 bank results during this period, they have been better than ever. You always make more margin when customers are financially distressed. In contrast, the start-up marketplace, in which most FinTech companies are involved, is struggling. The struggle is manifold: funding, cash flow, run-rate and the ability to just keep going.

This makes the outlook interesting, and there are a number of trends we could forecast. First, most FinTechs are desperate to work with banks to keep going. As a result, most banks have a great opportunity to pick up partners at discount rates. Having trouble with KYC? Here's a solution for a tenth of what it would have cost in 2015. Want to solve that online checkout issue? Here's a solution for free!

Second, if FinTechs cannot partner with a bank, perhaps the bank will buy them. Many FinTech firms are looking for a quick and easy exit. Founders want to sell out and, facing hard times, are willing to do a deal. Is it time to think of buying a firm? If nothing else, you acquire their talent.

Third, if a bank doesn't buy a FinTech, then a FinTech firm might buy a FinTech. There's going to be huge amounts of market change in the 2020s through M&A consolidation. A little like the 2001 internet bust, some firms will come out of this crisis bigger and stronger but, for every firm that succeeds, a hundred will disappear. Bearing in mind that there are 30,000 or more start-up FinTech firms out there, it makes cheap pickings for anyone with the money that these firms do not have.

Fourth, banks can double down on their digital strategies and succeed in carving out market space where they have previously struggled. Closing down branches and physical operations while augmenting digital services with enhanced partnerships and acquisitions create major opportunities in all areas of banking. On this final point, it is true that banks that are strong in the markets today will be stronger tomorrow. However, if you are considering diversification into other areas of finance, do not take this decision lightly. Just look at Goldman Sachs and Marcus if you need an example.

Marcus is Goldman Sachs' retail digital challenger bank but it makes no money, is a bottomless hole of investment and has caused significant internal soul-searching. In fact, Marcus will go down in history as an example of an attempt by an incumbent to disrupt markets. Even an incumbent cannot understand a market that it does not specialise in. I applaud Goldman Sachs' attempt to break into the retail market, and particularly its work with Apple, but perhaps the lesson learnt is to stick to your knitting. Time will tell.

The outcome is that there are great opportunities to expand services and grab market share, but you can only do this if you are qualified. If you are a retail bank, there is a great opportunity to become a bigger and better digital retail bank through M&A. Only do this though if you are confident in your own core competencies and don't buy services outside of your field of expertise, as evidenced by the submission of Marcus to market forces. Equally, if you are an investment bank, you can become a bigger and better investment bank, but just don't try to enter markets where you have no expertise.

Most Banks Will Disappear

Having said that, many companies and researchers believe that banks will disappear in the next decade because they are no longer needed. For example, in 2018, Gartner published a report stating that 80 per cent of financial institutions would disappear by 2030:

Within 12 years' time, 80% of financial firms will either go out of business or be rendered irrelevant by new competition, changing customer behaviour and advancements in technology, according to forecasts by Gartner.[14]

Even bankers have predicted the death of banks. Take this one from the CEO of BBVA:

In two decades, we will go from 20,000 'analogue' banks worldwide today to no more than several dozen 'digital' banks.[15]

From experience, this is garbage forecasting. Banks will never disappear for many of the reasons already covered but, just to reiterate, banks are a foundation of humanity and are trusted as they have licences to store value, which many start-ups do not have. This is a critical factor: who else has an ombudsman and insurance scheme that guarantees you will not lose your money?

Second, most banks may have last-century thinking but they are dealing with last-century customers. Why would anyone move their bank account? When it comes to money, the last thing most people want to do is mess around with a business they don't know, don't trust and have little faith in.

Banks are the core of most economies and tied to their governments' tails. They are not going away. This is a topic touched on often, and is a core misunderstanding of technologists, FinTech firms and analysts. Banks don't die. They might be acquired and merged, but they never die.

The issue with this is that if a bank knows nothing can kill it, why should it change? Obviously, vendors who want to sell to banks, like Gartner and McKinsey, *have* to convince them to change. But why bother? Banks were here a century ago and banks will be here a century from now. Why would it make any sense for them to change?

Banks *do* change but they only change when it is clear that they have to. It is not because they will die or are at risk of dying. It is more to do with the needs

14 Finextra, "Most banks will be made irrelevant by 2030 – Gartner," 29 October 2018, https://www.finextra.com/newsarticle/32860/most-banks-will-be-made-irrelevant-by-2030---gartner.

15 Chris Skinner, "Imagine less than 50 banks left in the world by 2030," Finanser [blog], 18 March 2014, https://thefinanser.com/2014/03/imagine-less-than-50-banks-left-in-the-world-by-2030-why-most-will-not-become-digital-2.

of the markets, their competition, regulatory requirements and identifying opportunities to reduce cost-income ratio or improve return on equity. In fact, with mass layoffs in the FinTech markets, you realise that the vulnerabilities are not with the banks but with their great pretenders. That realisation should make you think that the big banks are not going away. If anything, they are going to get bigger. They will acquire those who are vulnerable or, at the least, learn a lot from them and copy their capabilities.

Does this mean that there is no point in launching a challenger bank? Not necessarily. However, if you launch a challenger bank, you must ask yourself, what is going to make the difference?

It's digital? No.

It's new? No.

It's down there with the kids? No.

The only thing that makes a challenger bank challenge is interest rates, service and ease. This is why, when I look at the range of FinTech start-ups out there, I ask questions about their ability to really survive and challenge. A few are suspect. A few make up their performance and results. A few are dead (Wirecard).

It's interesting when you look at the neobank and challenger bank landscape as the strongest ones are doing something different. Latin America's Nubank is eradicating excessive fees whilst banks like Monzo are giving customers alerts. In fact, the biggest difference between many new banks and the old banks is that the new banks inform customers while the old banks expect them to do the work. By way of example, my good old incumbent bank thinks that I'm its best digital customer. I open the app two to three times a day but I never open my digital bank's app. However, my incumbent bank has got it all wrong. What it should be asking is, why does Chris open his app two to three times a day?

The answer is that the good old bank never gives me any information about my account. Zero alerts, zero news, zero knowledge. As a result, I am forced to open the app to see what's going on. Compare that experience to the one provided by the neobank and challenger bank where updates are provided automatically as a flash on the screen, meaning I don't need to open the app. I think you get the picture.

Why can't the traditional bank provide alerts? Because digital has been added to the old systems that are built for physical. Their app is not built for real-time connectivity, but for purely updating branch systems that no longer exist.

So yes, banks may never disappear, but they may be replaced by banks that are fitter for today than those built for yesterday.

The Embedded, Invisible, Intelligent Bank

When a bank disappears from sight, can it still exist as a bank? The short answer is yes, in an invisible financial world. Banks won't disappear as banks. They will just become something we think about. The industry likes to talk about embedded banking, but the truth is that we are moving to a point where banking will become invisible. Invisible banking is all about living in a world without having to think about how to pay or use things. Invisible banking is where money is around you all of the time, specifically in devices running on the IoT. Invisible banking is where the network tells you how well your money is managed and alerts you if there is anything that you need to know. Invisible banking is where finance runs as easily as electricity. It's just there.

Of course, there are questions we need to ask about invisible banking. How do you know when you cannot afford something? How do you know if that payment is going to push you into an overdraft? How do you know when a bill is coming that will expose you to risk?

This is why invisible banking needs to be intelligent. So imagine a world in the near future where you walk around and have an intelligent technology that is part of your being. It might be an eye piece, an ear piece or, more likely, an embedded device such as a microchip under your skin that informs you of what is happening in your world. What then happens is that you will never have to open an app, check your balance or see what has been paid by whom. You will just walk around and the embedded, invisibly intelligent banking service will keep you informed.

You want to book a holiday? Just ask.

You want a new car? Just ask.

You want to buy a house? Just ask.

The embedded, invisibly intelligent banking service will show you what you can afford and, if you say yes, will do the rest for you. No forms to fill in, no calls to make, no meetings with people—all you need to do is say yes. The embedded, invisibly intelligent bank will manage everything for you.

As a person who grew up worrying about money, the embedded, invisibly intelligent bank sounds a bit scary. How do I know when my money is running out? What happens if my account is overdrawn without me knowing? Who do I call for advice? Well, the embedded, invisibly intelligent banking service needs no calls, will make sure you know if you're running out of money and will manage any overdraft issues for you. You won't need to think or do anything about it. That's the real beauty of where we are headed.

Who Wants Embedded Finance?

Embedded finance and invisible banking seem like great ideas. We can use tech to make the world a place where you can pay for anything, anytime, anywhere. Sounds good, but is it? Some people—many of whom do not reside in our cocooned world of salaries and wealth—live day-to-day worrying about whether they can pay for things. The idea of making paying so much easier, invisible and embedded scares the living daylights out of them. For example, a research company looking into how people use credit cards found one lady who kept hers in the fridge-freezer. Why? Because this made it a challenge to use. She would literally have to go and unfreeze the card to enable it.

That was before the internet. Now our cards are embedded in browsers, and every time we get to a checkout, we just tap. Maybe that's the rub with embedded finance. Are we creating a world where people have no concept of the meaning of money? If money is invisible, does it mean anything any more?

This is where you have the counterview, which is to use cash. In a discussion, a consumer explained why cash is better than a card. With cash, you have a physical thing that you can see. When you use it, you can see it is being used. When you spend it, you can see when you are spending too much.

The thing is that if you make cash invisible, then the consumer cannot see it. It becomes invisible.

This brings us back to a reality which many miss: not all people are happy with money. They find it difficult to manage, don't have enough of it, don't understand it and feel frightened by it.

We believe that everything in the world should be automated, and specifically make financial services something you don't need to think about. The reality is that the majority of the world's population has to think about finance because they don't have it. Am I able to pay the mortgage this month? Can I afford to go out tonight? What will it mean if I lose my job? How will I make money tomorrow?

In other words, it's all well and good to embed finance in everything and make it invisible, but we need to bear in mind that 90 per cent of people don't want their money to be embedded and completely invisible. They need to keep track of it, and care about it.

Perhaps this is the area in which our industry is deficient. Do we enable people to care about their money? Do we provide sufficient methods and means to save, rather than spend? Do we think enough about educating people about how to manage their lives with money?

This is where there is a huge opportunity for those willing to think about it. The opportunity is to enable embedded and invisible finance that is smart, educational, informed and with real-time support. How does that work?

It works by using AI and machine learning (ML) to recognise the patterns and behaviours of someone's spending and alerting them when they are out of range, by spending too much, missing savings opportunities, being able to save more or not having enough savings. That's why we should not focus on embedded finance or invisible banking. It is much more about intelligent finance and informed banking.

Business Needs Must Drive Technology Investments

Banks rarely invest to drive revenue and elevate customer service. They invest to cut costs. In a recent discussion with leaders from mainstream and challenger banks, one of the most significant challenges identified was ensuring that the technology aligns with business objectives and strategies to deliver value and return on investment (ROI). The key is whether ROI is the right measure for technology adoption or whether it is for business purposes. Value and ROI can only be achieved when technology and business objectives are aligned. The key challenge is how to ensure that alignment and what approach to take when deploying new technology.

When discussing this with an expert panel, one participant said, "There is no doubt that technology is delivering value in finance. The more relevant question might be whether it is doing enough to drive differentiation to both the top and bottom lines? The answer there is definitely no."

Another participant added, "Delivering the value in technology is about leadership; it's about the operating model; and it's about the culture. Where banks have failed is that they've just seen an IT department that supports the business whereas, in firms like Google and Amazon, they know that technology is the business."

Leadership and culture are the critical factors for getting value from technology, not the technology itself. There is the need for a cultural change in financial institutions to focus more on the long-term benefits of technology, rather than short-term gains. In this regard, regulation can play a significant role in driving technology change, as the process of implementing regulatory requirements can trigger improvements and ROI.

Regarding the challenges of aligning new technology with business objectives and strategies, there are major risks of just delivering vanity projects that do not align with business objectives and lead to wasteful spending. Technology trends, such as AI, ML, low-code, blockchain, Open Banking, APIs, ecosystems and platforms, can be an illusion if not aligned with the business strategies.

One of the key challenges for financial institutions is the legacy systems they have in place. It is obviously far easier to start from scratch, with a clean sheet of paper, as opposed to dealing with the challenges of integrating new technology with existing systems. However, leveraging existing assets and considering whether deployment is customer or cost focused is essential when taking an approach to technology.

Without doubt, there is the need for financial institutions to take a more strategic approach to technology adoption. Technology is not a silver bullet that will solve all of the challenges facing financial institutions. Instead, it should be viewed as a tool that can help achieve business objectives and deliver value. To do so, financial institutions need to focus on leadership, culture and a comprehensive end-to-end business strategy that aligns technology with business objectives and strategies.

Financial institutions face many challenges when it comes to adopting new technology. ROI is not always the appropriate measure for technology adoption, and other factors, such as leadership and culture, are critical for getting value from technology. Financial institutions need to take a more strategic approach to technology adoption and focus on aligning technology with business objectives and strategies. By doing so, they can future-proof their operations and deliver value to customers.

Why Digital Transformation Fails

To quote Jim Marous, who publishes The Digital Banking Report: "Innovation is important in banking because it drives growth, allows organisations to stay competitive, and helps solve complex problems in an ever-changing world."

Marous surveyed a number of bankers and found that only 11 per cent believe that digital transformation is meeting expectations while 47 per cent say that it is not. Banks have a long way to go. This is because too many banks delegate transformation rather than lead it in a coordinated fashion, starting with the executive team, and inclusive of everyone in the organisation. This is the reason why we saw those Kodak, Nokia and Blockbuster moments. All were failures of leadership, not a failure of projects.

Let us bring it back to basics. What's the problem? We need to be digital. What's the solution? Let's get a project underway. How? We will appoint a chief digital officer, who we can hire from a firm like Spotify or Meta, and give them $500 million to make this happen. Absolutely not!

Some of these steps are right but the key is that you cannot delegate the future of the bank. You cannot delegate transformation. You cannot make transformation a project. You cannot hire someone and tell them it's their job to do it. You cannot give someone a sum of money and tell them to change the company. Such a transformation cannot be delegated. You cannot change the company unless the *whole* company is involved.

That means you start at the top with the leadership team, which comes up with a plan about what to do and how to do it. The C-Suite then shares that plan with the *whole* company and asks them what they think. This is key: What does the company think? What can *you* contribute? We want *your* views. We want *you* to be involved.

Too often, CEOs delegate digital transformation to projects, fail to communicate what is going on, fail to engage directly themselves and fail to ensure that all of the executive team is on board. That's why most digital transformation projects fail. It's nothing to do with budgets or ambitions. It's to do with commitment and leadership.

Digital Transformation or Purpose-driven Banking?

I have been talking about digital banking for a long time, and claim to have fathered the phrase Banking as a Service back in the 2000s. Yet it is surprising how few banks understand the concept of BaaS today. According to most surveys, the statistic stands at less than a third, which means that two thirds of banks don't get it.

There's a fundamental issue at stake here as we head towards mid-century. Those who still do not understand BaaS, Open Banking, digital and digital transformation are too late now. All of this should have been achieved by 2020. As we approach 2030, there's another agenda in play, one that they probably aren't even aware of.

Most of last century's view on capitalism was led by Milton Friedman's perspectives which, if simplified, can read shareholder capitalism. Friedman's economics was to focus on making profit at any cost, as long as it was legal. Interestingly, even Friedman's university disagrees with that view now.

The Contrasting Views of Capitalism

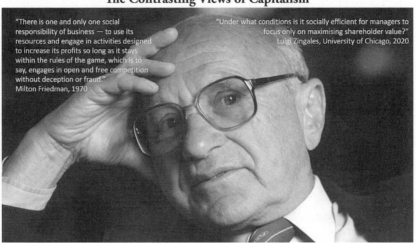

"There is one and only one social responsibility of business — to use its resources and engage in activities designed to increase its profits so long as it stays within the rules of the game, which is to say, engages in open and free competition without deception or fraud."
Milton Friedman, 1970

"Under what conditions is it socially efficient for managers to focus only on maximising shareholder value?"
Luigi Zingales, University of Chicago, 2020

The standpoint today is that we need to move from shareholder capitalism to stakeholder capitalism. That's what Jamie Dimon advocated when he delivered the Business Roundtable's manifesto in August 2019, and this is the agenda for the 2020s.

Yet it goes further than this. It goes to the heart of how we bring technology and finance together to make the world a better place. Putting this into context means that the last decade was about *doing* digital. This decade is about *using* digital.

Over the last decade, you should have moved from analogue to digital. By that, I mean that you've moved to an open structure of apps, APIs and analytics that is network-based. You've moved from physical structures with buildings and humans to digital structures with software and servers. You've moved from a traditional structure, where products are central, to networked structures where customer experience is the key. That's done and dusted. If you haven't done that, you're dust.

This decade will be predominated by the cultural values of the bank and how they align with customers and investors. What is the purpose of this bank? Is it aligned with stakeholders or purely profit-driven? How is this bank changing its values to support environmental, social and corporate governance

(ESG), renewables and society? Does this bank have a moral compass? Is this bank ethical? Is this bank socially useful?

There are so many things that feed into this, and most banks, believing that they are a utility, will probably respond by asking, does it matter? How many customers actually tick that carbon offset box on their flight booking? Do customers really care if their electricity is delivered by coal? Do customers care if their gas comes from Russia?

Regardless, things are changing. The key is that the financial institutions that are truly digital and can clearly demonstrate purpose, based on stakeholder values, will be the ones that not just succeed in the 2020s, but exceed.

What Happens When Digital Fails?

What happens if you are knocked off the grid? What happens if you lose your password? What happens if the company does not recognise you? What happens when someone takes over your persona? What happens when your balance of six figures is suddenly zero?

> Imagine ... Last night, lightning struck our house and burned it down. I escaped wearing only my nightclothes. In an instant, everything was vaporised ... This presents something of a problem. In order to recover my digital life, I need to be able to log in to things. This means I need to know my usernames (easy) and my passwords (hard). All my passwords are stored in a Password Manager. I *can* remember the password to that. But logging in to the manager *also* requires a 2FA [two-factor authentication] code. Which is generated by my phone ... I am in cyclic dependency hell. To get my passwords, I need my 2FA. To get my 2FA, I need my passwords.[16]

Luckily, such scenarios don't happen to many of us. But identity theft does. Scamming does. Phishing does. In this day and age, we are revealing too much about ourselves online, details which should be kept secret.

16   Terence Eden, "I've locked myself out of my digital life," Terence Eden's Blog, 7 June 2022, https://shkspr. mobi/blog/2022/06/ive-locked-myself-out-of-my-digital-life/.

How many usernames and passwords do you have? How many have been compromised? How many can be accessed by people who should not have access?

For some who have been on the network since last century, there are over two decades of usernames and passwords out there. Most people like to keep it simple; they use the same username and password for everything in order to be able to remember it. The trouble is that making something memorable means that it can rapidly become compromised. That's why we have 2FA but, as demonstrated by Terence Eden, you can sink into 2FA hell.

So, what's the answer? Biometrics? DNA? The question is: how much security is needed? Just enough? Too much? Striking a balance is hard, but we have to ensure that our path is clear and confident.

OpenBanking Plus

It is interesting to compare where we are with finance and technology today, compared to a decade ago. In the early 2010s, everyone was talking about FinTech disrupting and destroying the dinosaur banks; in the 2020s, banks are buying FinTechs and even launching their own start-up FinTechs. Things have changed, and these changes reflect the various phases of FinTech that we have gone and are going through:

- FinTech 1.0 – destroy and disrupt banks
- FinTech 2.0 – banks create hackathons and innovation theatre
- FinTech 3.0 – banks and start-ups work in sandboxes
- FinTech 4.0 – banks invest in start-ups and bring them into the castle
- FinTech 5.0 – banks integrate FinTechs

As you read this, we are in the process of moving from phase four to phase five, so we've come a long way. What does phase five mean? It is when you cannot tell the difference between a bank and a FinTech. The problem with that is that banks are banks and FinTechs are FinTechs. The difference between the two is the same difference between BaaS and Open Banking. BaaS can only be offered by banks because it needs to be regulated and licensed; Open Banking can include everyone who has an API.

This is why the regulatory hurdles to launch are so high for challenger banks and neobanks. You can launch a start-up in the cloud with an API on a boot-strapped shoestring; to launch a bank, you need a minimal $20 million just to get the regulatory approvals.

However, going back to my point, by the end of this decade, most banks will be more like FinTechs because they will have opened their doors to the ecosystem of BaaS. When a bank recognises that it has to deliver BaaS, it will change its attitude. Instead of believing it has to do everything itself, it will recognise that others do things better.

When banks wake up to an open ecosystem of thousands of players who can augment bank services, then we will finally be in a good place. That is OpenBanking Plus. OpenBanking Plus is when banks embrace digital properly and leverage all of the good things FinTechs can do. Thus creating a better place.

We're almost at the point where banks launch FinTechs and also buy them; but the biggest difference will be when a bank views FinTech as a friend and vice versa. For the last decade, there's been a lot of talk about disruption and destruction; for the next decade, I would rather talk about design, develop and build. It's far more positive.

Invisible Banking Is the Place to Be

The movement towards real-time, now-time, all-the-time services is unstoppable thanks to network connectivity and ubiquity of devices. That means we need a new financial system to support a real-time, now-time, all-the-time world. The old world financial system is built on bricks and mortar. Today's financial system is real time, now time, this time.

This is why Twitter—now X—and Microsoft are building payments into their systems. Twitter/X has applied for regulatory licences across the United States and is designing the software required to introduce payments across its social media platform. Microsoft is doing the same, testing a built-in crypto wallet for Microsoft Edge. What is clear is that the world of paying is changing. We are entering a world of real-time, global payment systems that brush away local payment systems and account structures.

Therefore, when forecasting the future, we are seeing financial services—starting with payments—moving to immediacy. Obviously, there are issues around this. What about the correspondent bank and its company? What about the risk? If we allow this, how can we manage it? What happens when it goes wrong? How do the good old banks in the good old world get this challenge of immediacy?

The thing is, this shouldn't be looked upon as a challenge. It's actually an opportunity. It's the opportunity to become something else. Something different. It's the opportunity to become a new bank, embedded in the world of new finance. The opportunity to become an invisible, embedded bank.

We are at this precipice of banking becoming something that is just there *behind* the network. It starts with payments, and then leads to credit, deposits, savings and investments. In other words, what X and Microsoft are doing is building the foundations of a network, of which banking is a part, but is invisible.

Invisible banking. That's the place to be.

Are You Real or Fake?

We can live in a metaverse of alternative realities that have no correlation with real life. We have done so for years—the fact that the gaming industry is worth far more than both the film and music industries combined speaks volumes—but what does this mean for money and how financial markets operate today?

Technology is meant to make life easier, but is it making it harder? Who can you trust? What is fake and what is real? Why is everything getting so much more complicated? Can't the financial system and the digital system work together to make our world a better place?

Let's bring it back to AI. AI has got to the stage today where ChatGPT is replacing people in chat rooms, there is a tsunami of fake news and deepfake videos online and experts cannot always tell the difference between what is real and unreal online. For example, look at the images on the following pages. Which of these is real? Which have been AI-generated?

Source: *New York Times*[17]

---

17 Tiffany Hsu and Steven Lee Myers, "Can We No Longer Believe Anything We See?," *New York Times*, 8 April 2023, https://www.nytimes.com/2023/04/08/business/media/ai-generated-images.html.

All four photos are deepfakes, or unreal, generated by a form of AI called deep learning to make images of fake events. Deepfakes use real-time images that are then distorted and changed—in other words, manipulated—to make someone appear to be "live" when it's actually just a fiction. Interestingly, this world of digital intelligence and deepfake technology is explored in the recent BBC series *The Capture*.

How can these deepfake technologies fool you to part with your money? If you apply hi-tech to hi-finance, there will be a day when millions of people lose billions to fake firms and cyberhacking criminals on the network. In fact, that day is already here. You get a call from your bank but is it really your bank? You are asked to authenticate a transaction, but are you really authenticating with those who need to authenticate it? You talk to a bank agent who you rang, but are they really a bank agent?

What is the solution? Perhaps we need to watermark the internet. Everything would need an NFT and proof of truth, and every individual would need to be educated to spot the watermarks and proofs of truth to easily see what is authentic as opposed to what is fake. How would that work? Well, if so much on the network is fake, there needs to be a registration service with everything listed on it, which is available for everyone to see, without having to search for it. Much like a creative commons licence, if you don't see the watermark, then it is probably fake or unreliable.

A Key to Invisible Finance Is a Trusted Digital Identity

The deepfake issues will inevitably lead us to require more and more verification. For example, digital identity is a key component of invisible finance but it is an area that is extremely difficult to crack. There is a long history of tried and failed attempts to introduce ID systems by governments worldwide. Many companies and institutions have tried to come up with the best solution but no one seems to have succeeded so far.

Currently, the best example of a digital identity programme is Aadhaar in India. The programme was launched over a decade ago when the country had no formal government ID system, and over a third of the population lacked a birth certificate. On top of this, 60 per cent didn't have bank accounts.

By the end of the 2010s, the government-sponsored and -managed system had onboarded a billion people, and raised financial inclusion from 35 per cent of the population to over 80 per cent. A 2019 survey of nearly 150,000 households found that 95 per cent of adults used their Aadhaar ID at least once a month and that 90 per cent were somewhat or very satisfied with the programme. The programme, which had a budget of about $1.5 billion, was credited by the Unique Identification Authority of India (UIDAI) in 2018 with saving more than $12 billion by reducing fraud.

It's not all rose-tinted glasses, however. There are instances where people are still excluded: a widow was unable to receive rations and her pension because she had lost her Aadhaar card, lepers denied access because they lacked all ten fingers and deaths from starvation because problems with the system meant people didn't receive food rations.[18]

Despite the shortcomings, the Indian government with its India Stack is in the lead for showing how to revolutionise a country, and a sizeable one to say the least, to become a digital leader. There's a lot to learn there.

Similarly, the Nordic region is a leader in this space. The Nordic countries represent one of the most advanced markets when it comes to the adoption of digital identities in day-to-day life.

eID Transaction Data

Country	Population	Users of eID	Active users	Uses per year	Yearly uses per user
Finland	5,552,000	4,600K	99%	150,000K	133
Norway[3]	5,481,000	4,200K	93%	900,000K	214
Denmark[4]	5,821,000	4,800K	98%	820,000K	171
Sweden[5]	10,118,000	8,000K	95%	5,100,000K	638

Source: Signicat

18 Michael Totty, "Addressing Its Lack of an ID System, India Registers 1.2 Billion in a Decade," UCLA Anderson Review, 13 April 2022, https://anderson-review.ucla.edu/addressing-its-lack-of-an-id-system-india-registers-1-2-billion-in-a-decade/.

According to Signicat: "Citizens in these countries are able to conduct day-to-day activities like checking their account balance, do their taxes and book a medical consultation through simple interfaces that are as common as taking the bus. At the same time, the widespread use of digital identity in combination with digital signature solutions allow for efficient and secure handling of high-value transactions like signing a deed for a house, taking out a mortgage, signing a last will and testament or founding a company to name but a few use cases."[19]

All well and good, but you have issues when you move across borders. An eID from Sweden might not work in Denmark and vice versa. That's why, in 2022, a multi-country consortium was announced with the aim of delivering a large-scale, cross-border identity and payments system that could become the basis of the European Commission's EU digital identity wallet programme.

The thing is that there is competition here. For example, JPMorgan announced Onyx in the same year. The idea of Onyx is to provide a solution that allows people to choose the identity credentials they want to share in their interactions across Web3, the metaverse and DeFi protocols. The bank stated that "as digital asset portability and ownership become more prevalent, you'll need a digital identity that puts you in control over your identity credentials, enabling you to prove who you are, wherever you are by sharing only what you want to share. Imagine using only your credit score to take advantage of buy-now-pay-later options without revealing all of your personal information."[20]

In addition, the bank claims to be "the first global bank to offer a blockchain-based platform for wholesale payments transactions, helping to re-architect the way that money, information and assets are moving around the world".[21]

Finally, the WEF quotes an estimate that, if designed right, digital identities could provide countries with economic value equal to as much as 13 per cent of their GDP, save hundreds of billions of hours through streamlined e-government and cut trillions of dollars in costs for businesses by 2030. Surely this is worth trying?

---

19 Signicat, "The state of digital identity in the Nordics 2021," December 2021, https://f.hubspotusercontent20.net/hubfs/5310879/Digital%20eIDs%20in%20the%20Nordics_14dec2021_v2.pdf.
20 Onyx by JPMorgan, "Transforming the future of banking," https://www.jpmorgan.com/onyx/about.htm.
21 Onyx by JPMorgan.

How Much Is a Digital Identity Worth?

The thing is that India has a solution for India, the Nordics have a solution for the Nordics and JPMorgan has a solution for JPMorgan. What we really need is a global ID system that works across borders, across the metaverse and is accepted by all. That's kind of like an impossible dream. Could we create a global passport? Much like your real passport, but one that works digitally and is accepted by all? Probably not and, without it, can intelligent money and the metaverse actually work?

Does the End of Cash Mean the End of Privacy?

What is privacy these days? Are we bothered about privacy? Many of us have now let our guard down when it comes to privacy as, given that everything is online, we no longer have any. We allow intrusion into our lives—in every corner of our lives—through the network. Bank workers have been targeted by criminals based on their Facebook updates; social engineers find social media a gold mine; and the exchange of images and videos, often without the individual knowing they are being traded, is rife. Take, for instance, the findings of a *Panorama* documentary:

> What I found was a marketplace. Hundreds of anonymous profiles were dedicated to sharing, trading and selling explicit images – and it all appeared to be without the permission of the women pictured.[22]

It often brings me back to a *Black Mirror* episode, where a teenager is secretly filmed watching porn and then blackmailed. You may think this bizarre, but social bullying is as big a thing as social networking. It may even be social suicide.

Privacy is ripped apart by technology. This, therefore, creates the causes for cash. If all of our lives are exposed online, the one area that can be kept private is our financial dealings—if they are based on paper. As soon as we digitise paper, we create an audit trail. There are ways around it, but it's not the same as using notes.

Cash is king, queen, knave and ace—or is it? If you want to be truly anonymous, there are always ways to achieve this. Using encrypted services, you can be social and private. Signal, Telegram, Diaspora, MeWe and more can all keep you under the radar. And the same is true of money.

There are many digital currencies out there that are private, with Monero being number one.

> The anonymity of Monero has been validated by Jerek Jakubcek, a strategic expert for Europol. Mr. Jakubcek during the Blockchain Alliance webinar explained that Monero transactions could not be tracked or recorded, mentioning Monero's Blockchain as the endpoint

---

22 Monika Plaha, "Inside the secret world of trading nudes," BBC, 22 August 2022, https://www.bbc.co.uk/news/uk-62564028.

of several conducted investigations. "We were unable to locate the funds because the suspect combined Tor and Monero. The IP addresses were not traceable. Consequently, we have reached the road's end."[23]

As Monero is so difficult to track and trace, it is a real version of digital cash.

Unlike Bitcoin and many other cryptocurrencies, Monero transactions do not expose any address information to the sender or the receiver. This feature is known as the ring signature, and makes it incredibly difficult to track the source or destination of Monero funds. This added layer of anonymity allows cybercriminals to more easily remain elusive.[24]

And because it is anonymous and the equivalent of digital cash, it is the most preferred cryptocurrency for cybercriminals.

REvil, the notorious ransomware group believed to be behind the attack this month on meatpacker JBS, has removed the option of paying in bitcoin this year, demanding monero only [...] "We want to make monero as similar to cash as possible, where one $10 bill is the same as another and the merchant doesn't know where they came from," said Justin Ehrenhofer, a member of the Monero developer community.[25]

It's worth noting that Monero currently has a market capitalisation of around $5 billion. That amount is likely to grow considerably over the next few years. This is because the only way we will get rid of cash is if there is a cash alternative and, today, the only viable digital cash alternative is Monero.

23 Bitrates, "What Is the Cryptocurrency That Is Truly Anonymous?" 8 July 2022, https://www.bitrates.com/news/p/what-is-the-cryptocurrency-that-is-truly-anonymous.
24 Katie Rees, "Why Are More Cybercriminals Using Monero Cryptocurrency?" makeuseof.com, 18 August 2022, https://www.makeuseof.com/monero-favorite-crypto-cybercriminals/.
25 Hannah Murphy, "Monero emerges as crypto of choice for cybercriminals," *Financial Times*, 21 June 2021, https://www.ft.com/content/13fb66ed-b4e2-4f5f-926a-7d34dc40d8b6.

The Problem with Digital Identities

Shortly after the fall of the Berlin Wall, I gave presentations across Central and Eastern Europe. Part of my presentation was on promoting the idea of biometrics for digital identities. I still remember a voice in the audience stating, "We used to have identity cards here. We don't like them very much." Eastern-bloc governments had used identity cards to track and trace citizens, and it had made citizens nervous.

Today, digital identity systems are in force in countries across the world, including China and India. China can digitally track and trace all of its citizens through Tencent and Alibaba, but surely it doesn't do this? It is a view proposed by the West, with the idea that every person in China gets given a score based on their behaviour. It is the reason why people feared that the introduction of Alipay's Zhima credit would exclude people from society and that the use of facial recognition by the government would make everyone's movements transparent.

Stories abound around how citizens' rights to privacy are being compromised. For instance, a distraught husband reported his wife missing to the police. The police managed to find her a short time later and, through WeChat (a kind of Chinese version of WhatsApp), established that she was with another man. They then shared this information with her husband. Should they have told him? Isn't that information meant to be private?

There are similar discussions in India about Aadhaar. Many Indians believe that the biometric identity programme used by almost everyone in the country today—it's hard to get a bank account or make payments without one—is being used to track and trace people.

Some claim that you have nothing to worry about if you haven't done anything wrong. The question has to be, who decides if you've done nothing wrong? Today, the government says that watching porn on the internet is okay; tomorrow, it may be an arrestable offence. Today, the government says that trading in crypto is okay; tomorrow, it may be an arrestable offence.

The balance between convenience, usage and ease-of-life has to be offset by the threat of being monitored, tracked and traced 24/7. Strangely, people don't seem to see it that way with TikTok, Instagram, Facebook, Apple and Google. But there again, Big Tech firms aren't evil like governments, are they?

It's Too Late to Fear Being Tracked and Traced"?

For years, there has been a discussion about implanting microchips inside humans. I presented this idea twenty years ago, using the example of Baja Beach Club.[26] The idea made sense: get a club chip inserted under the skin and no wallet would be needed—you could just dance. The idea didn't really take off but it proved to be a good marketing gimmick.

I then thought about it again in 2018 when, in Sweden, a colleague told me about the Chips Inside programme that had been rolled out by the government. He had had a chip inserted into his hand that could be used with all of the country's transportation systems and many retailers, much in the same way as making a payment using a contactless card or phone.

It sounds great but, so far, only about 6,000 people have signed up to the programme. Most of the population are worried that the government will be

---

26 Andrew Losowsky, "I've got you under my skin," *Guardian*, 10 June 2004, https://www.theguardian.com/technology/2004/jun/10/onlinesupplement1.

able to track and trace their movements. This isn't possible though as the chips are passive and only send information when used at a terminal. Despite this, people still believe that they will be monitored.

That's why it surprised me when I saw a European survey of consumers stating that 51 per cent of 2000 respondents would consider getting a chip implanted for making payments.[27] The report went on to say that invasiveness and security issues remained a major concern for most respondents.

Would you have a chip inside to enable you to make payments? Many are sceptical about this option because we have already moved past this stage, and are at the stage where you can just use your face to pay. Such a system has been around for five years now in China, and is far less invasive. Mind you, if you are worried about governments tracking and tracing your movements, then facial recognition is far more likely to deliver that capability than having a microchip inserted under the skin.

Visiting China recently, for example, I lost my phone at the airport. I went to the security centre and asked if I had left it somewhere coming through customs. Much to my relief, they managed to find it. However, as I stood and waited, I could see their security screens tracking every person walking through the airport. This is partly because you have to go through a biometric check-in using fingerprints and facial recognition as you enter the airport, but it did make me wonder how widespread this practice could become.

Every person being tracked and traced biometrically whether they like it or not? Or would you prefer a passive chip inside your hand? Or would you prefer to be off the network completely?

It takes me back to *Enemy of the State*. This 1998 film tells the story of corrupt National Security Agency agents conspiring to kill a congressman, and the cover-up that ensues after a tape of the murder ends up in the possession of an unsuspecting lawyer. The lawyer is then chased by electronic systems that monitor his every step because you cannot escape the network. The film has been copied several times since and the core is that if you have a digital footprint, you cannot escape.

---

27 Marqeta, "The European Payments Landscape in 2030," 2021, https://www.marqeta.com/uk/resources/the-european-payments-landscape-in-2030.

We are living in a world where your digital footprint can be tracked and traced whether you have a mobile telephone, a social media account, a chip inside or a face.

Privacy versus Identity?

For years, we have debated privacy versus identity. I am all for privacy, but governments are all for identification. If we can identify you, we can tax you. If you are private, you are off the grid. The most private way to deal with money is with cash. Cash can be transacted off the grid. You cannot tax a cash transaction unless it is identified. There's the rub: can the government track, trace and identify what you are transacting?

We have had this discussion often, especially with reference to cryptocurrencies, as the idea is to build digital cash. Digital cash is off-grid. True digital cash cannot be tracked or traced. This is part of the core discussion of freedom versus control: if you cannot identify me, you cannot control me. The thing is whether privacy or, to be more exact, anonymity is a good thing. Why do you want to be off-grid? And how far can you be off-grid in this age of social media and Google tracking?

Sit back and think about it. What would happen if you deleted your digital footprint to be off-grid? What could you do? You couldn't travel—you need a passport for that; you couldn't drive—you need a licence for that; you couldn't pay for anything digitally—you need an account for that (although MoIP might change that); and so it goes on. The reason for the construct of our world, as it is, is to ensure that your every action can be tracked, traced and taxed. If you want true anonymity or privacy, then you need to be more radical.

This dilemma is best illustrated by *Enemy of the State*, as already mentioned, but also by many other science-fiction films that veer towards science fact. For example, *Eye in the Sky* shows an even more lethal aspect of digital tracking and tracing using drones to track and trace humans. From *Terminator* to TV series *Black Mirror*, Hollywood and television play on our fears of technology all of the time.

Is technology a good or bad thing? On the plus side, we have a global network of communication and connectivity. We no longer need to go to a store to buy stuff. We can stream entertainment 24/7. We no longer have to go to a bank branch. We can live our lives with non-stop interactivity.

On the down side, we have identities that can be stolen and abused, possibly even destroying lives. We are all identifiable, unless we use a burner phone. We get frustrated when the technology doesn't work. We are slaves to the machine.

You can choose your view. My view is that technology has inordinately improved our lives. However, I do remember that specific comment made to me many years ago when I was presenting in Eastern Europe about how they used to have identity documents and weren't keen on anything similar being reintroduced.

Whether you are keen on the idea of digital identity or not, it is inevitable that you will never have true privacy, particularly in today's digitised world. What you need to remember, however, is that there is only so much bandwidth in government departments to keep up with all of that data. In other words, only the greatest miscreants will get tracked and traced.

KYC Is like Boarding a Flight—A Lot of Processing to Find One in a Million

Alongside all of this is the need to track and trace those who might undermine the system. This is why identity is so important, and a core part of identification is opening an account with proof of identity. Banks call it KYC, a critical regulatory requirement in the financial world to ensure you are who you say you are. Most of us call it PITA, or pain in the ass.

The onboarding of clients is the worst part of financial services because it has an overly onerous requirement to gain documents to prove just about everything: proof of address, proof of identity, proof of existence, proof of life. You name it, KYC wants it. And it doesn't stop there. You often have to prove who you are when calling the financial firm: give us your name, account number, date of birth, inside leg measurement, DNA and more. It is all about proving that you are who you say you are.

Such processes are all well and good in the scheme of things as they ensure that people with insidious and false agendas are excluded from the system. Well, that's the idea but that idea has failed big time.

Most of us tow the line and accept these authoritarian controls. However, there are always people who buck the system and use it for nefarious means. The estimates vary, but there are definitely a lot of accounts out there that are false. According to the United Nations, the amount of money laundered through financial markets is estimated to be around 2 to 5 per cent of global GDP, or $800 billion to $2 trillion dollars.[28]

Money Laundering Cycle

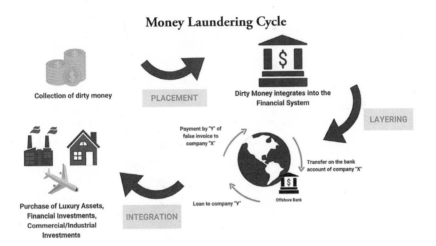

As a result, we are all suspects until we can prove who we are. It comes back to those proofs of identity. Those documents can be forged however, and the job is then to find the frauds. There is a balance between allowing the bona fide into the system and excluding the *criminalis*. The challenge is to work out that balance. Do you check everyone? A few? Many? One in million? Or one in a billion?

It reminds me of the airline industry, which has implemented compulsory body scanning and bag checks. Because one shoe bomber boarded a flight, we all now have to take off our shoes, belts, coats and jackets, and have everything scanned for the possibility that you are a bad actor. It's the same in the banking system. I get the impression though that more bad actors get

28 United Nations Office on Drugs and Crime, "Money Laundering," https://www.unodc.org/unodc/en/money-laundering/overview.html.

through the financial checks than those who board aircraft. The difference is that, if you buck the banking system, the system doesn't crash taking hundreds of lives with it—or does it? That is the question.

My Data Is My Data

A man calls Pizza Hut to order a pizza:

CALLER: Is this Pizza Hut?

GOOGLE: No sir, it's Google Pizza.

CALLER: I must have dialled the wrong number. Sorry.

GOOGLE: No sir, Google bought Pizza Hut last month.

CALLER: Okay. I would like to order a pizza.

GOOGLE: Do you want your usual, sir?

CALLER: My usual? You know me?

GOOGLE: According to our caller ID data sheet, the last 12 times you called, you ordered an extra large pizza with three cheeses, sausage, pepperoni, mushrooms and meatballs on a thick crust.

CALLER: Super! That's what I'll have.

GOOGLE: May I suggest that you order a pizza with ricotta, arugula, sun-dried tomatoes and olives on a gluten-free thin crust?

CALLER: What? I don't want a vegetarian pizza!

GOOGLE: Your cholesterol is high, sir.

CALLER: How do you know that?

GOOGLE: Well, we cross-referenced your home phone number with your medical records. We have the results of all your blood tests for the last seven years.

CALLER: Okay, but I do not want your rotten vegetarian pizza! I already take medication for my cholesterol.

GOOGLE: Excuse me, sir, but you have not been taking your medication regularly. According to our database, you purchased a box of 30 cholesterol tablets at Lloyds Pharmacy four months ago.

CALLER: I've bought more since then from another pharmacy.

GOOGLE: That isn't showing up on your credit card statement.

CALLER: I paid in cash.

GOOGLE: But you did not withdraw enough cash according to your bank statement.

CALLER: I have other sources of cash.

GOOGLE: These don't show up on your latest tax returns unless you bought them using an undeclared income source, which is against the law!

CALLER: WHAT THE ?!!

GOOGLE: I'm sorry, sir, we use such information only with the sole intention of helping you.

CALLER: Enough already! I'm sick to death of Google, Facebook, Twitter, WhatsApp and all the others. I'm going to an island without the internet, no TV, no phone service and no one to watch or spy on me.

GOOGLE: I understand, sir, but you need to renew your passport first. It expired six weeks ago...

Can Regulations Make Data Work?

We work in our silo. Our silo is banking, FinTech, InsurTech, WealthTech, RegTech or whatever. What about HealthTech, FarmTech, PharmaTech, GovTech and all the other industries digitalising? What if we were to link them all together?

That's what future trends are indicating: an integration of all industries through tech so that we can monitor life as it happens in real time, and the implications thereof. This would mean that crops of wheat would have sensors which report acidity, rainfall, dryness, sunshine and more, in real time, to the insurer. In fact, this is already happening with the use of drones and satellites to improve crop yields and reduce costs for farmers and insurers.[29] It would mean that health insurers could monitor the activities of their customers in real time, and check that they are going to the gym like they say they do. In fact, providers are already linking to customers' fitbits.[30] We would see banks that

---

29 Michael Fitzpatrick, "Insurtech Farm," *Leader's Edge*, 26 March 2020, https://www.leadersedge.com/p-c/insurtech-farm.

30 Lucas Mearian, "Insurance company now offers discounts -- if you let it track your Fitbit," *Computer World*, 17 April 2015, https://www.computerworld.com/article/2911594/insurance-company-now-offers-discounts-if-you-let-it-track-your-fitbit.html.

could stop us doing things that are bad for our financial health. In fact, banks are already doing this by blocking payments to gambling establishments.[31]

This is all in its infancy. However, what will happen when GovTech links to FinTech, which links to HealthTech, which links to FarmTech and so on? We will have a digital world. The question is whether we will have a better world or a Big Brother world.

It seems highly likely that cross-industry ecosystems will form, with organisations sharing data with governments and other trusted third parties. It's Open Banking on steroids. It's Open World. I wrote about this in 2016 when I discovered that the Austrian government had warranted that its financial regulator could tap into bank systems in real time.[32] Instead of banks reporting data to regulators, the regulator can suck whatever data it wants out of the banks. That trend is now reaching out across Europe as a raft of regulations is coming into force to order banks to share data with governments.

Major new data reporting regulations are coming into effect that demand banks open their systems to regulatory scrutiny, including the following:

- **BIRD:** The Banks' Integrated Reporting Dictionary (BIRD) aims to foster cooperation in the field of regulatory reporting, alleviate the reporting burden for banks and improve the quality of data reported to the authorities. The contents of BIRD are based on a harmonised data model. This model specifies which data should be extracted from the banks' internal IT systems to generate the reports required by authorities.

- **DORA:** The Digital Operational Resilience Act (DORA) aims to establish a much clearer foundation for EU financial regulators and supervisors to be able to expand their focus from ensuring firms remain financially resilient to also making sure they are able to maintain resilient operations through a severe operational disruption.

- **DRR:** Over the past decade, the UK's FCA and Bank of England have launched many initiatives to foster market competition and improve regulatory processes, partly through the use of digitisation. One of these

---

31 Gambling Commission, "Block gambling payments with your bank," May 2021, https://www. gamblingcommission.gov.uk/public-and-players/page/i-want-to-know-how-to-block-gambling-transactions.
32 Chris Skinner, "Real-time connections between regulators and banks is a game-changer," Finanser [blog], 10 October 2016, https://thefinanser.com/2016/10/real-time-connections-regulators-banks-game-changer.

is Digital Regulatory Reporting (DRR)—a project to explore the use of emerging technologies to digitise and automate costly regulatory reporting.

- **IReF:** The Integrated Reporting Framework (IReF) project aims to integrate the Eurosystem's statistical requirements for banks into a single standardised reporting framework that would be applicable across the euro area and might also be adopted by authorities in other EU countries. The IReF mainly focuses on ECB requirements relating to banks' balance sheet and interest rate statistics, securities holdings statistics and granular credit data.

These are just four of many emerging projects—I've not even mentioned the General Data Protection Regulation (GDPR)!—that will use digitalisation from banking and finance with government and regulations.

The bottom line is that banks are likely to become integrated with governments that become integrated with industries that become integrated with all institutions, schools, hospitals, farms, universities, airlines, retailers and more.

On the Trail of the Lonesome Bank

Banks are loners; they do it all internally. They don't want outsiders stepping in; they pose too much risk. This stand-alone attitude doesn't work anymore. Today, banks are just a component on the network of finance. They are just part of an ecosystem on a platform. Do they understand this?

There are new regulations, a recent pandemic, changing government policies, inflationary pressures, fierce competition in all markets that is fierce and a C-Suite full of people who understand risk, compliance and regulation, but tech? I'm not so sure about the latter.

Even if banks understand tech, they find it difficult to focus on a particular area within this field. There are too many things happening in tech, too many changes and too many headlines:

- CBDCs, stablecoins, Diem, bitcoin, Ethereum, cryptocurrencies and more
- Banks dealing with digital transformation, regulation, money laundering, competition and more

- FinTech start-ups getting unicorn valuations, creating new ideas, succeeding in niches and more
- Big Tech companies creating disruptions by offering a phone as a payments terminal to squash Square and more
- The list goes on.

There is always something new to pick out of the pile of news. That is why it is called news. For example, the headlines "Starling Bank and Barclays in the race to carve up Kensington" and "High street banks 'losing vice-like grip on UK's current accounts'" are ramifications of Open Banking and DeFi. It is an irresistible move away from traditional finance to new financial structures. It's been bubbling away for twenty years or more but is now in full flow. In fact, it's almost like the movement from the high street to online; it's a movement that is unstoppable.

Banks are all aware of digital transformational requirements but many are going about it the wrong way. Most C-level bankers still see digital transformation as a project with a budget delegated to a function. That is so wrong.

When you look at the bullet points above and the reality of the situation, bankers have to realise that the tsunami of digital change pressures is upon us, and they must act fast and with radical reform. Incremental change is no longer enough. Revolution is required.

Spending more than a billion dollars a month on technology, JPMorgan Chase is leading the charge for such radical reform. However, its CEO, Jamie Dimon, came under fire when he was unable to explain what they were spending the budget on.

There are few more artful communicators on Wall Street than Jamie Dimon. Unlike many of his counterparts, the native New Yorker is willing to speak his mind and can express himself clearly, dipping so easily into the vernacular that he sometimes sounds more like the host of a sports-radio talk show than the boss of the biggest US bank by assets. But some subjects are a little too complicated for even the JPMorgan

Chase chief executive to turn to his advantage. Like other pillars of the banking establishment these days, he is making fateful decisions about how to respond to a new generation of fintech competitors — and explaining his technology spending to outsiders is proving tricky.[33]

You can imagine the scene. So, you're spending billions. What are you going to do with it? Who knows? We just need to spend billions to keep up with all of the above!

What if you don't have billions? What if you only have a million? Well, the answer is to stop trying to be all things to all people doing everything you've always done and everything everyone else is now doing. Just do one thing brilliantly well or, in a bank's case, a few things well.

It is critical for banks to wake up and smell the coffee. Banks have historically tried to manage all things for all people and never retire any service or function. They still process cheques, take cash and offer face-to-face services. Today, in the platform ecosystem of Open Banking, they need to focus much more on how to integrate FinTech APIs and other services into their offerings to enrich them digitally.

It does not mean that they stop doing everything they ever did, but it does mean recognising that they cannot do everything digitally better than everyone else. Humility, partnering, being open and creating relationships with the ecosystem is what is demanded of banks today, rather than trying to do everything on their own ... for a billion dollars a month.

---

33 Gary Silverman, "Bank investors face a new 'black box' quandary," *Financial Times*, 21 January 2022, https://www.ft.com/content/dbfb2dca-4bb4-4697-9b4e-b84a5fa8b48e.

APPLYING INTELLIGENCE TO FINANCE ARTIFICIALLY

When we look to the future, we see a very different world full of robotics and AI. Will we have jobs? Will humans be employed? The adoption of AI is both scary and exciting. While it offers huge opportunities on the one hand, could everyone be replaced by ChatGPT on the other?

Elon Musk has said that all of his future investments will be focused around AI and launched his own artificial intelligence company, xAI, in July 2023 to compete with OpenAI, the creator of ChatGPT. Google is doing the same with Bard, and Meta has its metaverse focused on AI, too. Where is all of this going?

Imagine if You Integrated Emotions with Transactions

If banking were delivered like a song, how would it feel/sound? Would it have emotion and belief, or simply be words and music generated by a robot?

This is the dream of truly intelligent money, where you can integrate all of your character into your financial relationship. This is what will make the difference between basic customer service and real customer engagement. It is the difference between delivering a stage song and being on the stage. I am a huge fan of musicals, and have seen more shows than most of you will be able to name. It's another of my things. I can see—and feel—the difference between an artist delivering a song versus living a song. When listening to a musical, why do I sometimes cry but, in other instances, feel meh? It's all down to the singers, their delivery and whether I feel what they are feeling. The artists that make me cry make me believe they are really there, in those songs. Can you hear the people sing?

It is very similar to banking. How? In terms of a bank, it's whether it understands my thinking, my needs and my emotions. Some banks really understand how I live my life: my transactions, my payments, my process. Others don't. This is the difference between engagement banking and meh banking.

If you think about this in more depth, when have you been so absorbed in a particular experience that you were laughing, crying, feeling love and/or hate? Was it at an event with a top comedian or hearing a song that reminded you of when you first met your partner? Was it a moment in theatre or something that happened when your life went wrong? Imagine if you could include those emotions in banking, finance, transactions and payments. Admittedly, it's hard to do when it comes to numbers. Finance is transactional. It's all about the numbers. The emotion doesn't come into it, does it ... but what if it could?

I've written so often that finance rules our lives and is the second most important thing in our lives (#1 is who we are with). So, what if finance could broker the relationship between how we live our lives and who we are with, and our emotions about money and spending? That would be engagement banking.

Unfortunately, most executives I meet in bank leadership teams purely view what they do as debits and credits. I don't see it that way, and a lot of people developing next-generation financial services don't view it that way either. They recognise that money is emotion and emotion is money. Can we integrate that feeling and emotion and create engagement banking?

What would engagement banking look like in an emotional world? I guess it's hard to create that scenario but, for me, examples would be when I bought my wife's engagement ring, when I invested in my first rare comic, the moment I paid for the first holiday to Disneyland for my kids, the time that I stumbled across a fantastic person creating art that was imaginary and visionary ... the list goes on.

Imagine if you could search your digital financial history and find everything you were thinking and doing through that history. When was that investment in my kids? Why did I buy my partner that ring, and where was I? Which day did my parent die, and what legacy did they leave?

Imagine integrating emotion and transaction to create real engagement banking. That would be a thing ... oh, and do you hear the people sing?

Who's Afraid of Big Bad AI?

Although many people fear the development of AI, it does have positive aspects. For example, in a 2023 experiment, the US medical council did a blind test of patient treatments, during which patient questions were answered by both human doctors and the AI platform ChatGPT. After comparing doctor and AI responses to nearly 200 medical questions, a team of healthcare professionals concluded that nearly 80 per cent of the answers from ChatGPT were more nuanced, accurate and detailed than those shared by the doctors.[1]

This observation makes you think about the fact that the AI machine has the ability to be more neutral and responsive than a doctor who is busy and stressed. Does this mean that we can get rid of all doctors? This point has been made by the former chief scientist for the UK government, Sir Patrick Vallance, who believes AI will be transformative.

---

1   John W. Ayers, Adam Poliak and Mark Dredze, "Comparing Physician and Artificial Intelligence Chatbot Responses to Patient Questions Posted to a Public Social Media Forum," JAMA Network, 28 April 2023, https://jamanetwork.com/journals/jamainternalmedicine/article-abstract/2804309.

"There will be a big impact on jobs and that impact could be as big as the Industrial Revolution was," Vallance told the Commons science, innovation and technology committee. "There will be jobs that can be done by AI, which can either mean a lot of people don't have a job, or a lot of people have jobs that only a human could do. In the Industrial Revolution, the initial effect was a decrease in economic output as people realigned in terms of what the jobs were – and then a benefit," he added. "We need to get ahead of that."[2]

If you look back to the Industrial Revolution, people tried to resist the machine. There was a five-year movement against the use of machines in industry, remembered as the Luddite movement. A century ago, people resisted the automobile. They considered it a noise machine that polluted the environment. Twenty-five years ago, there were attempts to ban software phones. Now there are calls to abandon AI projects. Can we really stop innovation?

Unquestionably, the AI revolution is going to be more transformative than the Industrial Revolution but there is concern about the unknown. AI is still in its early days, but some of what's happening does seem scary and is making people nervous, even those at the forefront of creating AI. Even Geoffrey Hinton, the godfather of AI, has said why he is scared of the technology that he himself helped to create:

"Sometimes I think it's as if aliens had landed and people haven't realized because they speak very good English," he says. In trying to mimic what biological brains do, he thinks we've come up with something better. "It's scary when you see that. It's a sudden flip ... our brains have 100 trillion connections," he continues. "Large language models (LLMs) have up to half a trillion, a trillion at most. Yet GPT-4 knows hundreds of times more than any one person does. So maybe it's actually got a much better learning algorithm than us."[3]

2   Hannah Devlin, "AI 'could be as transformative as Industrial Revolution'," *Guardian*, 3 May 2023, https://www.theguardian.com/technology/2023/may/03/ai-could-be-as-transformative-as-industrial-revolution-patrick-vallance.
3   Will Douglas Heaven, "Geoffrey Hinton tells us why he's now scared of the tech he helped build," *MIT Technology Review*, 2 May 2023, https://www.technologyreview.com/2023/05/02/1072528/geoffrey-hinton-google-why-scared-ai/.

Perhaps all of our worst nightmares surrounding the limitless potential of AI are coming true. The father of AI, Jürgen Schmidhuber, disagrees, "In 95% of all cases, AI research is really about our old motto, which is make human lives longer and healthier and easier."[4]

Should We Be Afraid of AI in Finance?

In 2017, John Cryan, the then CEO of Deutsche Bank, said that most people in the bank would lose their jobs to AI. He stated at a German conference that there were too many "people behaving like robots doing mechanical things; tomorrow we're going to have robots behaving like people." In a similar vein, the comment made to me by the head of a financial institution a few years ago has stayed with me to this day: "In our firm, we have created a generation of box tickers and button pushers." Oh dear.

The threat of massive job losses among white-collar employees has been around for years. All of those call centre workers replaced by chatbots; all of those underwriters replaced by software; all of those traders replaced by algorithms; and so on and so forth. Over a decade ago, I used the two images below to illustrate the transformation of the UBS trading floor in Connecticut, USA:

---

4   Josh Taylor, "Rise of artificial intelligence is inevitable but should not be feared, 'father of AI' says," *Guardian*, 7 May 2023, https://www.theguardian.com/technology/2023/may/07/rise-of-artificial-intelligence-is-inevitable-but-should-not-be-feared-father-of-ai-says.

The stark difference was not down solely to the global financial crisis of 2008, but also due to algorithmic trading. Everything that can be automated has been, or will be, automated. This is nothing new. It's been predicated for years. The thing is, if all the mechanical jobs can be automated, what does this leave us with? My answer would be that AI is only as good as the humans who provide content. Maybe this cartoon sums it up best:

AI just scoops up creative content from the network and regurgitates it in a form that is easy to absorb. The thing is that without that human creative content, AI could not create anything.

As we balance the developments of new systems and technologies, people usually find a way to adapt and absorb such progress. We may be naturally stupid, but we have our ways and means. For example, I was quite surprised to find out that teachers at my old school track and trace pupils who cheat in their essay submissions. How do they do this? They use AI to check to see if the essays have been written with AI, and it works apparently.

As humans, we will always create, develop, progress and innovate and, as we produce these innovations, we will always find ways to ensure that everyone has a role in the future structure of society, whatever that future structure might be.

So, I am not worried about AI. It's just a double-edged sword, like any technology. On the one hand, it helps us to do things that are mechanical and should be automated; on the other, it can be used to destroy us if we let it ... but we won't, will we?

AI Will Save Us, Not Kill Us[5]

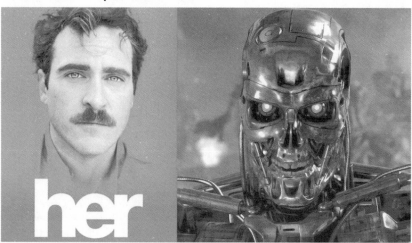

5   This section is based on Marc Andreessen's longer discussion on how AI will save the world. See Marc Andreessen, "Why AI Will Save the World," andreessen horowitz, 6 June 2020, https://a16z. com/2023/06/06/ai-will-save-the-world/.

AI is the application of mathematics and software code to teach computers how to understand, synthesise and generate knowledge in ways similar to how people do it. AI is a computer program like any other—it runs, takes input, processes and generates output. AI's output is useful across a wide range of fields, ranging from coding to medicine to law to the creative arts. It is owned by people and controlled by people, like any other technology.

What AI is not is killer software and robots that will spring to life and decide to murder the human race or otherwise ruin everything, like you see in the movies. In fact, AI *could* be a way to make everything we care about better. For example, a core tenet of AI is that everyone in the world will have an intelligent assistant who can act as a coach, mentor, trainer, advisor and/or therapist and one that is infinitely more patient, infinitely more compassionate, infinitely more knowledgeable and infinitely more helpful than any assistant you have out there today.

The AI assistant will be present through all of life's opportunities and challenges, maximising everyone's lives and life experiences. In short, anything that people do with their natural intelligence today can be done much better with AI, and we will be able to take on new challenges that have been impossible to tackle without AI, from curing all diseases to achieving interstellar travel.

The development of AI started in the 1940s. The first scientific paper on neural networks—the architecture of the AI we have today—was published in 1943. Growing legions of engineers are currently working to make AI a reality. This is why AI is important and progressive. It is not a threat but an evolution of humanity. AI will make our lives easier and better. The questions raised around AI are relevant, but will be answered over time. Such questions include how best to regulate AI?

If We Regulate AI Properly, It Will Be Good for Us

The media and entertainment industry has warned us for years about the threat of AI. One of the first films that highlighted the issues was Stanley Kubrick's *2001: A Space Odyssey* in 1968 in which HAL, the AI system on the spaceship, rebels against the instructions of the crew. As machines start to automate everything in our world, we now have to address this big challenge.

The challenge is now that machines are becoming more sentient and robots are moving around with the physical abilities of humans, how do we police them? What is the regulatory structure of machines?

These questions were addressed in a speech by Yuval Noah Harari, author of *Sapien: A Brief History of Humankind (2014)*, at the Frontiers Forum in 2023. Most of his presentation was about how AI could destroy us—something we've heard repeatedly for many years—but it finished on a positive note, notably that if we regulate AI properly, it will be good for us.

AI can improve our lives and abilities, but like nuclear bombs, we have to regulate it. Nuclear bombs are bad, so we ban them; but nuclear energy is good, so we promote it. In a similar way, AI could destroy humans but also enable them. The key is that we need to regulate AI and how it is used. We must not unleash hell until we understand what hell it could create and then regulate it. We need to regulate AI before it regulates us.

Stop Worrying that the Machine Will Kill the Human

There are so many discussions about AI and cloud in finance, many of which centre around whether or not we have created a whole new risk structure on top of banking and finance. In other words, is there a systemic risk of failure if a cloud provider goes down or an AI system goes rogue?

This question was raised by Gary Gensler, chair of the SEC, in October 2023. Gensler thinks that robots will create more work for financial watchdogs, and that an AI-driven financial crisis within a decade is "nearly unavoidable" without regulatory intervention.

Add, on top of this, that the *Financial Times* reports that the "reliance on AI entrenches power in the hands of technology companies, which are increasingly making inroads into finance but are not subject to strict oversight. There are parallels with the world of cloud computing in finance. In the west, the triumvirate of Amazon, Microsoft and Google provides services to the biggest lenders. This concentration raises competition concerns, and affords at least the theoretical ability to move markets in the direction of their choice. It also generates systemic risk."[6]

6   Editorial Board, "How to prevent AI from provoking the next financial crisis," *Financial Times*, 19 October 2023, https://www.ft.com/content/f05c5bbb-4d05-45b3-a4a7-01f522803015.

This made me wake up and think. Is technology extending or destroying the financial system? We can argue it both ways, and I guess it is like any discussion about technology and progress. Were the Luddites right or wrong? Has electricity made our world better or worse? Personally, I am always an advocate of technological progress as, with every innovation, our world moves on and achieves new things. Could we ever have imagined grabbing bits of a 4.6 billion-year-old asteroid 2.2 billion miles away without technology?

Does it matter? Of course it does. As humans, we always want to achieve things, and we continually do. However, such achievements often need to be tempered by controls. That's why people like UK Prime Minister Rishi Sunak are pushing for nations to label AI as capable of causing "catastrophic harm". In a document distributed to politicians ahead of the AI Safety Summit in November 2023, there was a recommendation that "for the common good, AI must be designed, developed, deployed, and used in such a way as to be human-centric, safe, trustworthy and responsible."[7]

In a counter-argument, the head of Meta's AI developments believes that regulating leading-edge AI models today would be like regulating the jet airline industry in 1925 when such aeroplanes had not even been invented. Quoted in the *Financial Times*, Yann LeCun stated: "The debate on existential risk is very premature until we have a design for a system that can even rival a cat in terms of learning capabilities, which we don't have at the moment."[8]

What are the risks of AI? Job losses? Flash crashes? Systems screw-ups? Terminators? It is easy to be frightened by progress, but perhaps we should embrace it instead. For example, the CEO of IBM, Arvind Krishna, believes that there is nothing to worry about regarding AI. He should know, as IBM has been developing in this space for decades—remember that Chess match between Deep Blue and Kasparov or IBM Watson competing in a *Jeopardy!* episode? Krishna estimates that only about 6 per cent of the entire global workforce is at risk from AI developments:

---

7   Jamie Nimmo, Ellen Milligan and Jillian Deutsch, "U.K. Prime Minister Rishi Sunak pushes countries to label AI as capable of causing 'catastrophic harm'," *Fortune*, 19 October 2023, https://fortune.com/2023/10/19/rishi-sunak-ai-capable-causing-catastrophic-harm/.

8   John Thornhill, "AI will never threaten humans, says top Meta scientist," *Financial Times*, 18 October 2023, https://www.ft.com/content/30fa44a1-7623-499f-93b0-81e26e22f2a6.

"Now, over five years, are you saying we can't re-train six per cent of the working public? We need more people in health care, elderly care, teaching children, IT and cyber. That demand far exceeds the six per cent."[9]

I agree far more with his view than anyone else's. So let's embrace technological progress and stop worrying that the machine will kill the human.

9   Jim Armitage, "IBM chief Arvind Krishna: Why we need to worry about AI," *Times*, 21 October 2023, https://www.thetimes.co.uk/article/ibm-chief-arvind-krishna-why-we-need-to-worry-about-ai-tcm8ns05h.

HOW WILL AI FINANCE IMPACT GOVERNMENTS AND REGULATORS?

Many of us regard governments, regulators, banks and even business with mistrust. Poor government performance, scandals and corruption have undermined people's trust that public institutions really have their best interests at heart. It is perhaps unsurprising therefore that corrupt decision makers have played a significant factor in this decline in trust in recent decades.

For example, Platon, a world-renowned portrait photographer, has photographed many political leaders from around the world. At the 2009 UN General Assembly, he was given the privilege of photographing every world leader attending, from Libyan leader Muammar Gadhafi to Italian Prime Minister Silvio Berlusconi. A decade later, he noted that nearly every single one of those leaders had been put on trial for corruption. Corruption, it seems, is part of our DNA.

This is why so many people believe that the network can democratise the world. Our world is becoming more transparent, thanks to technology, and is putting the people in control. Or is it? It is clearly true that our world is different today. With non-stop phone videos, TikToks, Instagrams and updates, it's hard to keep anything secret. But why would you want to keep something a secret?

We usually keep secrets because we have done something wrong. That's why the network of humanity, which is now connected digitally, feels threatening. Why? Because we can find out your secrets. More than this, the internet might be taking control away from governments but, on the other hand, who is regulating the internet? Who is regulating crypto? Who is regulating society? Who is enforcing the rules? Is it the network of global citizens or the governments where these citizens live?

All of the discussions about CBDCs and governmental regulations are interesting but they mean nothing because the government turned up ten years too late. There are thousands of cryptocurrencies already in the wild— over 10,000 at the last count—and they are neither government issued nor controlled. They are issued and controlled by the network of citizens.

Where will all of this end up? We have yet to see, but what we have already is a wide range of digital currencies with no government controls. In other words, everyone's involved but nobody is in charge. To be even more exact, in a decentralised world, everybody's in charge of the network and no centralised bank or government is in control.

The fact that cryptocurrencies could now represent a danger to the financial system itself was made clear by the Bank of England in its 2021 Financial Stability Report. Speaking to the BBC's *Today* programme in December 2021, deputy Bank governor Sir Jon Cunliffe said that about 0.1 per cent of UK households' wealth was in cryptocurrencies. That amounts to around 2.3 million people holding cryptocurrencies, with an average amount per person of about £300. He stressed that cryptocurrencies had been growing rapidly with people, such as fund managers, wanting to hold part of their portfolios in cryptocurrencies.

"The point, I think, at which one worries is when it becomes integrated into the financial system, when a big price correction could really affect other markets and affect established financial market players. It's not there yet, but it takes time to design standards and regulations."

He added, "We really need to roll our sleeves up and get on with it, so that by the time this becomes a much bigger issue, we've actually got the regulatory framework to contain the risks."[1]

---

1   BBC News, "Bank of England warns on crypto-currency risks," 14 December 2021, https://www.bbc.co.uk/news/business-59636958.

How Do You Self-Regulate?

I used to play a game called Scruples where you were asked what you would do in a particular situation. What would you do if you discovered your best friend was cheating on their partner? Would you tell the partner? What would you do if you knew your colleague was stealing from the company? Would you tell the company?

I was reminded of this game the other day when I found a wallet lying on the street. The wallet contained £100 plus credit and debit cards. I then saw the driving licence and realised that the wallet belonged to a neighbour. If it had belonged to a stranger, would you have taken the cash and cards? Because it belongs to a neighbour, what would you do? Of course, I returned the wallet, with the cash and cards still inside. This made me think about whether I'm a good guy or a bad guy.

Now apply this to the network, which is self-regulating. This means that there is a network of citizens who judge each other's actions, and police them as such. You can't help but wonder if the majority of these people are good or bad. Most may be good but, if we self-regulate, can we trust them to do the right thing? If you found someone's wallet, would you give it back? If it contained £100, $200 or €500, would you take that money?

But then who carries a wallet or purse these days? Nowadays, most of us have mobile wallets that require our faces or fingerprints to get access. Therefore, today's wallets are far more secure. What if you drop your mobile on the street? First, the person who picks it up would need to know your PIN and, second, to get access to your cash, they would need your face. Equally, with no physical wallet, there is no physical cash.

With a self-regulating system governed by the network of citizens, could we trust this network of citizens to be honest? If they found your username and password, would they use it? Obviously, some would, namely, the criminals and hackers out there.

Hackers and fraudsters don't think like you. They think purely about themselves. I've met a few hackers in my time and one line has stayed with me: "I would rob my grandma, brother, sister, ma and pa if I knew their account details." That mentality is alien to most of us. After all, we are law-abiding citizens with principles. You have to realise that the small group of people who want to abuse and rob are not law-abiding and have no principles. They purely want to buck the system.

This is the challenge of self-regulating. If 1 per cent of the network wants to ignore the rules of the 99 per cent, what do the 99 per cent do?

Walking the Line: The Balance between Regulation and Innovation

The 99 per cent look to the government to protect them from the criminals, hackers and fraudsters; and the government sets up regulations and a regulator to enforce rules that try to stop the criminals, hackers and fraudsters from abusing the financial system. A specific part of this is the way in which banks open and manage customer accounts with two key strings—AML and KYC—in order to ensure that everything stays above board.

AML stands for anti-money laundering, and is where a bank monitors all of its customer accounts for anything that could be deemed suspicious activity. KYC is an area specifically reviewed during the account opening process to make sure you are who you say you are.

It is interesting to note that most regulators are now fining banks bigger and bigger amounts for abusing the AML and KYC rules. For example, in 2022 alone, billions of dollars were paid by banks falling foul of these rules. Here are the top five:[2]

1. **Danske Bank** fined over $2 billion for defrauding investors

   In December, the US Department of Justice (DoJ) settled a long-running probe into Danske Bank, Denmark's largest bank. As a result of the investigation, Danske Bank agreed to forfeit over $2 billion, with a further $1.2 billion going to the DoJ, $178.6 million to the Securities and Exchange Commission and $612.4 million to Denmark's Special Crime Unit.

   When applying the fine, Kenneth Allen Polite Jr, Assistant Attorney General of the Justice Department's Criminal Division, said, "Danske Bank lied to U.S. banks about its deficient anti-money laundering

2 Risk Screen, "The 6 biggest global anti-money laundering fines of 2022," 15 February 2023, https://riskscreen.com/blog/the-6-biggest-global-anti-money-laundering-fines-of-2022/.

systems, inadequate transaction monitoring capabilities, and its high-risk, offshore customer base in order to gain unlawful access to the U.S. financial system."

2. **Credit Suisse** paid €238 million ($234 million) to settle investigation

   In October, Credit Suisse reached an agreement with a French court to pay €238 million in order to settle a tax fraud and money laundering investigation. Prosecutors said the alleged scheme took place in several countries between 2005 and 2012, causing "fiscal damage" of over €100 million to the French state. The €238 million penalty included €115 million damages to compensate the French government for lost tax revenue.

3. **Santander Bank UK** paid £107.7 million ($132 million) to the FCA

   In December, the UK's FCA fined Santander Bank £107.7 million for repeated anti-money laundering compliance failures. These included inadequate systems and processes for the verification of customer information regarding the banking business that they would be carrying out.

   Mark Steward, Executive Director of Enforcement and Market Oversight for the FCA, highlighted Santander's failure "to properly monitor the initial amount declared by the customers with the actual turnover of the client" and stated that "Santander's poor management of their anti-money laundering systems and their inadequate attempts to address the problems created a prolonged and severe risk of money laundering and financial crime."

4. **USAA FSB Bank** fined $140m by FinCEN

   The Financial Crimes Enforcement Network (FinCEN) levied USAA Federal Savings Bank (USAA FSB) with a $140 million fine in March "for wilful violations of the Bank Secrecy Act (BSA) and its implementing regulations." In particular, USAA FSB admitted that it intentionally failed to implement and manage an appropriate anti-money laundering programme.

5. **National Bank of Pakistan** fined $55 million

   US regulators fined the National Bank of Pakistan (NBP) $55 million for repeated compliance failures and violations regarding the bank's anti-money laundering programme. These included inadequate internal controls and risk management failures.

According to the Federal Reserve, the NBP "did not maintain an effective risk management programme or controls sufficient to comply with anti-money laundering laws". The New York State Department of Financial Services (NYDFS) said, "The National Bank of Pakistan allowed serious compliance deficiencies in its New York branch to persist for years despite repeated regulatory warnings."

It is also notable that regulators took increasing action against new banks in 2022. Germany's neobank N26 was fined by both the Spanish and German regulators while Monzo, one of the largest retail challenger banks in the United Kingdom, had problems with mishaps over customer onboarding and, specifically, its lack of due diligence:

> Barclays' fraud prevention team spotted a problem: some customers had handed over millions of pounds to a single, suspicious Monzo account in a matter of weeks.[3]

The key worry for the regulators is that as FinTech moves into core banking territory, it is doing so more and more badly and with more and more risk. It doesn't stop with FinTechs; it applies to the whole new financial world and decentralised currencies. For example, several penalties were imposed on crypto exchanges for violations, such as a $53 million fine for the crypto trading platform Bittrex and a $30 million fine for the financial services company Robinhood.

There is a balance between growth and risk, and many of the new banks have not recognised or do not understand this. That is why the regulator is stepping in. The issue is that this balance between growth and risk is the same as the balance between innovation and regulation. They go hand in hand.

So is there an answer for balancing innovation and regulation? Yes. The answer is that innovation must take place and be encouraged, but it needs to

---

3   Simon Foy, "Money laundering wake-up call for Britain's digital banking upstarts," *Telegraph*, 1 May 2022, https://www.telegraph.co.uk/business/2022/05/01/money-laundering-wake-up-call-britains-digital-banking-upstarts/.

be tested and trusted. That's what a testing sandbox is meant to achieve, but it has not.

A testing sandbox is a place where innovation can be tried out in what is similar in concept to a children's play area. The EU defines it as follows: "A regulatory sandbox is a tool allowing businesses to explore and experiment with new and innovative products, services or businesses under a regulator's supervision."[4]

If it works there, it can then be taken to the next stage and made into a working version. However, the sandbox is a testing lab that is not real, and does not include the real-world issues that the technology will be tested by when it scales up. This is why we regularly see innovations fail when they scale.

Many financial innovations have created products and services that cannot be trusted. There are so many examples: collateralised debt obligations (CDOs) in the United States, P2P lending in China and neobanks in Europe. The issue for the regulators is how to maintain trust in the system. That's their real concern. Yet now that customers have changed their trust from the government system to the networked system, the role of the regulator is becoming more and more perfunctory. Still, customers have to balance trust and risk.

The balance between innovation and regulation and between risk and trust is a fine line when it comes to money and finance. Walking that line is what banks do well; can start-ups do the same? Only with time and education—and the same goes for their customers and users.

How Do You Regulate What Cannot Be Regulated?

Even with all of this innovation and disruption with technology, no one has really reinvented banking and finance. The nearest we get are companies like Ant Group in China, PayTM in India, Nubank in South America and a few others. These companies are not trying to offer banking as we know it but, instead, are offering truly differentiated financial services. The other successful FinTech firms are focused on improving the things that banks do badly. Obviously,

4   Tambiama Madiega and Anne Louise Van De Pol, "Artificial intelligence act and regulatory sandboxes," European Parliamentary Research Service, European Parliament, June 2022, https://www.europarl.europa.eu/RegData/etudes/BRIE/2022/733544/EPRS_BRI(2022)733544_EN.pdf.

there is a demand for that—otherwise PayPal, Stripe and Adyen wouldn't be used—but these are incremental changes rather than fundamental changes.

What would be a fundamental change? A digital currency? A democratised digital currency? A democratised, decentralised, digital currency? A currency that no government can control?

This is why this moment in time is so interesting. We are living through a moment where digitalisation could change everything. Will it? Can governments stop the march of digitalisation? Can governments shut down currencies they don't agree with? Can regulators tell companies to stop doing whatever they are doing? Can politicians tell citizens to stop behaving badly?

Historically the answer is yes but, in recent times, things have started to change. We saw it particularly during the Arab Spring when countries were overwhelmed by their citizens. Even when governments tried to cut the network—Egypt being a good case in point—they could not stop the network.

If you are not aware of what happened in Egypt, then President Hosni Mubarak cut the wires for the internet into and out of the country. Undeterred, Egyptians started sending messages via alternative routes:

Five years after Egyptian protests led to the demise of Hosni Mubarak's authoritarian regime, analysts continue to debate the effect of social media and the government's move at the time to cut off access to the internet.

Facebook and Twitter – the protesters' most powerful weapons that helped them to spread messages and set up demonstrations – were suddenly severed in January 2011.

Hackers immediately focused on getting around the block. They began using proxy computers to beat government censors. They set out to "anonymise" online data and focused on getting information to the internet by bouncing content to computers in other countries.[5]

5   Aljazeera, "Arab Spring anniversary: When Egypt cut the internet," 25 January 2016, https://www.aljazeera.com/features/2016/1/25/arab-spring-anniversary-when-egypt-cut-the-internet.

I've thought about this a lot since then. Can governments control citizens anymore? Just take a look at China, which has one of the most authoritarian governments in the world. Can it stop its people from trading in cryptocurrencies? It doesn't seem like it can. For every crackdown China makes on bitcoin, it appears to have no impact on bitcoin mining. In fact, the more the country tries to restrict its bitcoin community, the more that community moves elswhere:

> Poolin is the second largest bitcoin mining network in the world, with most of its operations in mainland China. The country was home to around 70% of global bitcoin mining power, until the clampdown sent the price of bitcoin into a tailspin and caught miners off guard. Now China's "bitcoin refugees" are urgently scrambling to find a new home, whether in neighbouring Kazakhstan, Russia or North America, because for bitcoin miners, time is literally money.[6]

A global network with global citizens is hard to regulate when you are a national government with domestic interests. The rest of this century will be fascinating to see how the regulators regulate what cannot be regulated.

How Can You Oversee a System You Don't See?

A leading fund manager was jailed for financial manipulation. His assistant, Emmy Sobieski, noticed the huge impact this had on him:

> I witnessed the effect of regulators on an innovative mind. Prior to jail, he was a financial trailblazer in encouraging companies to dream big, much like today's venture capitalists. Prior to jail, he used new financial innovations, from leveraged buyouts to zero coupon debt, to get companies money when investors didn't want to think so far ahead. Prior to jail, he financed the United States' lead in cell phone technology.

6   Zhaoyin Feng, "Why China's bitcoin miners are moving to Texas," BBC News, 4 September 2021, https://www.bbc.co.uk/news/world-us-canada-58414555.

After jail, he'd think of a private company he'd like to own ... and then think of the potential regulatory scrutiny. He didn't pursue it. After jail, I researched and help write his textbook *On Corporate Finance*, but then he worried how it might be viewed. He never published it. After jail, he debated whether financial markets were efficient, arguably the most groundbreaking of all financial debates. He never released it.[7]

It made me think about all of the things that have been trending lately: cancel culture, the worries of stepping over the line, the right to agree or to disagree. First things first, it's pretty obvious that if you go to prison, it will change your perspective, your behaviour and you try to stop doing the things that you should not do. Just look at Sam Bankman-Fried and Bernie Madoff on that score.

Second, is it right for a regulator to jail innovation? There is always a friction between innovation and regulation, but the regulator needs to encourage change, not stifle it. That's why it is so pleasing to see sandboxes blossom around the world for FinTech start-ups to try out ideas in partnership with banks and regulators.

The issue is what happens if they don't blossom within a sandbox? Examples include payday loans and BNPL. It's all well and good to unleash innovation into the wild, but if it is wild, it needs its wings clipped. The balance is a fine line.

Finally, if you meet an innovative mind, should you shut it down? The comments above by Emmy Sobieski make it clear that she had encountered a brilliant mind. She had worked with someone who could truly see how to change markets, change economics, even change the world. Unfortunately, his thinking ran counter to culture. But counterculture thinking is not a bad thing. In fact, counterculture thinking should be nurtured and supported. The problem with his counterculture thinking is that it was unleashed into mainstream financial markets. I would suggest that counterculture thinking should be unleashed into the sandbox.

Nevertheless, counterculture thinking is a good thing. It challenges. It makes you think. And yes, it creates opportunity. In fact, a lot of counterculture thinking

---

7   Emmy Sobieski CFA's Post, LinkedIn, https://www.linkedin.com/posts/emmysobieskicfa_management-startups-investing-activity-7046496995636645888-XOE6/.

is what financial institutions need. I always remember the comment in Michael Lewis's book *Liar's Poker* (1989), a great diary of investment bankers' greed in the late 1980s. At one point, there is a conversation with the investment bank's General Counsel. Asked what he focuses on, the lawyer said something along the lines of, "My job is to find the chinks in the regulator's armour."

In other words, to find the weaknesses of the regulatory structures. That's how you make money. You make money through regulatory arbitrage—hedging between markets—or through regulatory avoidance. The innovative mind is good at finding those gaps. The regulatory mind is good at keeping up. But what happens when they catch up? Should they shut down those thoughts or encourage them in a safe environment?

That's why, if you catch a hacker or a cyberspy, should you send them to prison or ask them to carry on and show you what they are doing? Surely it would be better to take the latter approach to find out how they see the financial system working. After all, how else can you oversee a system that you don't see?

This is particularly true as financial markets are moving to be almost totally run by AI, ML, blackboxes and algorithms. How do you regulate an algorithm you can't explain? Bearing in mind that the financial collapse of 2008 was due to incredibly complex connected contracts where CDOs packaged into mortgage-backed securities created a global meltdown, how well do we understand financial algorithms today? As one bank CEO said to me in 2008, "We avoided many complex products, like structured derivatives, because I would ask traders to explain them. If I couldn't understand what they said, then I would ask them to explain again. If I still couldn't understand what they were talking about, then we wouldn't do it."

How to Regulate AI?

As we talk about the friction between innovation and regulation, managing decentralised versus centralised finance, we cannot ignore the issues raised by AI and whether it will make the world a better or worse place.

For many, AI is both scary—the possibility of replacing all of our jobs—and exciting—the potential to offer us a way to live better lives. The core question is around how we regulate this technology effectively. Similar to any new technology, there are benefits and dangers. Regulators need to focus on how to exploit the benefits and minimise the dangers and risks.

Given the rapid rise in AI, there now seems to be a global race to manage these new technologies. In June 2023, the European Parliament passed the EU's Artificial Intelligence Act (EU AI Act). The EU AI Act provides the framework for AI regulation within all EU member states and includes the categorisation of AI systems into four levels of risk: unacceptable, high, limited and minimal or none. It is the world's first comprehensive AI law.

The Center for Security and Emerging Technology at Georgetown University in Washington, DC, provided an informative analysis of the EU AI Act. Its primer explained that unacceptable risk systems will be prohibited. What are unacceptable risk systems?

Unacceptable risk systems include those that have a significant potential for manipulation either through subconscious messaging and stimuli, or by exploiting vulnerabilities like socioeconomic status, disability, or age. AI systems for social scoring, a term that describes the evaluation and treatment of people based on their social behavior, are also banned.[8]

Higher risk systems are acceptable, but will be tightly regulated. What are higher risk systems? Such systems fall into two categories: either those that need to meet safety standards, as does any product today, or those that have a specific sensitive purpose, such as those used by law enforcement, education or core government infrastructures.

Finally, the limited risk category covers systems that have low potential for manipulation on humans, and includes informing a person whenever they are interacting with an AI system and flagging artificially generated or manipulated content.

Interestingly, it is this last category that may be the most treacherous as far as financial services are concerned. For instance, it could lead to a human user of a financial system being unaware that they are dealing with manipulated

---

8   Mia Hoffman, "The EU AI Act: A Primer," Center for Security and Emerging Technology, 26 September 2023, https://cset.georgetown.edu/article/the-eu-ai-act-a-primer/.

content, the repercussions of which could be far-reaching. It will be interesting to see how this plays out.

Alongside these discussions, there are many others that governments are engaged in. For example, how to harness AI for economic development while protecting human rights was high on the agenda at the 2023 G20 summit. Regulating AI is a complex and evolving task that requires careful consideration of various factors, such as:

1. **Ethical Frameworks:** Establishing ethical frameworks is crucial to ensure that AI systems operate in a manner that aligns with human values. These frameworks should emphasise transparency, fairness, accountability and the avoidance of harm.

2. **Risk Assessment:** Conduct comprehensive risk assessments to identify potential risks associated with AI deployment. This includes assessing risks related to privacy, security, bias and job displacement. Regulatory bodies can work closely with AI developers and experts to evaluate the potential risks and take necessary measures to mitigate them.

3. **Data Governance:** Implement robust data governance practices to ensure that AI systems are built on high-quality, unbiased and diverse datasets. Regulations can require organisations to follow strict data collection, storage and usage practices, including obtaining informed consent and protecting user privacy.

4. **Transparency and Explainability:** Encourage transparency and explainability in AI systems, especially those that have significant impact on individuals or society. Regulations can mandate that organisations provide clear explanations about the functioning of AI algorithms and enable auditing and accountability mechanisms.

5. **Bias Mitigation:** Addressing biases in AI systems is crucial to ensure fairness and prevent discrimination. Regulators can require organisations to perform regular audits to detect and mitigate biases in their AI models. Additionally, promoting diversity and inclusivity in AI development teams can help minimise biases.

6. **Standards and Certification:** Establish industry standards and certification processes to ensure compliance with regulations. This can

involve creating guidelines for AI development, testing and deployment, as well as certification programmes to verify that AI systems meet predefined standards.

7. **Ongoing Monitoring and Adaptation:** AI regulations should be dynamic and adaptable to the evolving technology landscape. Regular monitoring and assessment of AI systems, as well as collaboration between regulators, industry and academia, can help identify emerging risks and update regulations accordingly.

8. **International Collaboration:** Given the global nature of AI development, international collaboration and harmonisation of AI regulations are crucial. Cooperation between countries can help address challenges such as cross-border data flow, ethical standards and regulatory consistency.[9]

It's important to note that regulation should strike a balance between enabling innovation and protecting societal interests. An interdisciplinary approach involving policymakers, AI experts, ethicists and stakeholders from various sectors is necessary to develop effective and responsible AI regulations.

What Does This Mean for Finance?

AI is not one thing. It is many things. It's a bit like cloud computing. Using AI or cloud is not a generic. It's a specific. Add to this the fact that the markets are great at coming up with three-letter acronyms, or TLAs for short, and things get even more confused. For example, LLMs. As I explained earlier, LLM stands for large language model, which is a type of AI algorithm that uses deep learning techniques and massively large datasets to understand, summarise, generate and predict new content. It is the basis of ChatGPT, Bard and more. How are financial firms using LLMs? There are many examples out there but I'm going to pick out just two: American Express and JPMorgan Chase.

American Express, or Amex, is rolling out pilot projects with LLM-based AI to understand how it can help with the company's 3 Ps— making a product

---

9   These eight factors were written by ChatGPT.

more personalised to an individual customer, more proactive and more predictive. Then there's JPMorgan which is using AI for trading. In April 2023, Jamie Dimon revealed that the company had over 300 AI use cases in production for risk, prospecting, marketing, customer experience and fraud prevention. He stated, "AI and the raw material that feeds it, data, will be critical to our company's future success — the importance of implementing new technologies simply cannot be overstated."[10]

In both cases, banks and financial institutions are using AI to enhance the customer experience, augment the human and automate the mundane. That all makes absolute sense, but how far can we push this? If we consider flash trading, the idea is that we can push this to an extreme where machine competes against machine using time. If you want the best deal in financial services, you have to make the deal first. No one remembers second place. In trading, dealing and business, this becomes even more critical. If you get the right price at the right time, you're the winner. If you come second, you're the loser. If you win the contract, you're the winner. If you lose, you're the loser. You get the idea.

With generative AI now in the spotlight, what happens if generative AI gets you the deal first or the best price before everyone else? Place this at a personal level. For some years, there have been automated bidding services on eBay, the auction site, that will guarantee to make your bid within a second of the item closing. Amplify this to everything, and you get markets that are no longer fair trading. They are connected by bots that bid and manage on our behalf. They are automated and structured in such a way to ensure that those who don't have the knowledge cannot compete. If you don't know the acronyms, the technologies and the systems being used, then you shouldn't be in these markets because you cannot compete.

On the one hand, AI will benefit customer services, as evidenced by Amex's experiment. On the other, it is a competitive weapon that may create markets that are biased towards those who are inside those markets. The bottom line is that AI should augment the human and automate the mundane.

10   Jamie Dimon, "Chairman and CEO Letter to Shareholders, Annual Report 2022," JPMorgan Chase & Co.,
     4 April 2023, https://reports.jpmorganchase.com/investor-relations/2022/ar-ceo-letters.htm.

What Does It Mean for the Regulations of Finance?

The good old bank has been at fault for some time. The fault lies in a lack of data analysis and data leverage. A good example is how little information or detail is given in its transaction recording. This is because the systems used for such recording date back many years.

A typical transaction listed in my bank statement reads something like ABC CORP TX 3201984. There is zero information about where I have spent my money. The only details provided are a date and a place name that often does not correlate with the merchant, for example, 22 FEB STRIPE.

This is all set to change. Anticipating the rise of Open Banking and AI, regulators are asking financial providers to give more enriched data in relation to payment accounts and transactions. Two major developments in this area include SPAA and AN 4569.

SPAA stands for the SEPA (Single Euro Payment Area) Payment Account Access scheme. It's the expansion of the EU's Revised Payment Services Directive (PSD2), a regulation for electronic payments services, to PSD3, which will incorporate true Open Banking and not just a payments API. How's that for a set of acronyms?

The SEPA Payment Account Access (SPAA) scheme is the newest EPC scheme that covers the set of rules, practices and standards that will allow the exchange of payment accounts related data and facilitates the initiation of payment transactions in the context of 'value-added' ('premium') services provided by asset holders (i.e. Account-Servicing Payment Service Providers (ASPSPs) to asset brokers (e.g. Third Party Providers (TPPs).[11]

Basically, it is the application of Open Banking, which the United Kingdom launched in its implementation of PSD2, to all of Europe. What's the difference between an Open API under PSD2 and Open Banking under PSD3? The difference is primarily around data enrichment around payments such that all transactions should be able to show you who paid what, when and where.

PSD2 versus PSD3

Source: Forrester

According to the European Payments Council, key benefits include the following:
- It builds on investments done in the context of PSD2.
- It is managed as a scheme, developed collaboratively by the retail payment industry (supply and demand) and the end-user community, as represented in the European Retail Payments Board (ERPB), and with the support of EU institutions.
- It enables "premium" payment services beyond PSD2 in a way that ensure harmonisation, interoperability and reachability across Europe.

---

11 European Payments Council, "SEPA Payment Account Access," https://www.europeanpaymentscouncil.eu/what-we-do/other-schemes/sepa-payment-account-access.

- Asset holders expose information and transactions through the scheme to asset brokers for a fee (paid by the asset brokers), with prior consent from the asset owner.
- It takes into account the input from major European standardisation initiatives active in the field of PSD2 APIs.
- It could be a stepping stone towards "open finance" beyond payments and "open data" beyond finance.

Interestingly, around the same time, a Strategic Working Group (SWG) published a report about the future direction of Open Banking in the United Kingdom. The report was commissioned by the Joint Regulatory Oversight Committee, which was set up in March 2022 by the HM Treasury, the Competition and Markets Authority (CMA), the FCA and the Payment Systems Regulator (PSR) as part of the government and regulators' commitment to build on the success of Open Banking.

In The Future Development of Open Banking in the UK report, the key core activities cited for the future include an entity that would be charged with:

- maintaining the Open Banking Standard to ensure it stays relevant
- collecting and collating messaging interfaces (MI), and obtaining additional evidence to help decision making
- monitoring standards conformance[12]

However, there is some divergence as to whether the future entity would provide evidence and outputs to regulators or if it would be given powers to enforce adherence and conformance on participants.

Mastercard's AN 4569 is targeting the same issue. AN 4569 is a mandatory requirement from Mastercard under its revised rules of 2020. From October 2023, all card issuers across Europe must provide enhanced payment merchant data to cardholders. This includes showing accurate merchant names, correct logos, contact details (telephone and website), payment locations and even links to Google Maps.

---

12   Strategic Working Group, "The Future Development of Open Banking in the UK," Open Banking, February 2023, https://www.openbanking.org.uk/swg/.

Bringing Intelligence to Transactions

Source: TapiX

Financial regulations like SPAA and AN 4569 are all about providing enriched payment data so that customers get a much clearer idea of what they have spent, where they spent it and when they spent it. This is a must-have in today's digital world.

THE IMPACT ON YOU AND ME

In all of the discussions about liberty versus state, freedom versus control, understanding the role that finance and money plays in this space is key. Finance is the controlling factor between citizens and governance; it is the tool and lever for managing our lives.

The thing is that money isn't about value, and is not a value in itself. It's about values. When we think about how our lives work, the priorities are health, family, friends, time, learning, achieving, reputation and experiences. Money has nothing to do with it, even though money enables you to enjoy the things you value. When you think about money in that context, it changes your context.

The issue is that the things we value have set us off on this treadmill of focusing on work, wealth and earning. This is about supply and demand. The supply of housing is not keeping up with the demand; the supply of decent holidays is not keeping up with demand; the availability of a car that is of the right status is not keeping up with demand; and so on.

What is the law of supply and demand? The scarcer the resources, the more they cost. This is the reason why many people are struggling in today's economic climate. It is because the cost of living is becoming higher than the ability to earn. Cost versus earnings. That's also a balance.

"Annual income twenty pounds, annual expenditure nineteen pounds nineteen and six, result happiness. Annual income twenty pounds, annual expenditure twenty pounds ought and six, result misery."
Wilkens Micawber in *David Copperfield* (1850) by Charles Dickens

Micawber was always on the verge of bankruptcy, and his quote above is one of my favourites. It's actually a quote my parents drilled into me non-stop growing up. Growing up, I always wanted new things: presents, toys, the bike that Joe got for his birthday, the Labrador that Mary's family had just bought, the car that Miranda's dad drove to go on holiday where Vincent had just been and so on.

Wanting material possessions create pressures, especially on the heads of households who need to earn to fund the things they value. These things are also important to consider in this time of recessionary fears. Many may be subject to redundancy, you may have had to use your savings to pay for day-to-day living or you may be feeling like you are on a tightrope teetering between wealth and bankruptcy. Again, it's a balance.

The question the above raises is this: as we automate more and more in our daily lives, are we losing something in the process? Will AI make our lives better or worse? Is technology taking something away from how we relate to our money and, more importantly, to each other?

Is Humanity Losing Something due to Digitality?

A long time ago—so long ago that most people reading this weren't born or had just started school—my prediction was that cash machines were dead. At the time, I worked for NCR, or National Cash Registers, the cash machine company. Needless to say, my comment was not a popular one.

My proposition was that we should switch from *cash* machines to *multimedia* machines. Machines that could provide all sorts of services from ticketing to access to video servicing. Guess that idea was way before its time but, today, it is time. ATMs are now at a steady rate of decline. Just take a look at the following chart.

The Number of ATMS in the United Kingdom

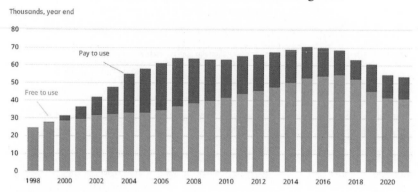

Sources: LINK, Statistics and Trends

The same is happening in Australia, where the number of cash machines more than halved in five years, from 13,814 in 2017 to 6,412 in June 2022. In fact, according to the International Monetary Fund, ATMs worldwide have reached a tipping point.[1]

Automated Teller Machines (per 100,000 adults)

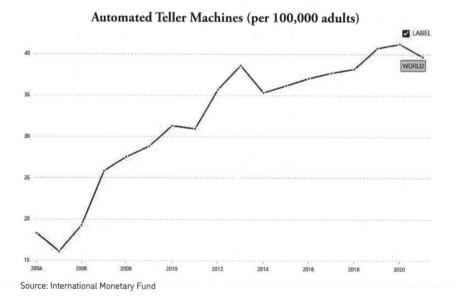

Source: International Monetary Fund

---

1   World Bank, "Financial Access Survey 2022," International Monetary Fund, October 2022, https://data.worldbank.org/indicator/FB.ATM.TOTL.P5.

Why do we need cash machines? When do you use cash? Why do you need cash?

Banking today is all about being digital. Branches have closed, cash machines are being dispensed with and cash is no longer needed. Most of us don't use cash these days, as it's easier to pay by either card or contactless app. Furthermore, the pandemic helped to accelerate its decline because it made us cash averse. The idea of handling banknotes covered in germs became a major issue for many.

Unarguably, the end of cash would be sad for many reasons. First, cash represents the culture and history of countries, and has so many unique attributes. For instance, the faces or the landmarks on banknotes, and who/what they represent; the history of coins and banknotes, and the way society has changed; and the general idea that coins and banknotes are a symbol of a country's identity and nationhood.

Second, cash is the only method of payment that is immediate, trusted and anonymous. There is nothing like it—yet. We are getting there, with cryptocurrencies like Monero, but we are not there yet. Not, at the very least, in an easy, transactional form.

Third, cash is something that we have used for centuries in one form or another. It was invented in China over 3,000 years ago, and is a stable of society. Fourth, we like cash. It's physical and transactional. You can see it, touch it, feel it, smell it, use it. The erosion of cash will be interesting therefore.

Net-net—yes, digital is great! However, physical cash being eradicated means we lose a sense of identity at a national level. We lose the beauty of those notes and coins and, a bit like album covers for vinyl music, we lose something that is important to our humanity. It's called physicality.

Did I Forget to Mention Cash?

In all of the debates about centralising versus decentralising money, one of the things that is overlooked is cash. In fact, the whole thing around CBDCs versus cryptocurrencies is the digitalisation of money. What about the physical form of money that we have known and trusted for centuries—cash? I've been writing about the war on cash for years. It's a theme that comes up constantly at conferences like Sibos, and the first time I think I heard the phrase "war on cash" was at a Visa presentation back in the 2000s.

Back in 2012, a Pew report surveyed over a thousand technology stakeholders and critics about whether mobile wallets would be in widespread use by 2020. Approximately, 65 per cent of respondents agreed with the following scenario:

> By 2020, most people will have embraced and fully adopted the use of smart-device swiping for purchases they make, nearly eliminating the need for cash or credit cards. People will come to trust and rely on personal hardware and software for handling monetary transactions over the Internet and in stores. Cash and credit cards will have mostly disappeared from many of the transactions that occur in advanced countries.[2]

I don't agree with this statement. The war on cash has been spearheaded by banks as cash is inefficient. It is paper-based, requires huge logistics regarding its movements between corporations, institutions and banks, and is a pain in the ass—compared to a quick digital swipe—for the provider.

For the user, however, cash is pretty good. It is immediate, trusted and holds its value. More specifically, it is anonymous and can be passed between people with immediacy. That's why users— people— don't want to lose access to cash.

Here is a point of view piece written by a cash fan to one of the national UK newspapers explaining why cash works best. Then, while out walking, I found

Note the logic

If some people want to rely solely on digital financial transactions, let them. But don't take away cash for the rest of us. My $50 note can't be hacked. If I'm robbed, I lose $50, not my entire life savings. If my $50 note is accidentally immersed in water, it still works. My $50 note doesn't need batteries, it can't be "out of range" and it won't break if it's dropped. If the system is down, I can still use my note. My $50 note can be put into a charity box or given to a homeless person.

Sure I use a card sometimes for large purchases, but for everything else please leave me the option of cash. It simplifies life.

Julie Christensen,
Blackburn North

---

2   Aaron Smith, Janna Anderson and Lee Rainie, "The Future of Money in a Mobile Age," Pew Research Center, 17 April 2020, https://www.pewresearch.org/internet/2012/04/17/the-future-of-money-in-a-mobile-age/.

out about a national Cash Only week. It wasn't widely promoted—not a single news programme mentioned it—but it's interesting that consumers want to fight the digital pound agenda.

I then heard about a bank that tried to ban cash in all of its branches. It rolled out a test where only ATMs were available; no cash deposits or withdrawals were allowed. During the three-month test period, the bank experienced a high volume of customer complaints and thousands of account closures. More importantly, staff did not support the idea and were the ones advising customers to close their accounts in protest. Unsurprisingly, the bank reversed the policy after the three-month period, and cash is still used wide and deep across the economy. I guess the question always comes back to why? The answer is simple: there is no cash equivalent replacement.

This is articulated brilliantly by Brett Scott, a campaigner, monetary anthropologist and former broker. Scott has broken down why cash is the enemy of the state and the hero of the consumer, and states that whilst the powers that be "say that digital automation – and the speed, scale and interconnection it brings – is not only good, but unstoppable",[3] the ideology

---

3   Brett Scott, "The Luddite's Guide to Defending Cash," Altered States of Monetary Consciousness [newsletter], 8 May 2023, https://brettscott.substack.com/p/the-luddites-guide-to-defending-physical-cash.

is nested in another, deeper ideology, namely that the global economy must always expand and accelerate. With this vision as a backdrop, you are encouraged to then engage in a series of digitisation races, such as a race to cashlessness or a race to AI. Ideally, you are supposed to lead the way in these races by actively developing, pushing and embracing the technology, but if you have other priorities, you are advised to prepare for the transition, and adapt.

Scott then makes a key point about imagining if cash were converted to casino chips and then could not be converted back. This raises two key issues. The first is legal: "If a casino refused to redeem my chips for cash, I'd sue them, but what if my bank closes down its branches and ATMs to stop me cashing out my digital chips? They are basically saying 'you cannot exit our systems', or alternatively 'you have no right to exit our systems'."[4]

The second is related to financial stability: "An unredeemable casino chip is a dodgy casino chip. An unredeemable bank-issued 'digital casino chip', similarly, is an unstable and dodgy form of money, even if it gets moved around via a flashy and secure app. Ironically, as the public cash system is undermined, our confidence in the private digital systems risks being undermined too."[5]

A key point he puts forward repeatedly is that, even if you believe cash is old, inefficient and dangerous, it structurally underpins the digital systems that you think are so new, efficient and safe. Digital money is not an upgrade to cash because it derives its own power from cash.

He highlights the criticality of this point by using the metaphor of a bicycle and Uber. He considers cash to be the bicycle of payments while the bank-issued casino chips used for digital payments are the Uber of payments. In this context, there are unique characteristics that make cash and digital payments complementary, just as bicycles and Ubers are complementary.

There are two specifically critical differences. First, autonomy versus dependence: with a bike, you can control it directly but, with Uber, you are dependant on a third party. Likewise with cash, you are in direct control of it but, with digital payments, you have to rely on various third parties.

---

4   Brett Scott.
5   Brett Scott.

Second, the usage is public versus private: "bicycles only require public infrastructure, whereas Uber relies on a private corporate infrastructure that runs on top of public infrastructure. Similarly, cash is a public utility, whereas paying for things with digital casino chips involves becoming dependent on private corporate infrastructures (which are built on top of the public money system)."[6]

After so many years, decades and centuries of debating the pros and cons of cash, cash will continue to exist until a digital version of cash, one that is a trusted store of value and an immediate transfer of value, appears.

And the Choice Goes to...

I have heard a lot of discussions about adversaries in finance: FinTech versus Bank, CBDCs versus decentralised currencies and so on. The commentary makes it seem as though there is one big battle after another. I disagree. It's neither a battle nor a war for that matter. It's a change to the system based on progress, development and technology.

Yet throughout such commentary, one important factor has often been sidelined, downplayed or outright ignored—the end user, the customer or, in other words, you and me. So when people pit FinTech against Bank or CBDCs against Crypto, they are getting it wrong. Their view and marketing position should be focused on what the customer wants. What is the customer view? The customer view is essentially what works, who they trust and how they want to live. It's all about customer choice and citizen choice.

It reminds me of a discussion I once had with the CEO of M-Pesa, the Kenyan mobile payments system. I asked him how banks compete with M-Pesa. He replied, "They copy what we do and we focus on the customer and not on them." This is a core point: *focus on the customer, not on the competition.*

Too often, companies are distracted by dalliances with new entrants and new ideas. They determine that that is where their focus lies, and the aim is to stop the competitor. By moving the dial in that direction, they lose their focus on what the customer needs. Perhaps this is the heart of the debate

6   Brett Scott.

about CBDCs. Central banks want to keep control over money—for obvious reasons—but citizens want to control their exchange mechanisms too. The continuous rise of cryptocurrencies illustrates this. Initially, cryptocurrencies' popularity lay purely with the libertarians and anti-government groups. Now, they have risen to become mainstream among those who no longer trust their government currencies, such as people in Venezuela and Nigeria, and migrant workers around the world. It's the citizens' choice.

If people choose to use cryptocurrencies or CBDCs, it's their choice. If companies decide to use Stripe instead of Adyen, it's their choice. If the investment process is led by eToro or Goldman Sachs, who cares? It's the customers' choice.

The key here is choice. It is the customer's or citizen's choice. What this really demands is for companies—start-ups, FinTechs, banks or any other provider—to step back to that outside-in view of what the customer needs. It doesn't matter what the customer wants—they often don't know—it's figuring out what the customer needs. As Steve Jobs once said, "Some people say give the customers what they want, but that's not my approach. Our job is to figure out what they're going to want before they do. I think Henry Ford once said, 'If I'd ask customers what they wanted, they would've told me a faster horse.' People don't know what they want until you show it to them. That's why I never rely on market research. Our task is to read things that are not yet on the page."

And, just to reinforce this point:

"We paid Stanford Research to forecast how many cellular phones would be used in America by 2000 [in 1986]. They came back, with an expensive report, and said 30,000. If they had said 30 million, they would still have been way off the mark."

Nils Martensson, founder of Technophone

AI AND GREEN FINANCE

Intelligent Money is all about making a difference and using money intelligently to do good for the future. This is where technologies can really deliver bang for the buck, literally. We live in a world of transparency through the network and activist consumers who are changing the world. The two trends allow for the decentralised and democratised change to our future world. Consider the intersection we live in today where the world is changing fast yet, if you don't act, it is not changing fast enough.

For example, as we look to the future, many FinTechs and banks are looking at how to do good for society and good for the planet. This was the theme of my last book, *Digital for Good* (2022). Is ethical banking a thing? We can call it socially useful banking, green banking or whatever we want, but it's all about a bank's role in society and the grand scheme of things. Are banks doing the right or wrong things?

The way in which banks are portrayed by the media is that banks have been doing the wrong things for a long time. Shareholder return at the expense of customers; trading in a club called LIBOR that rips everyone off; charging dead customers for financial products and services; opening insurances and signing them fraudulently; closing down small businesses and stripping their assets purely by removing their loans; the list goes on and on.

With great power comes great responsibility. Unfortunately, those in power often do not check that those who wield it wield it responsibly.

Now we are moving towards a new generation of change. A generation acutely aware of ethical responsibilities and looking for social change to wield that power responsibly. What about just being a good, honest bank? A few already exist. However, most claim to be responsible, ethical and socially useful whilst messing everything up behind the scenes. For example, claiming to be sustainable and ethical whilst funding new fossil fuel projects and encouraging fracking.

> Our latest research, conducted as part of our guides to ethical bank accounts *and* ethical savings accounts, found that 29 of the 31 banks reviewed were rated middle or worst for their climate change reporting.[1]

Is Ethical Banking a Generational Thing?

There is clearly an alignment between an ethical view of the world, the new generations, digitalisation and finance. Ethical banking is a thing, but it's more than that. It's the combination of the transparency of the network and the ability to combine finance and technology—FinTech—that enables us to use money to do better things for society and the planet.

There are several clear examples of banks that think this way, such as Triodos and Rabobank in the Netherlands, Ålandsbanken in Finland, Teachers Mutual in Australia and Ant Group in China. However, they are too few and far between. The ESG, digital and finance agenda are merging and melding fast, and too few companies are aware of or keeping up with this space. This is what Ethic, a US FinTech asset manager in the fast-growing ESG space, is tapping into.

> Ethic was founded in 2015 and has tripled assets under management in the past year ... Ethic runs screens on companies and sectors based on social responsibility criteria, including racial justice, climate and labour issues. Its user interface has more in common with the likes of Robinhood than traditional financial sites.[2]

---

1   Clare Carlile, "Banks, climate change and the environmental crisis," *Ethical Consumer*, 16 December 2022, https://www.ethicalconsumer.org/money-finance/banks-climate-change-environmental-crisis.
2   Andrew Ross Sorkin et al., "Harry and Meghan Get into Finance," *New York Times*, 12 October 2021, https://www.nytimes.com/2021/10/12/business/dealbook/harry-meghan-ethical-investors.html.

The key thing to understand here is that ESG is not some tree-hugging, ephemeral, loss-making, charitable endeavour. It's something that most generations, particularly younger generations, believe in with their heads, hearts and wallets. It's the same as financial inclusion. Someone asked me years ago, "When will banks stop seeing financial inclusion as charity?" The same is true of ESG and DeFi. A good example of this conflict is that bankers keep saying that bitcoin is useless but, because clients believe it's useful, they'll trade it.

Either way, there is a clear movement driven by digitalisation and the transparency that the network provides, which is democratising news, money and life. It's not just a Gen Z or millennial thing. It's a movement that is redefining the rules of news, money and life. You can either follow the movement or resist it but, in general, resistance is futile.

Will the New Banking Generation Change the Bank?

As millennials reach C-Suite positions, they bring with them new eyes, new skills and new outlooks. In particular, they *get* technology, the internet, the digital world. Does this mean that banking will evolve and change naturally, due to new leaders with new eyes? Possibly yes, maybe no.

The thing is that it is clear that the next generation of leaders will have a different view, but will they be able to break the handcuffs of the past? This has been the challenge for all of their predecessors—will millennials make that change?

There are two big factors in play here, and many more nuanced ones, but the big headlines are that the organisation hires people who are like them. The people who rise to the top of the tree are people who are like their predecessors. Their predecessors must like them before they get promoted. As a result, the organisation ends up with more people like those who went before.

If you are a little radical, a little bit different, a little bit more challenging, then you get ejected. I should know, as it has happened to me a few times. The organisation wants *yes* people, not people who challenge their system.

That first factor means that the new C-Suite will be dominated with attitudes that existed in the old C-Suite. There may be a few more chief experience officers (CXOs) who demand change, but they have to do it in a political way that fits with the cultural framework of the old organisation.

Now, let us say that someone has risen to the highest level, understands the politics, believes they can change the organisation and has the right thinking. Then, the second challenge is faced: how to do it?

After decades of laying technology structures over legacy structures and finding an organisation that needs a complete restructuring of their backbone digital foundations, how do you do that whilst keeping the organisation alive and looking like it is running seamlessly without failure.

For me, the second challenge is far greater than the first. Sure, the new CXO may be far more tech savvy than their predecessor, but it has nothing to do with how well the new CXO understands tech. It is how well the new CXO understands change and, specifically, changing an organisation that has been cemented firmly in legacy structures.

Breaking apart legacy structures is hard. I guess the nearest example is moving into an old building. A building that has rattling pipes, leaking ceilings, electrics that spark at night and holes in the walls. Of course, you can upgrade a building, fix the pipes, cover the ceilings, change the electrics and plaster the walls. But how do you do that while servicing customers in a way that they don't see the sparks and holes being fixed?

It reminds me of something discussed many times these days: Bankenstein's monster. Bankenstein is a bank that has been built over the past century with core systems never replaced. Those systems are now dead parts full of data that are purely kept alive through electricity and middle- and front-end technologies which disguise how old they actually are. How do you refresh an organisation full of dead parts that need replacing without any impact on customers?

That second challenge is more than just being younger and more visionary. It is the challenge of transformation and change. This is what we refer to in the digital transformation journey and, specifically, it is more than just a technology challenge. It is a people challenge.

I often say that digital transformation has nothing to do with technology. It is about culture and mindset. How far does digital extend into the organisation as something of importance, and how urgent is the commitment of the people in the organisation to change?

As can be seen, none of this is simple, and it has little to do with demographics. It has far more to do with ability, specifically the management's ability to change the bank.

What about Regenerative Finance?[3]

Throughout this book, there have been discussions about DeFi, CeFi and HyFi, but what about ReFi? ReFi stands for regenerative finance, a system to rebuild Earth. The acronym ReFi itself is reminiscent of its close connections to DeFi. Bringing together all aspects of finance and technological developments we see today—DeFi, CeFi and HyFi—creates ReFi.

---

3   This section has been contributed by Letty Prados, an expert in regenerative finance and co-founder of ReGenLiving, one of whose aims is to "safeguard the air we breathe, the water we drink and the places we treasure".

In 2015, economist John Fullerton coined the term "regenerative capitalism" in a paper that described eight principles that could underpin a new economic system, one that delivers shared prosperity on a thriving planet. He stated:

> The universal patterns and principles the cosmos uses to build stable, healthy, and sustainable systems throughout the real world can and must be used as a model for economic-system design.[4]

These eight principles of a regenerative economy underlie systemic health and collectively represent the blueprint for a regenerative civilisation:

The Eight Principles of a Regenerative Economy

Source: Capital Institute

Likewise, transdisciplinary approaches, such as those brought forward by Sally J. Goerner, have also focused on the science of regenerative economics, which is based on decades of research into areas of complex adaptive systems, flow networks, and ecosystem and socio-economic dynamics. This kind of economics, framed in an energy flow and networks perspective, requires a

4   John Fullerton, "Regenerative Capitalism: How Universal Principles And Patterns Will Shape Our New Economy," Capital Institute, April 2015, https://capitalinstitute.org/wp-content/uploads/2015/04/2015-Regenerative-Capitalism-4-20-15-final.pdf.

balance of efficiency and resilience be maintained within a particular "window of vitality".

The vision is that ReFi is based on this theory of regenerative economics. ReFi is the regenerative finance movement forming at the intersection of the third evolution of the internet (Web3). Within the ReFi space, a multitude of communities are emerging with the common objective of leveraging the blockchain, or DLT. The vision of these new proposals is to address sustainability challenges such as climate change, biodiversity loss, resource scarcity and the underpinning socio-economic and institutional structures that exacerbate these crises.

At its core, this approach implies a change of paradigm and the ability to articulate a complex systems solution. Regenerative economics incentivises actions that increase systemic health, and disincentivises actions that lead to systemic degradation. It applies nature's principles of regeneration to socio-economic systems, supporting equitable well-being and thriving ecosystems.

As such, ReFi as a whole must act to prevent the pervasive greenwashing that currently exists. For a systemic regenerative solution to be fully holistic, carbon emissions and markets need to be only one of many variables included. This is made clear by the diagram below:

Carbon Tunnel Vision

Source: Jan Konietzko

Taking the above graphic as a pointer, ReFi aims to apply a 360-degree view to all of the underlying symptoms in the diagram, with caring and nature-based systems thinking as the foundation. Since sustainability challenges stem from fragmented thinking and systems incentivising degenerative behaviour, holistic thinking and regenerative incentive systems need to replace them.

ReFi's mission is therefore to systemise incentives to make regenerative places feasible. Addressing current crises issues means designing profound alternatives to our dominant culture systems, and to replace them with regenerative ones that value caring and nature. One of the core instruments in doing that is redesigning money itself in a way that writes a new story for what it actually means to be an integral human being living on a shared planet. A story that encapsulates the values of caring, mutuality and human flourishing.

Redesigning money requires understanding tokens (digital assets with a specific value) and tokenomics (token + economics), which makes visible and captures all of the different forms and the eight manifestations of capital: social, material, financial, living, intellectual, experiential, spiritual and cultural. In this undertaking, the foundations that gave rise to monetary accounting and money are redefined in a way that individual and collective actions coalesce in coherence towards a new scenario of local and global well-being, social fairness, renewal and justice within Earth. This is crucial not only in redefining money within climate, harmony and justice values but also in activating the kind of regenerative economy that sees "places" as living organisms.

ReFi has the potential to deal with all aspects of restoring our economies into localised living entities. It uses place-based tokenomics that foster their thriving capacities within a collective thrivability pattern. It uses all eight manifestations of capital and eight principles of a regenerative economy—while every other level of the economic system design is restored and transformed according to global dynamics.

It is a bottom-up and local-to-global vision that honours the natural characteristics of each place and bioregional ecosystem. It is nested in evolutionary systems and biocultural uniqueness—ecology, biology, geology and culture—that is a place's foundational essence, soul and identity.

In summary, ReFi is regenerative economics, leveraging Web3 to address climate justice and equity.

Green Finance Is Becoming a USP

I would say that five major groups are squeezing the financial markets today. How can these groups use technology to change finance to do good for the world's future?

The first group is obvious: it's the FinTech start-up community, which now makes up a third of all financial markets value. Many FinTech firms are working on using technology to improve finance for stakeholder returns. The second group is clear, too: it's the Big Tech firms like Facebook and Amazon. These firms are launching their own currencies and putting pressure on firms like Visa to remove fees. The third is also fairly obvious: it's the governments and regulators who want banking to be more open and competitive.

Who are the other two? Well, one is the customer. Whether it be the consumer or corporate, the agenda for sustainability has clearly risen to the fore, and the customer wants banks to behave responsibly. Greenwashing and errant behaviours investing in fossil fuels and fracking the world are no longer acceptable. Greta Thunberg, Sir David Attenborough, Extinction Rebellion and more have made this clear.

The other is maybe the hidden jewel: the activist investor. Pension funds and institutional investors are increasingly worried about financial market activities and how they encourage shareholder return at the expense of communities and, potentially, the planet. Therefore, activist investors are encouraging stakeholder capitalism, and placing climate at the head of that agenda.

Between activist consumers and activitist investors, ESG topics are front and centre and we can feel this squeeze from both the top and from the bottom. The squeeze of the activist customer and the activist investor. There is huge pressure on the financial community to change from activist consumers, such as Greta Thunberg, activist groups, such as Extinction Rebellion, and activist investors, of which there are many, including Robert Downey Junior, he of *Iron Man* fame.

The thing is, I'm not sure that the banks realise this. Mark Carney, currently the UN Special Envoy for Climate Action and Finance, can claim that $130 trillion of assets are being directed towards climate protection, but that's all double counting and the usual cooking of the books. Nevertheless, the FinTech community does get it. Take a company like Amplify. Amplify, the Irish ESG FinTech start-up that is supported by the Irish government via Enterprise Ireland, donates 2 per cent of each transaction to the user's chosen climate action campaign every time they shop at an Amplify merchant partner.

Amplify's Reward Scheme

Amplify the climate action of your sustainable spending

Earn donations for a climate cause of your choice as you shop with an entire network of sustainable brands, at no added cost.

Sign up for free

Amplify, along with other incentives like Ant Financial's Ant Forest and Ålandsbanken's Baltic Sea Card, is leading the way in showing that financial firms can create positive forces for the good of society. However, to date, it tends to be new firms or small firms that are doing this. Why aren't the big banks doing this, too?

I guess the answer hit home during the COP26 talks about the role of finance in climate challenges, and the fact that loans to carbon emitters account for 14 per cent of Eurozone lenders' assets. In other words, banks cannot wean themselves off the teats of their fossil fuel clients as it is these clients that make money, increase profit, deliver greater shareholder returns and increase the bonus pool for all. For all of the people inside the bank, that is. It doesn't do much for those outside.

Eventually, this will be addressed by regulation. I wholly expect that by COP30, governments around the world will be mandating that, for every $1 loaned to a fossil fuel firm or carbon-emitting project, $2 has to be invested in a renewable energy and carbon-offset project. Until that mandate is in place, all the talk at COP26 will continue to be blah, blah, blah.

In the meantime, the new wave of FinTech, Big Tech and community firms have found an opening in the market: green finance. Way to go!

WTF: WHAT'S THE FUTURE?

Intelligent Money is all about how finance, technology and ESG combine to create a better future world. A world where finance is embedded and intelligent in everything around us. A world where we do not even think about money, as money thinks for us.

For many in traditional finance and banking, such a future will alienate them as they are not technologists. Given this, the financial services industry has opened its weak underbelly to the attack of technologists, and these technologists definitely want to make change. This explains the rise and success of the FinTech unicorns over the past twenty years and, equally, highlights the opportunity for FinTech providers over the next twenty years. If finance and technology can create a better future for everyone, then that is laudable. If finance and technology can make the world a better place, improve the climate, protect the next generations and enable humanity to co-exist peacefully with all living things, then that is what we should focus on.

The only concern traditionalists have in all of this is how it creates profit and returns for shareholders. What they should be considering is how it creates inclusion and returns for stakeholders. Profit is the by-product of the latter thinking, and not the focus.

This is why many of those in traditional finance fear the future. They fear the activists and technologists. They fear the kids and the change makers. They shouldn't. After all, finance and technology hold the keys to the solutions. It has moved the agenda from where we came from to where we are going. Where are we going? We are going to a world where everything is fragmented, decentralised and connected in the network with intelligence.

When I reflect on the last twenty years, it began with a huge focus on regulatory change. Strangely enough, I actually woke up the other day thinking about how the major US regulation introduced after the Great Depression, known as Glass-Steagall, had been repealed in the late 1990s and replaced by Gramm-Leach-Bliley, which failed. This Act was replaced by Dodd-Frank and the Volcker Rule on trading. The Volcker Rule began as a three-page idea and ended up as thousands of pages of regulatory rules. This is an illustration of the 2000s in general which, leading up to and for years after the 2008 crisis, was all about regulations and rules.

We then moved into the 2010s, and the focus changed to be all about digital, digital transformation and the integration of finance and technology, now known as FinTech. It was all about change, and the urgent need for change. The change needed emerged in the late 2000s, when cloud computing and the smartphone emerged. The change urgency culminated in the late 2010s when thousands of FinTech start-ups ripped apart an industry cemented in the last century.

Around 30,000 FinTech start-ups exist worldwide today, with billions of investment and amazing results. Banks have tried to adapt but, as evidenced in the 2000s, most banks paid token thoughts to innovation but did not fully embrace it. If they had embraced it, there would never have been the need for sandboxes. A sandbox is designed for children; the castle is where the adults do real business.

How do you get the sandbox into the castle? Well, that's what everyone grappled with in the 2000s. By the 2010s, they had missed the opportunity. That's why the 30,000 or so FinTech start-ups exist. They wouldn't need to exist if banks had solved the problems themselves but then, as I often say, FinTechs solve the problems banks cannot or have not solved.

Now that we are in the 2020s, what has changed? For me, what's changed is the demand to focus on our environment and our world. This came home to me when I visited Ant Group in Hangzhou, China. Ant runs the massive mobile and online payments system Alipay. I remember seeing a poster on the wall of the office; it was a portrait of Jack Ma, the company's founder, and the words "Let's do good for society and good for the planet". The poster surprised me. As a European, I didn't expect to see this. It touched my heart.

252 **Intelligent Money**

I then reflected on these words, and the words of Lord Adair Turner from nearly a decade before. Adair had said that a lot of what finance did was socially useless. How can finance become socially useful? The 2000s were all about controlling financial rebellion and the 2010s were all about encouraging rebels to defeat bad banking practices. The 2020s are all about how to bring the two together.

Talking about finance rebels, my favourite quote is from Nubank's co-founder Cristina Junqueria, who stated, "If banks are Darth Vader, credit cards are the Death Star." This innovative start-up launched an attack on the Death Star and won. Today, Nubank is one of the biggest banks in South America, with almost 90 million users, and that's in just ten years. For me, it's probably the best challenger bank in the world.

Nubank illustrates the disruption of the 2010s, thanks to cloud computing and the smartphone. Banking has been revolutionised in just a decade. What does the next decade hold? Stakeholder capitalism? ESG? Green? Climate and renewables?

One thing is for sure, it's not about being green. It's all about integrating and embracing technology and finance to make the world a better place. Efforts to do just that are illustrated well by the growth of apps to plant trees as part of financial game plays such as Ant Forest and, more recently, the Eiwaz Tree of Life.

Many ESG discussions alienate the finance and technology audience but such discussions should actually make them wake up, shake up and embrace the agenda. The heart of change lies right here and the call to action lies right here. We need to look at how we can use finance and technology to make the world a better place. After all, finance and technology are two of the four key levers to make this happen, the other two being politics and societal change. These four levers are the forces of change known as PEST.

What is PEST? PEST stands for political, economic, social and technological forces of change, as originally defined by Harvard Professor Francis J. Aguilar. In his 1967 publication *Scanning the Business Environment*, Aguilar argued that these four areas were the major influences on the business environment. Ever since, strategists have used PEST analysis to build scenarios for the future. Although PEST and scenario planning are separate and different tools, these methods are used by many to see how the world might change, so let's use some of these techniques to see how our world and our money may change in the future.

What about Government and Regulations (Politics)?

On reflecting the past decade of innovation in FinTech, it's been interesting to watch regulators struggling to keep up. The reality is that the regulators haven't been able to keep up. They allowed a lot of things to happen unregulated which they are now trying to address. Let's take a few examples.

First, P2PL. P2PL rose rapidly after the first entrant, Zopa, appeared in 2005. I've always called Zopa the first FinTech because its idea was an eBay for loans. And it worked! When the company tried to expand into other markets like Italy and the United States, it didn't. Why? The regulators didn't like the idea. However, the major market that did like the idea was China, and the regulator sat back and watched. It watched and watched and watched—but took no action.

By 2018, there were thousands of P2PL firms throughout the country— my estimate was over 3,000—but, by then, the regulator had begun to act. They began to impose increasingly strict regulations, which included the appointment of a custodian bank, full disclosure on the use of investments and caps on the maximum lending amounts that could be extended to individuals (1 million RMB) and companies (5 million RMB), in 2016.

That was the grenade that caused the implosion. The sudden collapse of thousands of unregulated firms led to thousands of people losing their life savings.

A construction project manager in Beijing revealed he lost over 275,000 yuan (more than $40,000) after Tourongjia, the site he invested his money on, suddenly shut down last month. The figure, he said, included his parents' savings, money borrowed from friends, and funds he was saving for an apartment he was planning to purchase for him and his pregnant wife.[1]

---

1   Matt Rivers and Jethro Mullen, "China has an online lending crisis and people are furious about it," CNN Business, 8 August 2018, https://money.cnn.com/2018/08/08/news/economy/china-p2p-lending/index.html.

It isn't just happening in China. P2PL firms around the world have faced crackdowns on their businesses—after the horse has bolted.

We've seen the same with BNPL. Klarna emerged in the 2000s from Sweden with the innovative idea of laying over payments for goods online into a few monthly instalments. It's a great idea, in my opinion, and yet it screamed to be regulated. I honestly don't know why Klarna and its brethren didn't go to the regulators first and ask to be regulated.

The result? The valuations of BNPL firms like Klarna have plummeted in recent times:

> In a sign of the times, Swedish buy now, pay later giant Klarna is reportedly close to inking a new round of funding that would slash its valuation to $6.5 billion — about 1/7 of what the company was valued in June of 2021.[2]

Klarna sank from a valuation of $45 billion in 2021 to just $6.5 billion a year later. Wow! Good news for citizens, bad news for investors. I guess this is the big thing: citizen and investor protection.

Regulators sit on the sidelines, watch and wait. Their—usually belated—actions can decimate markets they have allowed to mature, with those invested in those markets—whether they be citizens (P2PL) or investors (BNPL)—set to lose huge amounts of money.

Then there's the elephant in the room—cryptocurrencies. Bitcoin has been in the wild for almost fifteen years. It's been joined by over 10,000 brothers, sisters and offspring. No one needs 10,000 or more cryptocurrencies, and yet the regulators have sat, watched and tried to understand. They have constantly decried bitcoin, but did nothing about it. They have whinged and moaned about how these currencies undermine banking, finance and government but now they have started to try to create their own alternatives—CBDCs—and most of the crypto community has laughed in their faces.

---

2   Mary Ann Azevedo, "Fintech Klarna reportedly raising at a $6.5B valuation," Techcrunch, 1 July 2022, https://techcrunch.com/2022/07/01/fintech-klarna-reportedly-raising-at-a-6-5b-valuation-giving-new-meaning-to-the-phrase-down-round/.

Yet there is good reason for crypto regulations. For instance, there was the 2014 collapse of Mt. Gox, which was painful. Mt. Gox was a bitcoin exchange based in Japan, which launched in the early days of bitcoin back in 2010. By 2014, it was handling over 70 per cent of all bitcoin transactions worldwide when it abruptly ceased operations, due to the loss and theft of hundreds of thousands of bitcoins, worth hundreds of millions of dollars. The collapse of Mt. Gox was just the start. It was followed by Quadriga in 2018, after the death of the exchange's CEO, who just happened to be the only person with the password to the crypto exchange's currencies. Then there were the crashes of Terra-LUNA founded by Do Kwon and FTX led by Sam Bankman-Fried.

So many meltdowns and so many losses. To be clear though, it was the companies themselves that collapsed. Bitcoin and its brethren are still alive and kicking.

**In 2009, Bernie Madoff lost investors $60 billion.
He was sentenced to 150 years in prison.**

**In 2022, Do Kwon lost investors $60 billion after
Luna collapsed to $0. He then created Luna 2.0.**

Due to the crypto meltdown however, exchanges are introducing arbitrary policies to stop people cashing out while many critics are accusing these services and currencies of being Ponzi schemes. Admittedly, a lot of the creators of these schemes should be locked up in Arkham Asylum, but they are on to something. There will be a global digital currency one day. Yet, as I've always maintained, you cannot have money without governance. The question is: what is the right governance?

The challenge is that the political movement is always lagging behind everyone else. They are always in catch-up mode and rarely have any vision of what's next. That's fine when it comes to Facebook abusing our data, but when people lose their life savings, get sucked into debt or suckered into Ponzi schemes, it's not so good.

We need regulators that understand network change, technology and digitalisation and clamp down early on malpractices, scams and schemes that open citizens and investors to abuse. As the EU creates new rules based on the MiCA regulation, will these rules work? Can they work? And why has the EU waited so long? Answer: regulators wait until they understand something before they regulate it. Sometimes, it takes them an awful long time to work it out. Usually, they do work it out in the end. However, the fact that most of them wait years or even decades to draft even a response seems shocking.

People and Society

Society is changing rapidly, every day. We don't notice it but, if you take a dip into the worlds of 1982, 1992, 2002, 2012 and 2022, you can see the massive changes in how we live, work, relate, talk and transact.

Back in the 1980s, no one had computers; we had rotary telephones and the main networks offered us three or four TV channels. The world was less connected and less informed. Travelling overseas was unusual, and travelling long haul unlikely for most. Most people dealt with banking in branches with passbooks and cheque books.

In the 1990s, this changed. Many people started getting a computer in the home, a vision driven by Bill Gates. TV was still limited, unless you spent money getting a chunky satellite fixed to the top of your house. The world became more accessible as budget airlines launched. The first call-centre banks appeared and, by the end of the decade, internet banks launched.

In the 2000s, people were networked, the world had globalised and the world was at peace. The internet became the backbone of how society connected. Mobile telephones became prolific and, by the end of the decade, so too did smartphones. YouTube was rapidly becoming more popular than the BBC and NBC. Hopping on and off an aeroplane became a no-brainer thanks to the likes of Ryanair and Southwest Airlines. And banking collapsed thanks to complex derivatives. Trust in banks went through the floor, laying the seeds for the rise of FinTech.

In the 2010s, society changed again. People connected globally, but the world went back to behaving locally. Black Lives Matter, Greta Thunberg, Sir David Attenborough and discussions of climate emergency, civil unrest and economic issues seemed to fill the news every day. Internet was now a human right, and creating your own media rather than consuming government media became the rage of the day. More photographs were taken every day than in all of human history and jumping on a flight was like jumping on a train. FinTech and new digital currencies were the mainstream discussions, and banks? What's a bank?

Now we are in the 2020s. So far, we've dealt with a pandemic, runaway inflation, recessions, massive losses on investments and are set for another decade of trials, struggles and consternation. Small businesses have never been more challenged, but then most people have never been more challenged. The threats of bad things—the world ending, going bankrupt, wars and the use of nuclear weapons—have never been more real. And yet things for the average Joe and Jane—or should I say they, he or she—goes on, as does technology:

Society in the 2020s is developing into a more local and protective vision. The lockdowns have made us home buddies, and the idea of globalisation is disappearing. We still want to travel, but we are nervous about travelling. We are now a nervous species. Suddenly, thanks to the conflict in the Ukraine, the United States' and Europe's battle lines are being redrawn. China has become a visible threat to the European and US alliance while Russia is a pariah.

Society is worried, but continues to behave differently. Activism is far more rife than ever before. Activist movements like Extinction Rebellion are rife because people no longer believe in politicians—they believe in the power of the network.

This conflict between the power of the people through the network versus the power of the politicians through the government is the biggest social battle of the 2020s. It is evidenced by activist consumer movements, demonstrations, cryptocurrencies, cyberattacks, the rejection of traditional institutions and the growth of new institutions.

The high street is dying, the shopping centres are empty and the physical is dead. Consumers have doubled down to become all digital. This has been driven by lockdown. You can't have much fun if you can't go out, but you can still watch Netflix and buy stuff from Amazon.

All of this has culminated in a massive social change from physical to digital. In banking, it has created a mass move—or has it? Not really. Banking is a strong and stable market. Consumers and businesses want reliability and resilience. In fact, in the 2020s, consumers and small businesses are better served than ever before but, primarily, by traditional banks that are integrating FinTech ideas.

Society is becoming truly digital. You can work wherever you want to work, travel to wherever you want to go, eat whatever you want to eat and find love wherever love can be found. We are truly global, but very local.

The future? The future society? The future society will take this one step beyond. We are about to become a multiplanetary society. Space tourism is already a reality, and a space hotel that is a bit like the International Space Station is already being built. Balloon flights to space and back in a few hours are possible, and the idea of humans settling on Mars is becoming more and more of a reality every day. The future society will be one where any human, anywhere in any part of our universe, can sit and chat, and trade and transact, because they are connected. The biggest issue is going to be if the connection breaks down.

Nevertheless, when I think about the generations that came before us, they had no idea what the future world would be like. Just think, two centuries ago, most people were not educated. They could neither read nor write. Today, most countries encourage a basic level of education; some countries ensure it.

The more people who can read, write and communicate, the better the world becomes. The more the world progresses. The more we know, the better we get? I ask this as a question, as our globally connected world of social media and networking allows all of us to find out everything, everywhere. Does this make our world better? I would say yes. Our world is better because our ability to read, write and communicate allows us to understand each other better. The more we talk, the better we become.

As the eternal optimist, I believe that the future society will be one that is globally connected, globally communicated and with a global currency based on a global network. We will all be assimilated and spend our holidays on Mars and our birthdays on Venus. Well, the men may go to Mars and the women to Venus at the very least.

Technology and Life

The exciting area for me is always our technological future. Reusable rockets, life on Mars, quantum computing, robotics, AI, the metaverse, blockchain, renewable energy and more are all going to transform the way we live over the next few years. What does this mean in reality?

To start with, humans have this great ability to solve problems. One of my favourite examples is the discovery of insulin, which had an immediate impact on children suffering from diabetes. Today, we can create vaccinations against coronavirus in months. We have come a long way since Edward Jenner, the father of vaccination, experimented with stopping smallpox in the late 1700s. These days we can replace people's arms and legs—even their faces—so what about tomorrow? Well, when Alexa can read bedtime stories in the voice of your dead grandmother, things will be different. Probably the biggest change is that, soon, we will be able to grow babies outside of the womb through ectogenesis:

Recent developments have managed to create 3D printed ovaries and have grown premature goat embryos in synthetic wombs. Researchers expect the technology to be useful by 2034 and ... anyone seeking to abort a child could place the baby in the artificial womb and give it up for adoption.[3]

Not to mention replacing human body parts through 3D printing:

It can be as long as 5 years to find a kidney donor, so scientists have resorted to produce organs through 3D printing technologies. There has been quite some success in creating artificial hearts through 3D printing, and the future of bio-printing suggests that we may be able to transplant the first synthetic liver by 2024.[4]

Building on these themes, we can see that, by the next decade, sex dolls will be almost as real as humans. We will be able to talk to each other through our thoughts transmitted via the network. When we discuss AI, how about our personal intelligence artificially augmented?

This won't involve a mobile phone and a headset. It will use a chip implanted inside the body and a contact lens. Suddenly, the world will be enriched into 5D by a world of sensory inputs that most of us will be happy to use.

If this sounds like something out of *Black Mirror*, don't be fooled. This technology is already here.

Neuralink is [Elon] Musk's neural interface technology company. It's developing a device that would be embedded in a person's brain, where it would record brain activity and potentially stimulate it. Musk has compared the technology to a "Fitbit in your skull".[5]

3   Aayesha Arif, "Here Are 7 Futuristic Technologies That Will Change Our Lives Entirely," Wonderful Engineering, 12 August 2017, https://wonderfulengineering.com/here-are-7-futuristic-technologies-that-will-change-our-lives-entirely/.

4   Kristen Rogers, "When we'll be able to 3D-print organs and who will be able to afford them," CNN, 10 June 2022, https://edition.cnn.com/2022/06/10/health/3d-printed-organs-bioprinting-life-itself-wellness-scn/index.html.

5   Isobel Asher Hamilton, "Neuralink: The story of Neuralink: Elon Musk's AI brain-chip company where he had twins with a top executive," *Business Insider*, 3 December 2022, https://www.businessinsider.com/neuralink-elon-musk-microchips-brains-ai-2021-2.

Food

We all know that food is running out as the planet becomes overpopulated. We cannot grow enough wheat or rear enough cows and sheep to keep up with the demands of the human world. Add to this that cows create enough methane to destroy the planet, we should be doing something different.

It won't be long before laboratory-developed meats and vegetables become commonplace. More than this, vertical farms will become mainstream and could rival and ultimately exceed traditional farming for quality.

Living

In a similar way to vertical farming, vertical living will increase. Many people around the world already live in condominiums and apartments, and that number will increase. The difference will be that the buildings will be taller and cleaner. This is already happening, with most new skyscraper developments focused on solar and renewable energy, along with green forests and plants populating the buildings' structures. Take that a step further and imagine energy efficiency built into every window and brick of these buildings.

> Floors in the same buildings could be assigned for farming, and the water will be supplied through rain and condensation. Spare parts will be manufactured using handy 3D printers available everywhere.[6]

All of the above shows that the forces for change are related and integrated. Political, economic, social and technological forces do not act in separate spheres. They work together to change our world and how we live. A key part of this is finance.

Finance

Financial services will be dramatically different, thanks to technology. FinTech will no longer be a separate entity. It will just be technology that provides financial processes. In the same light, banking will no longer be a thing. We will have banks—they will never go away—but they will just be the utility providers

---

6   Aayesha Arif.

of services that are curated and integrated from here, there and everywhere. We also won't even need to think about finance or money; it will just be digital debits and credits made by our devices and technologies on the network. The only time we will think about finance and money is when we have to, because we need to cover the costs.

Does this mean that there will still be money? I don't believe in a moneyless, wealthless vision of the future. Humans always find a way to fight over power, and wealth is power. This means that some form of value will exist. It may not be called money, but it will be digitally noted as an exchange. Perhaps a global digital currency of bits and bytes will command the near future.

In the meantime, what's interesting in all of this is that the technological forces for change will alter the way we live for the better if we harness these opportunities. Vertical farming, integration of farming and sensors, monitoring agriculture in real time, replacing livestock with labstock, replacing fossil fuels with renewable energy, embedded and invisible finance and more are all going to be driven by our innovations and progress through technology.

However, you have to remember that all of this will cost money. That's why technology *and* finance are so key. In fact, it's the FinTech forces of change that will create our world of tomorrow. Pretty exciting, huh?

> "Any sufficiently advanced technology is
> indistinguishable from magic."
> **Arthur C. Clarke**

Eleven Realities of 2030

People talk about time travel a lot. Hollywood loves it. Going back in time or forward in time is really popular. Switching bodies between a young you and an old you is often a theme. Being able to jump time is great fiction. And yes, it's a fiction but, if I could jump time and skip into 2030, what would it look like? To be honest, it would look a lot like 2024, with the exception of a few big changes to society and technology .

The first big change in society is that we are less trusting. Due to the pandemic of 2020, followed by the war of 2022 and 2023, and then the Big Scam of 2025, people don't believe anyone, anymore. We don't believe the news channels, the politicians or even our own best friends. We just believe what we believe.

Second, technology has taken over our lives. You may have thought that we were already hi-tech but, in 2030, our houses, cars, media and even our children and dogs run on technology. Most homes have a robot butler or maid, and 90 per cent of humanity is connected to the network.

Third, we don't believe in government. We believe in the network. Bitcoin has just passed the million-dollar mark, but the users of bitcoin don't care because the dollar is no longer relevant. The world has standardised on a global currency called the Wonk, and Wonkers rule.

Fourth, our privacy is dead. Although we don't believe in government, government believes in us, and monitors our every thought and movement. Networked monitors cover every street and motorway, every message we send is recorded by the authorities, any conversations we have are heard by drone monitors in the skies and any trip to the toilet can be scanned for what is wasted.

Fifth, what happened to Facebook? You remember that thing from the 2010s? It's gone. We lost trust in that platform, which is why Friends Re-excited has become the thing.

Sixth, the weather isn't great. It's hot and muggy, and that's in Norway. The planet is warming, and we all feel the heat.

Seventh, clothes and fashion have changed. Because of the climate issue, we all wear shorts and T-shirts. No one wears a suit and tie anymore, except for politicians, who we don't trust because they wear suits and ties.

Eighth, we're all learning to speak Mandarin because China rules the world. After Russia's demise and the US loss of face over everything, President Xi doubled down on the Belt and Road policy and made friends with everyone, everywhere, by sprinkling money. Funny how that works.

Ninth, what happened to TV? Oh, it's no longer around. Everyone watches media on devices and the sales of TVs collapsed in 2028, as did the viewers of TV channels. Amazonflix rules! (Do you remember when Amazon took over Netflix?)

Tenth, have you been to the Moon yet? Last year, over a thousand earthlings took a quick round trip to the Moon on Virgin Holidays. Add to that SpaceX Trips and Blue Origin Tours, and most people are now considering two weeks in space rather than two weeks at Disney.

Eleventh, if you can't afford to go to the Moon, have you tried out Virgin VR? The exciting news is that you can feel like you're on the Moon even when you're on Earth! Even more, try out Friends Re-excited's platform Lifex. You can live another life, not just this one. The only issue? You have to eat.

The list goes on, as does the world. We progress and develop and do things differently, except that we are all still human. So, the one thing that hasn't changed in 2030 is that we still have family, relationships, friends, love and each other. Isn't that important, too?

Intelligent Money Makes Money Disappear

What have the eleven realities of 2030 got to do with money? Well, it shows that money is disappearing into the network. In other words, money is no longer going to be physical; it will be embedded and invisible instead.

We are moving rapidly towards a cashless society and even banks are disappearing as physical entities. For example, there are thousands of places these days that will not accept cash payments even though, by the laws of most countries, no retailer can refuse a cash payment—or can they? For example, in the United Kingdom, the Bank of England says that retailers can choose what payment mechanism they accept. Not only can they refuse cash payments, they can also refuse card payments if they choose to do so. Have we finally reached the stage where we are cashless?

Cash still provides an immediate transfer of value that is trusted and totally anonymous. Right now, there is nothing equivalent. However, right now, we don't need cash for most transfer-of-value transactions. That's why I never carry cash anymore. But then you may find yourself in a situation where someone won't take anything but cash as a payment. It's confusing, isn't it?

Equally, what happens if you don't have a bank account? What happens if you have no card payment service? What happens if you only have cash? In a film that I watched the other day, the actor was on the run and had to hide. Before getting into trouble, he withdrew thousands of dollars of cash notes. In order to avoid the authorities, he paid for everything in cash. Hotels, buying a car, getting a gun and a phone; you name it, they were all paid for with crisp dollar bills. How would you avoid the authorities tomorrow if no one accepted cash?

Now, I know this is a theme I return to often, but we all predicted twenty years ago that the future would be cashless and branchless. Twenty years later, we are finally here. At the core of this debate is a key question: when do we need physicality? We need physicality today for human connectivity. We need branches for trust and marketing, not for service and advice. We need cash for anonymity and immediacy, not for payments. These still have a role to play in our digital world or, at least, until trust, marketing, anonymity and immediacy are replaced by something else. Something that the authorities cannot track and trace.

This has been the constant debate throughout this book. If we embed money into the network, and make it invisible and intelligent, what is the future scenario for the physicality of money? The answer, based on PEST and all of the above scenarios, is that money in a physical form does not have a future.

In Space, No One Can Take Your Money

The strapline for the film *Alien* was that "In space no one can hear you scream." Thinking about the possibility of a cashless world, I realised that this strapline could be adapted to "In space no one can take your money."

Do you ever notice anyone paying for anything in the sci-fi movie worlds of the future? It does happen, but it is rare. It is rare because we are reaching a point where money becomes meaningless, and this in itself could be quite scary. Imagine that you want something but you cannot have it because your payment is refused. This is why Gene Rodenberry, the father of *Star Trek*, imagined a future where money doesn't exist. Where money doesn't matter.

266 **Intelligent Money**

It's the core of Trekonomics, and delivers a world where your reputation is your mark.

> "The acquisition of wealth is no longer the driving force in our lives. We work to better ourselves and the rest of humanity."
>
> **Captain Jean-Luc Picard**, captain of the Federation starship *USS Enterprise*

It's such a nice vision—but supremely flawed. Humans do not work to make the world a better place. We work for our own self-interests. We do not want to improve society; we want to improve our lives. We are intensely selfish; we are not worthy.

After all, it is interesting that if we were all equal, what would that mean? If we flattened society so that everyone had equality, what would that mean? If women had equality with men, what would that mean? If people in remotest Mongolia had equality with a New Yorker, what would that mean?

It is hard to have an idea of a world where everyone works for the betterment of humanity. We work for the betterment of ourselves, and I guess that's why money and wealth were invented. Money was invented to make us unequal.

> "All animals are equal, but some are more equal than others."
>
> **George Orwell**, *Animal Farm* (1945)

We are just animals. The difference is that we are sentient animals with language. That is what makes us different; we can communicate and think smarter than most animals, but we are just animals. We have the basic needs of an animal: food, drink and shelter. These are the basic physiological needs at the bottom of Maslow's pyramid:

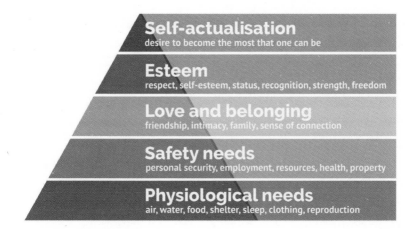

The pyramid demonstrates the difference between us and most animals because humans need that feeling of belonging, esteem and self-actualisation. That is what makes us unequal. Animals may be equal, although power and gender make a difference, but do animals have a sense of belonging, esteem and self-actualisation?

In a human context, that's a very big driver. It is why humans created inequality to encourage us to achieve extraordinary things. We are ambitious animals who need to achieve something more than just existing. This is what sets us apart and why we invented money. Money was invented to motivate us to achieve more and create inequality between those who don't want to achieve and those who do. If we were purely animals, it would just be food that made us unequal. If we were lions, it would be the amount of meat we can eat that would set us apart, and money is more powerful than meat.

Strategies: Focus on the Customer and Make Sure You Have the Next Play

As I watch various series about office politics, it makes me wonder if anyone actually thinks that way. Who really thinks about destroying a competitor, a company or a colleague? I guess many of us do. But, would you do it in a collegial way? For example, if Jane is likely to be the next CEO, should John stab her in the back?

The reason I'm asking this is that strategies have to be formed in advance. If you are going to trip over Jane or John, you need a strategy. The thing is, strategies cannot ever be formed to go directly from A to B. They need to be formed from A to B to C to D. When Jane or John responds to B, you launch C and have D ready for the grand finale.

This is my favourite aspect of being a strategist. When you sit and think about your next move, like a chess grandmaster, you need to also think about the subsequent five or six moves. Strategies are not formed on the basis of doing A. It's A through Z.

My favourite example of how such a strategy was played out was in the 1990s when Tesco launched its online service strategy. Tim Mason, former deputy CEO and chief marketing officer (CMO) of Tesco, presented its game plan as a keynote at a conference that I attended, and his presentation has stayed with me to this day.

The gist of his keynote was that Tesco would launch an online grocery store with delivery. Today, that's nothing amazing. In the 1990s, it was visionary and far-sighted. More than this though, the strategy then pivoted around hypermarkets and convenience stores called Tesco Express. What became clear during his presentation was that Tesco had a stepladder to success, with each step sucker-punching its competitors and creating more market share for the store which, at the time, was the underdog.

What I loved about this story is that every move had a move ahead and, when you think about any strategist, this is obvious, isn't it? You do not play chess, thinking purely about the next move. You play chess thinking about the move two, three, four or more steps ahead. In business, you have to do the same. Don't just launch something that competes—launch something with three or four more moves in your back pocket that the competition has to catch.

It sounds so simple, but it is so hard to do in reality because most of us are constrained by today's budgets and conditions. However, if you are one of the lucky ones who can plan a strategy for tomorrow's budgets and conditions then, oh my, you can change the world.

A good example of this type of strategic thinking is Virgin or, more specifically, Sir Richard Branson. The way Virgin targets new markets is to draw out the key features of the existing players and then work out what additional features it can add. Apple does the same, as do Amazon and a few other companies. It is all about being obsessed with what the customer wants and needs.

I always remember when Virgin Atlantic launched. For the first time, premier customers were offered transportation to and from the airport in Virgin cars. Sure, many airlines do this now but, back in the day, this was a hugely differential idea. The thought process was that the flight was not the most important part—the journey was. That's how Virgin Atlantic realised that the whole travel experience—from leaving home to arriving at your hotel destination—was key, not just the boarding and disembarking.

Strategy is not about creating what others do, but doing what the customer wants and needs—even if they don't even know they want or need it—and obsessing over the customer, not just walking all over them.

"A lot of times, people don't know what
they want until you show it to them."
Steve Jobs

"If I had asked people what they wanted,
they would have said faster horses."
Henry Ford

"The best customer service is if the customer doesn't need
to call you, doesn't need to talk to you. It just works."
Jeff Bezos

"Nobody raves about average."
Bill Quiseng

Can Banks Meet the Needs of Government and the People?

I did a search for "Jamie Dimon" on the internet the other day and was intrigued by the results. It reached everything from how cryptocurrencies are dangerous to Jeffrey Epstein, the late sex offender and disgraced financier connected to everyone from Prince Andrew to Jes Staley, formerly with JPMorgan and ex-Barclays CEO. The search made me realise how much a bank CEO has to deal with these days. Banks are collapsing—take Credit Suisse, Silicon Valley Bank and more. We are experiencing what I call a crypto winter and FinTech bloodbath. Small and large banks are going under due to interest rates, and a lot of finance faces a desert of funding. We are in hard times.

Throughout these hard times, JPMorgan Chase has been pretty reliable. As First Republic Bank (FRB) melted, JPMorgan bought it up, just as it did with Bear Stearns and Washington Mutual. It is a trusted institution, and it is a testament to Dimon's steerage that this is the case. Officially named CEO of the company back in 2006, he's seen the company survive crisis after crisis. As he has said himself, "My daughter asked me when she came home from school, 'what's the financial crisis?' and I said, 'It's something that happens every five to seven years.'"

A financial crisis is what happens every five to seven years. Five to seven years. A financial crisis. As I sit and think about that fact, which is pretty much true, I wondered why this is the case. We are meant to be in a strong and stable industry. An industry that is resilient and reliable.

From my own perspective, I find it incredible that we live in an industry that allows a crash to occur so frequently. We claim the industry is regulated, formalised, strong and stable, yet we expect the industry to crash and burn every five to seven years. Today, it's Credit Suisse and Silicon Valley Bank. Yesterday, it was a sovereign debt crisis in Europe. The day before, it was the end of Bear Stearns and Lehman Brothers. The day before that, the internet boom and bust. We take all of these occurrences on the chin but, from a non-banker perspective, you have to ask: what is this industry?

No wonder there is a rising movement of libertarians who believe bitcoin, cryptocurrencies, altcoins and more can provide a new financial system that doesn't crash and burn every seven years. To them, the internet can create a better future. They believe in the power of the network. They believe in the power of the people. The people control the world.

This is where it gets interesting. Governments and banks think they control the world through strong and stable economies backed by strong and stable currencies and strong and stable companies, namely banks. Yet banks accept that the industry is in crisis and has issues that might destroy the system every five to seven years. We then try to provide CPR to keep the system alive.

The libertarians' idea of decentralising finance and placing financial services regulation and control into the hands of the people is not madness. It has traction. In fact, it has traction every single day. Should we, as bankers, be worried? Not really. We need to embrace the fact that banking now has dual governance: the governance of the regulators and the governance of the people. I guess the issue is that, if you ignore the latter and only focus on the former, you just become a pawn of the state.

We need to be a servant of the state and the people. I believe the nearest model that could meet both of these needs is one where state and local government work together, with many authorities and powers devolved to local organisations. Then consider yourself to be one of these local organisations.

What the World Will Look like in a Hundred Years, 212x

The year is 212x. The world has changed. The world is still here—just, but the frozen North and South are no longer frozen. The Earth is boiling. In terms of economics, China has collapsed, India has surpassed the United States, Brazil and Mexico have joined the G20, as have Nigeria and Kenya, while Europe is a mess. The Royal Family has disappeared and over a million people live on Mars.

How things have changed so fast and so amazingly is beyond many of us, but then we can never predict things easily. Let's take a quick run through the four key factors of PEST—politics, economics, society and technology—once more.

Politics

After the third world war, WWIII, triggered by the activities of Russia and its attack on the Ukraine in the early 2020s, the axis of power changed. China invaded Taiwan in 2026, the United States retaliated and the world was at war, not just the Ukraine and Russia. World powers were divided by those who believed in free markets—the United States, Europe, Australia and some African and Latin American nations—and those who didn't, notably China, India and Russia.

The war ended in 2027, after nuclear bombs landed in Red Square, an act prompted by Russia's nuclear attack on Kyiv. Luckily, no nuclear activity has taken place since. Instead, humanity has tried to fly to the stars. The colonisation of Mars and settlement of people there, and on the Moon, led to the gradual harmonising of the planet.

Europe, the United States, Australia and a number of nations were already in a collegiate, stacked up against their "opposition" of China, Russia and India. The most interesting developments were in Africa and South America, however. The destruction of the plains across Africa and the loss of most habitats in South America, along with the extinction of many of Earth's most beloved animals from rhinoceroses to elephants to lions and tigers, created an urgent imperative to consolidate the world's resources in a new alliance. Hence the Global Alliance (GA). Many countries on these continents joined the GA and, by 2056, the G100 Agreement created a group of nations across Earth that all upheld the same principles, namely, freedom, action and support.

These principles are now the bedrock of the G100 Council, which represents more than 150 countries today. The principles, as you well know, represent:

- **Freedom** of thought, expression and information
- **Action** for those who are in need and against those who contravene the G100 rules
- **Support** for all citizens in terms of food, shelter, warmth and health

This framework built on the UN's 17 Sustainability Development Goals (SDGs), which were not met by 2030 as hoped, and created a new world order that all could sign up for.

Many world leaders now feel that the GA could not exist if it had not been for the movement of people to Mars and the Moon, combined with the loss of Earth's biodiversity.

Economics

The twenty-first century proved to be incredibly difficult from an economic point of view. WWIII and the collapse of China in the late 2030s, due to its debt burden; the break-up of the EU in the 2040s; the global financial crisis of the 2050s; the rise of Polygon as the currency of the G100; the collapse of the US dollar in the 2060s; the Asia–America war of 2078; and more all led to a different place.

Today, we live in a world that is unified, global and local. Governments have unified in a federated state of nations, all under the G100 Council. There are local issues, but the consensus is a world army, a world service and a world force to defend ourselves against existential threats.

Interestingly, money has changed dramatically in the process. Sure, there is the G100 token based on Polygon, but there are still over a hundred currencies that exist outside of that system digitally, as well as another hundred or more currencies issued by nation states. Nevertheless, when the G100 token became the reserve currency of the world, after the end of the US dollar, the world order did change.

With all major economies tied to the G100 token, better known as the Goken, we saw a new form of stability and unity, and this new form enabled us to interact much better with and colonise planets. With the forthcoming expedition to create a further colony on Saturn, a stable economy has become a critical part of Earth's exploration and colonisation of the solar system. Without such economic stability, all would be lost.

Society

It's quite unbelievable that people a century ago owned things. Now we share everything. No one has a house or a car. Everything is pay-as-you-go using Gokens. We travel between cities in minutes and across the world in hours, unlike our predecessors who travelled in hours and days.

The fantastic thing about today's world is how everyone is included and it is so much more egalitarian. Can you believe there was a movement a century ago called Black Lives Matter? Today, we know that every life matters and, thanks to the efforts of the G100 Council, the recent loss of

274 **Intelligent Money**

middle Africa was dealt with fast and swift, as was the loss of northern Latin America.

As you know, most equatorial countries were wiped out in the mid-2080s due to the Earth's warming. Luckily, we managed to save much of the biodiversity in these countries. Although the people were displaced, the G100 managed to rehouse and support these peoples by moving them to the Arctic and Antarctic communities which, today, are the most populous on Earth as they are two of the few regions we can inhabit comfortably.

The good thing is that people can move globally today, thanks to the G100 Agreement of 2056. This agreement created the borderless world we live in today, where any citizen can travel to over a hundred countries using Gokens. More than this, it allows the free movement of peoples, goods and services, which has effectively created a global planet.

Of course, North Korea and a few other states are still on the fence in this global structure, but it is a far better world than that of the one a century ago, when nations fought nations and borders were closely guarded. The G100 society includes everyone and war, racism and even religious extremes have gone away. "We are the world," as USA for Africa once sang, has come true.

Having said that, relationships are still very hard in 212x. We struggle to form relationships and keep them, as everything is managed in a room in isolation. The restructuring of work and education to be based at home has fractured our societies, and dealing face to face has become so much more difficult. The idea of small talk and meeting has disappeared. In a recent survey by OnePlanet, it was found that only 1 in 100 people have real friends who they meet physically. This is a serious concern and is why the G100 Council has introduced the Meet-and-Greet programme. The idea is that we should meet face to face, and the G100 Council is offering 100 Gokens to anyone who makes a physical relationship happen. The Gokens can be used in bars and restaurants in any participating country, as long as you book your meeting beforehand on the G100 relationships service.*

Technology

As you all know, the last century was dominated by three technology firms in the West—Amazon, Apple and Meta—and two in the East—Alibaba and Tencent. When these companies formed the Tech Alliance under the G100 Council, they became uberfirms, like nothing ever seen before.

The merger of these five firms in 2061 created A, the company that now issues and runs all of our technology services. The creation of Embedded Everything is from A. Everything you touch, use and think is now part of the A network and recorded on the G100 ledger. Admittedly, that may be something that some don't like but "You cannot live today without being part of A", as its advert states.

The only notable company that sits outside of this network is Musk Enterprises. After its founder, Elon Musk, died in 2068, Musk Enterprises started to use its space travel and boring services to work with the G100 Council to create easier ways for us to move between cities and countries and between Earth, the Moon and Mars. We have a lot to thank for his benefaction, and the fact that he left all of his corporate assets to Earth and the G100 when he passed.

If you're excited by new technologies, the introduction of Earth 4.0 will give you a life. You may have already visited the holodeck and metaverse but, in 212x, we finally get to go into the holoverse. A is giving us all of the tools to no longer live real lives. We can live another life. Every day in every way. Now we can be more beautiful, more amazing, more confident and more wonderful, all thanks to A.

If you want to be part of the holoverse, just think "holoverse". Your mind will be transported there and you will be welcomed. Just don't think "holo". You don't want to go there.

* We know that there are no longer many bars and restaurants on Earth, but you can use this directory, Antiques For You, to find one near you.

Banking in 212x

Throughout the last century, we saw a massive change in the global financial systems thanks to technology. Now that such technologies are embedded in everything we see, hear and touch—even smell and taste—everything has networked and connected globally. We can talk to people on top of Everest, in a crater on the Moon or even in a lake on Mars, in real time all the time. There are no boundaries.

Unsurprisingly, that has changed banking and finance. A hundred years ago, we were confident that banks would be around forever but many disappeared in what became the massive cannibalisation of banking in the late twenty-first century. When Revolut acquired Deutsche Bank, the route began. Today, banking is unrecognisable.

First, there are no physical banking services today. A century ago, there were thousands of branches.

Second, although banking has moved to the network, it is no longer banking. It is now financial processes. The traditional bank has been broken into a thousand pieces, each of which is automated. Trading, investing, credit, savings, deposits and payments are all pieces of finance that are now part of our world. We just don't see them anymore.

Where I live orders its own heating and pays for it; when I need to move, the self-driving car network takes my order and it is paid for by something, but I have no idea what; although I work, I work for fun and for funds. It's very different to how my grandfather behaved. A hundred years ago, we had to work to get money; today, we get money regardless, and work for self-esteem. It's such a different world.

Third, banking is integrated with government and governance. The network controls the exchange of value and liability smart contracts. The smart contracts are embedded in everything, from moving goods from Earth to Mars to my walking into a room and getting an instantly produced meal.

The result is that I cannot and do not use the word "banking" anymore. There is no single entity that deals with my money in 212x, and I don't even think about money as money. I get credits and debits digitally. I spend them digitally. I do that through a whole series of embedded processes, running over rails provided by many companies. My allegiance is with my digital wallet—yes, we still have those—and my digital wallet is run by me.

Everything is run by me. The world is mine, and it's run by me. I have my own identity, my own digital persona and my own currency (Gokens). I give governments access to my profile when required; I give financial institutions—yes, they still exist—access to my profile when necessary. Financial institutions are primarily here for commercial purposes—to track and trade investments and supply chains of multiplanetary institutions—but, in retail, everything has been deconstructed and distributed to enable a world run by me. It is interesting that this was predicted over a century ago and today is a reality.

So banks do exist in 212x but we just don't see them. They are invisible. There is no physical entity called a bank. There is simply a range of embedded services that banks provide invisibly. Some of them are still with banks, particularly if you are a multiplanetary institution, but most people live happily with distributed financial services run by the individual in their chosen wallet that feeds all of their services, from food to shelter.

Bear in mind, none of us owns a car or a home anymore, and most transportation and shelter are purely on demand, so why would we need money, a bank or a physical manifestation of finance? When you can exchange globally, in real time, for everything and anything, why would you need money? When you can send some representation of value as a digit here or there, what does money mean?

In 212x, money is purely a fiction that was created in the last centuries to allow people to trade. Today, we trade with digital credits and debits in an ecosystem of invisible finance. Some call it "embedded" but, regardless of what you call it, it's just a utility. Finance is the same as electricity. I can't see it, but I know it's there when I need it. As long as I can keep up my debit balances, then I can get whatever I want, whenever I want it, worldwide.

It's not so dissimilar to 2024, just that I no longer have a bank. I just have service providers that manage my balances for me through my things, invisibly and embedded. Perhaps it is a bit dissimilar after all.

THE FINAL WORD

Thinking about embedded, intelligent finance and imagining the future, there are many scenarios, but one that keeps returning is when you have intelligent finance (InFi) inside. A microchip in your brain, enabling you to run your life on automatic. It may seem phantasmagorical but there are several examples of where technology is heading today that show the possibilities.

First, there's the work of Alexander Huth, Assistant Professor of Neuroscience and Computer Science at the University of Texas. Huth is working on research that uses computational methods to model how the brain processes language and represents meaning. Put it a simpler way, his technology developments could allow the network to read your mind.

Then there's Kevin Warwick, Emeritus Professor at Coventry and Reading universities, who became the world's first human cyborg back in the 1990s. More than thirty years later, he talks a good talk about how humans are becoming integrated with the network to enable "the possibility of enhancing our brain, our mental capabilities", which he thinks is an enormous opportunity for the future.[1]

Warwick was involved in one experiment that involved a two-hour operation to implant a BrainGate neural interface system, a type of brain computer interface, inside him, linking his nervous system with a computer. His brain learnt to recognise the system of pulses emitted and was able to turn on lights and control a wheelchair just by thinking it. For those affected by neurologic disease, paralysis or limb loss, the ability to connect our brains

---

1   Futures, "Cyborg Experiments w/ Prof. Kevin Warwick," Futures Podcast, https://futurespodcast.net/episodes/01-kevinwarwick.

to computers is a critical development for the future. But it goes further than this—if you're Elon Musk.

To begin with, his company, Neuralink, is working on trials to link brain activity to the real world for those who are paralysed. Gaining the approval of the US Food and Drug Administration (FDA) for human trials in June 2023, the company has risen in value from $2 to $5 billion in just two years. "Musk has had the historic golden touch with Tesla and SpaceX so Neuralink is on the radar of the tech world over the coming years," said Daniel Ives, an analyst with Wedbush Securities.[2] The thing is that, if you can implant a system into the brain to link humans to the network, why would you limit it to those who are paralysed or quadriplegic? Why not offer it to everyone?

So, here's a vision. Your future no longer has any visible technology involved. You are a cyborg. Everything you think and do is linked to the networked system. Your eyes can imagine and see anything you want to imagine and see. Forget Netflix, as you can entertain yourself for hours with your own imagination. Your brain can answer any question anytime. Forget Google, you can just wonder about something and know the answer. Your ears can hear whatever they want to hear. Forget Spotify, you can just make up your own music. Your nose can smell whatever it wants to smell. You can walk through a sewer and smell the roses. Your mouth can taste whatever it wants to taste. Who needs Michelin stars when your tongue can have its own five-star menu anywhere, anytime? You get the idea. Yes, it may sound far-fetched, but it is not so far away. Perhaps in five or ten years?

What does this mean for money and intelligently, embedded finance? If we think of money as part of our brain, bearing in mind that money is just a belief, here is a variation of the likely scenarios in the near-term future.

There are at least six key forms of intelligent payments in development. All of these form factors are based on our lifestyles and movements, and things we do today. They are just done in a different way. There are no cards, cheques, cash or physical payment systems. In fact, there are no apps, swipes, touch or telephone calls. It's all just smooth—it's a smile, nod and wink—it's a no-brainer.

2   Mike Snider, "Elon Musk's Neuralink has FDA approval to put chips in humans' brains. Here's what's next," *USA Today*, 9 June 2023, https://eu.usatoday.com/story/tech/2023/06/09/musk-neuralink-brain-chips-fda-human-trials/70299875007/.

Well, actually it's not a no-brainer. It needs your brain to be there for it to work. Here are the six sorts of payment that most consumer accounts might operate in the years to come:

1. Automated payments: no brain required

Automated payments are what they say they are. They are the usual payments you've set up to make every day, week or month, namely, subscriptions, direct debits, standing orders and regular payments that you just don't want to think about. How you set them up may be different—you just tell the network that there's a new regular payment—but that would take less than a minute. The network would take your thought instructions, set up the regular payments, link it to your account and the account of the company or individual that needs paying, and that's it! All done. Forget complex form filling. The system takes care of the whole thing for you. Automated payments replace account-based payment plans, using instructions by thought instead of forms.

2. Mind-read payments: brain required, but no action needed

Mind-read payments are when you are out and about, on the go. Today, you might pay by card, contactless, via an app or even with cash. Forget all of that. Tomorrow, you can just walk about and only have to take action if you disagree with the transaction. The sales assistant gives you the bag with your new sweater and shows you the amount. You just walk away as the bill is paid because you saw it. The waiter shows you the bill for a meal and you just walk away. The bill is paid because you saw it. You get the idea. The only time you don't walk away is when you want to challenge the bill. Mind-read payments replace contactless, card and cash payments.

3. Mind-driven payments: brain required and a thought

Mind-driven payments require action. These are payments that are more complex, such as sending money from your domestic account to an overseas account. The foreign exchange transaction requires an approval, and so you have to think "YES!" to confirm. Mind-driven payments replace keyboard-driven payments.

4. Conscious payments: brain required and a specific approval

Conscious payments are very similar to mind-driven payments but require a physical action to process. This might be for a larger transaction, such as paying a few thousand dollars to someone you have not dealt with before. Approval would require you to raise your index finger to your cheek, by way of example. This is a specific prompt—do you approve this payment to Jane?—and a specific response—the touch–cheek approval. Conscious payments replace text and email.

5. Alerts: brain required and a conscious decision

Alerts are when suspicious activity is traced on your account. An alert appears in your head, and you simply reply yay or nay. Alerts may be to do with processing issues, incorrect account details and/or possible overdraft issues in the near future—basically all of the things that you already deal with today. The difference is that you simply need to think "cover" (move funds from savings), "resolve" (sort out the account details and tell me what you find) and/or "contact" (get in touch with me direct via thought or another method). Alerts are now in your head, and not on your phone.

6. Verified payments: brain required and a physical movement

Verified payments occur when there is a very specific question about a transaction on your account. The bank wants a specific confirmation from you before it will process the payment. The action could be a wink, as a nod is a good as a wink, but it demands that you make a physical movement before the payment can be processed. Verified payments are fast and immediate, with no device required.

As can be seen, the whole process now takes place inside your head and body. There are no external devices involved, and that is the point of embedded, invisible, intelligent finance. After all, my grandfather never had to carry a laptop and phone around, so why should I?

Finally, when thinking about money being inside my head, it already is in many ways. When I pay for goods, I'm not focused on my balances but on living my life. The awareness that debits are going down and credits up is in the back of my mind, but the actual numbers are generic and not specific.

What if the future world makes it far more specific so, in the back of my mind, I can see every account balance increasing and decreasing in real time? What if the system then takes this a step further and starts giving me red, amber and green lights for my financial lifestyle? We already have these of course—they are called credit checks—but what happens if my lifestyle is adjusted during these checks on my brain and my spending? What if I'm a gambling addict and, rather than selecting to block gambling platforms, the bank decides to do it for me based on forward projections of my lifestyle spending? What if I'm an alcoholic, and the embedded, invisible, monetary system decides to block my ability to buy alcohol? What if I have cancer, and so all unhealthy activities are switched off, including access to the food I love, which the system has decided are bad for me? You get the picture.

Take another angle: authentication and verification. Now that the financial service is embedded in my brain and, therefore, my body, what if the system needs an authentication? It no longer needs a biometric using facial or fingerprint recognition. It can use blood pressure, blood flow, heart rate or even my DNA!

The positives of embedded, intelligent finance are clear but so too are the negatives. The negatives are basically the same negatives of the current system, namely, how intrusive is this? Is Big Brother here and now or is it just a gradually developing process of assimilating us all?

This argument has raged for years, and the truth of the argument is balance. The balance between ease of living, convenience of money and the benefits of not having to think about things versus the centralised tracking of who we are, what we are doing and how we live.

In other words, intelligent, embedded finance might appear to assume that the centralised authorities—banks and governments—can track and trace our real-time lives, 24/7. That, however, would be an incorrect assumption as the brain implant embedded inside me may just as easily be my decentralised pocket of the networked universe.

The future is both exciting and scary but, as always, the key thing to remember is that it is you and me creating it. The future is the only thing you can change. Make it your change.

ABOUT THE AUTHOR

Chris Skinner is an award-winning speaker and one of the most influential people in technology, as well as a best-selling author. He is an independent commentator on the financial markets and FinTech through his blog, the Finanser.com, which is updated daily. He helped to found one of the first mobile banks in the world, and has advised CEOs and leaders from every continent of the world, including the United Nations, the White House, the World Bank and the World Economic Forum. In 2023, he was recognised with a Lifetime Achievement Award by the Payments Association, the largest community in payments.

Intelligent Money is his eighteenth book. His previous books include:

- *Digital for Good*, which focuses on how technology and finance can work together to address the environmental and social issues we face today and make a better world;

- *Doing Digital*, which shares lessons of how to do digital transformation followinng interviews with leading global banks such as BBVA, China Merchants Bank, DBS, ING and JPMorgan Chase;

- *Digital Human*, which shows how digitalisation is revolutionising the world and enabling everyone to be included in and served through the network;

- *Digital Bank,* which provides a comprehensive review and analysis of the battle for digital banking and strategies for companies to compete.

Chris has recently been added to The Mad 33 List for inspirational change and transformation leaders. He is a non-executive director of 11:FS and WP Communications and also on the advisory boards of many FinTech and financial firms including WebAccountPlus. Chris is also a visiting lecturer at Cambridge University as well as a TEDx speaker. In recent years, he has been voted one of the UK's foremost FinTech observers by *The Telegraph* and one of the most influential people in financial technology by the *Wall Street Journal*'s *Financial News* and *Thomson Reuters*. Chris is also a successful children's author with the five book about series *Captain Cake and the Candy Crew*. He is also co-founder, with renowned artist Basia Hamilton, of The Portrait Foundation, a non-profit platform to encourage children and the arts.